From
Cowgirl
to
Congress

Journey of a Suffragist
on the Front Lines

Jessie Haver Butler

with

Mila Johansen

From Cowgirl to Congress

Journey of a Suffragist on the Front Lines

by Jessie Haver Butler with Mila Johansen

Published by Mila Johansen
with
Sierra Muses Press

Cover Design: Julie Valin, Self to Shelf Publishing Services
Editor: Dara Powers Parker
Photo of Mila Johansen, page 297: Dee Anne Dinelli, Nevada City, CA
Book Design and Production: Margaret Jean Campbell

This book is set in Baskerville Type Text.
Printed in the United States of America

First Edition: April 2020

ISBN 978-1-952508-00-4

Library of Congress Control Number: 2020905267

1. Suffragist   2. Suffragette   3. Women's Rights   4. Social Activism

For

My Beloved Daughter, Olivia

*And for all women, everywhere, to find their own voice
and know it's time to speak up.*

*Special thanks to my grandmother, Jessie Butler, for inspiring
me to bring her story forward in celebration of the
100th anniversary of women winning the vote.*

*Many hands worked together to make this book possible.
Beginning with my niece, Crystal Stanfill, who helped me
start searching the archives and organizing them.*

*Thank you to Sherna Berger Gluck for writing the Foreword.
Gratitude to my industrious writing group,
The Sierra Muses, who have met and encouraged one another
for the past seven years. My husband, Rich, who is always
supportive. My dear friend Penelope Fox, who encouraged me
all the way through the process. And last but not least, to my
four loyal dogs, who lay at my feet while I write.*

*Others who contributed are Mariah Miller,
who put together a lot of the nuts and bolts of the
manuscript; Dara Powers Parker, who did the final edit;
Julie Valin for the cover; and Margaret Campbell, who
designed and produced the book.*

*And, of course, to all the women who came before,
so bravely waving the flag for women's rights.*

You've always had the power.

- Glinda, the Good Witch

CHAPTERS

Foreword by Sherna Berger Gluck

Introduction.. 1

1. In the Beginning: Pueblo, Colorado................................ 7

2. Tragedies Strike 15

3. A Heroine Enters My Life.. 19

4. Three Miracles and Another Tragedy 25

5. Off to Smith College... 29

6. A New England Education 35

7. Career Woman in the Making....................................... 45

8. I Help Put Together the Pulitzer School of Journalism.............. 51

9. Minimum Wage for Women 57

10. Moving to Washington, D.C., and Joining the Suffrage Struggle... 61

11. He Walks into My Life and We Start a New Kind of Household... 73

12. My First Speech.. 79

13. I Become a Lobbyist... 83

14. 1918: Women Almost Get the Vote............................. 91

15. Dangerous Waters: Canoeing Down the Potomac....................... 93

16. Another Legislative Job and I Reveal a Crime 97

17. Hugh Will Never Marry.. 101

18. Two Suffragists Speak Across the West 105

19. Women Get the Vote! Put the "Rat" in Ratification................ 119

20. We Are Invaded 125

21. Tug of War: Career Versus Marriage 129

22. Immaculately Conceived... 135

23. Marriage and Moving to London................................ 145

24. George Bernard Shaw.. 151

CHAPTERS

25. Dressing Appropriately...155

26. The Business of Having Babies...................................157

27. We Go to a New Kind of School: The Fabian Summer School.. 159

28. I Meet Lady Astor..171

29. Baby Advice: She Arrives...177

30. Presentation at the Court of St James's: Queen Mary...............195

31. The Queen's Garden Party..203

32. The Queen Takes a Hint...209

33. Three Funerals and A Ball..211

34. Isadora Duncan, Maria Montessori, and I Get Homesick........215

35. A New Home Near Boston and Two Mrs. Butlers....................231

36. Getting Back on Our Feet in Washington, D.C.......................245

37. A President's Wife Lends a Helping Hand 249

38. A Deadline to Write a Book: *Time to Speak Up*...........257

39. She Speaks Up 269

Closing Thoughts..274

Appendix

    Additional Photos 276

    Letters Home to Family..282

    Suffrage Timeline...288

Photo Credits...292

About the Author, Mila Johansen 297

FOREWORD

BY SHERNA BERGER GLUCK

Fifty years ago, in celebration of the golden jubilee of women's suffrage, the new generation of feminists ferreted out our foremothers—women like Jessie Haver Butler. She, like some of the other foremothers who were featured in celebrations in 1970, did not simply rest on her laurels. Rather, she actively engaged with the new generation of feminists and, drawing on her own experiences as a mother while living in London, was a strong advocate for child care.

While building on the work of all the Jessie Haver Butlers—and the Sojourner Truths, Lucretia Motts, Susan B. Anthonys, Lucy Parsons, Carrie Chapman Catts, Rose Schneidermans, Ida B. Wells, Alice Pauls, and more—we were also forging new ground. So, at the same time we were grateful for and honored their work on behalf of women, we were sometimes impatient with these living foremothers. Rooted in their own historic experiences, they often were confounded by—and even critical of—the new paths we were breaking.

After cofounding the community-based Feminist History Research Project with Ann Forfreedom in 1972, I joined with other grassroots feminist activists, especially in the west, to "recover our past." I started my trajectory as a feminist oral historian by interviewing suffragists, including Jessie Haver Butler. Like her, none were particularly modest about their accomplishments, and each had their own unique view of their place in history.

To some extent, they were all storytellers, but Jessie was unique among them because she was also a highly accomplished public speaker who took enormous pride in the role she had played in training other women in public speaking. Among other things, this meant that she was often in a public speaking mode in her interviews with me. By contrast, her memoir, so creatively edited by her granddaughter, is often much more lively and conversational. This memoir, with all its accompanying photographs and letters, wonderfully captures the life of a feminist in early to mid-twentieth century, and utterly captivated me.

We owe a tremendous debt of gratitude to Mila Johansen for her work in bringing us this engaging story. It is a wonderful contribution to our celebration of this 100th year jubilee of the 19th Amendment.

Sherna Berger Gluck
Santa Monica, California

SHERNA BERGER GLUCK

BIOGRAPHY

Scholar-social activist Sherna Berger Gluck has been honored as a pioneer of feminist oral history. Her work has focused largely on women activists, both in the US and Palestine, and her books include *From Parlor to Prison* (in which Jessie Haver Butler is featured), *Rosie the Riveter Revisited: Women the War and Social Change*, *Women's Words: The Feminist Practice of Oral History*, and *An American Feminist in Palestine: The Intifada Years*.

Three of Jessie's public speaking students holding her book,
Time to Speak Up

Introduction by Mila Johansen

I've listened to my grandmother's stories since I was a toddler. I would sit for hours, enchanted by the rhythms of her voice, the fascinating way she wove together the threads of her life. When I was very small, I often spent the night in her guest room, which had one entire wall covered with large glow-in-the-dark stars arranged in astrological patterns. It was a magical sight for any child to fall asleep to. I'm talking about years ago, before there were glow-in-the-dark sticker stars. Those stars are an enigma for me to this day—I can't imagine where she found them—perhaps they were painted on.

In the morning, I would run into her room and hop on her bed, begging for another story. Those early tales were amazing, about the animals who lived on the Colorado ranch where she grew up. Other times she told me about how, as a little girl, she got herself into some mischief or another. I loved those stories best.

Some of the stories in this book, I have heard over and over again. She never tired of telling them, and I never tired of listening. Even when I was a teenager and young adult, I would knock on her door, flop into her comfy armchair, and ask her to tell me a favorite tale again. I even brought my prospective boyfriends over for a story to break the ice on first dates. They all loved her.

Jessie helped raise me, which made the woman I am today—a writer, historian, activist, and speaker. She encouraged me to write about her life, but I was young and busy in college. All of her archives were passed to me after she died, but they remained in two file cabinets during my years of teaching, raising a child, and writing over twenty-two plays and books. Included in the files was her vibrant, yet unpublished, memoir.

When I finally opened the file cabinets and began going through the copious archives, I discovered what might be the largest collection of suffragette memorabilia in the world about one very prolific activist. These included letters from Carrie Chapman Catt and Bernard Shaw, and photos of Jessie with Alice Paul and Gloria Steinem.

Totally inspired, I serendipitously began piecing this book together, and it was a few months before I realized that the 100th anniversary of women winning the right to vote in the United States was coming up on August 18, 2020. This book allows all women to experience the rousing front lines of the suffrage movement.

I also discovered a packet of letters between Jessie and Lady Astor. (Jessie made copies of hers, and Lady Astor's alone total nineteen—perhaps the largest collection worldwide). I didn't realize that Nancy Astor, an American from Virginia, became the first woman to sit in England's Parliament! Nancy Astor proved to be a major voice for women, children, and laborers for over twenty-six years. After participating in the struggle for women's right to vote in 1920, Jessie lectured in London beside George Bernard Shaw. That is where she met and struck up her lasting friendship with Lady Astor. The two women wrote back and forth for two decades.

I don't know how I had the presence of mind to do it, but in my early twenties, I returned from college to record Jessie telling her stories and life history for two hours a day for two weeks. She sat, very patient, answering all my questions. She happily retold each life event as if for the first time, every word the same as each previous telling. That's why, when you read this book, you will be hearing her tell each story exactly as it happened.

Jessie grew up in Pueblo, Colorado, on a large cattle ranch. Her early years were riddled with unthinkable tragedies. This book touches lightly on these events as they integrated into the psychological history and complex life of a very extraordinary woman. At the same time the tragedies occurred, the first major glory found its way to the forefront. Jessie was ten years old the day she looked up into the face of Susan B. Anthony, who was touring the West, speaking about women's rights from the back of a wooden wagon. That day, Jessie's life changed forever, and she found hope and purpose. She knew at that moment that she would grow up and follow in the footsteps of Susan B. Anthony.

That is exactly what she did. Against all odds, she attended Smith College in Massachusetts. One of her first jobs was to help establish the Pulitzer School of Journalism at Columbia University. Her second was to help set the first minimum wage for women in America, from four dollars a week to eight. She was the first official woman lobbyist at the Capitol in Washington, D.C., proudly carrying the torch handed to her by Susan B. Anthony that fateful day in Pueblo. She wrote a book called *Time to Speak Up*, the first public speaking textbook specifically for women, and taught speech classes to hundreds of women, including the wives of senators. Eleanor Roosevelt supported Jessie by speaking at the opening of each of her lecture classes.

She was one of the major players in the Equal Rights Amendment and the minimum wage law for women. Alice Paul, an extremely radical feminist, tried to enlist Jessie into her movement. Although she respected Alice Paul's efforts, often dining in her home, Jessie believed she could accomplish more by giving well-orchestrated speeches on platforms that included men. She believed that men needed to be liberated from the social restraints imposed upon them by other men's own insecurities. So, she joined Carrie Chapman Catt's parliamentary movement and toured the country as the second speaker on her platform. Carrie then appointed Jessie as the lobbyist for the League of Women Voters, which she founded in 1920, the same year that women received the vote.

Just weeks after women celebrated the right to vote on August 18, Jessie's fiancé, Hugh Butler, received an assignment with the American Embassy in London, where they commissioned him to write a one-thousand-page book on the pros and cons of coal. While in London, the newly married couple regularly sat at the Fabian Summer School's Round Table with George Bernard Shaw. Shaw, impressed with Jessie, invited her to lecture with him throughout London. Jessie and Hugh spent eight years in England, where they gave birth to a daughter and a son. They were presented at the Court of St. James's, where Jessie procured the only write-up the next day in *The Times of London* about her gown that, unbeknownst to all present, she purchased used at a consignment store for forty pounds.

Jessie had a rare gift of unquenchable energy that carried her throughout her career to the age of ninety-three. That year, she made her last speech in Hollywood, sharing the podium with Gloria Steinem, Marlo Thomas, and Jane Fonda, and she took me along. I was also there when Sherna Berger Gluck interviewed her for the book *From Parlor to Prison*.

When I returned to this book, to fill in those early years of Jessie's life with her own words, it was tough going because of all the tragedies my grandmother endured. I left many of the harsher ones out. (You can ask me about them in person someday.) I read through each chapter several times, shortening and adjusting the stories to get them just right. I conducted copious amounts of research to get the timelines and facts exact. I am a research hound and love doing it.

Tears fell as I typed, and I felt closer to my grandmother than I had since her passing in 1985. It is amazing to me that she escaped the drudgery and certain death of the pioneer life to a world full of extravagances and possibilities, which allowed her to be a leader on the front lines of everything important. You and I and every woman can thank Jessie and the other women who broke ground for us with their perseverance and bravery. The events of Jessie's life and the history of the struggle for women's rights are like that wall of stars in her guest room. These stories glow brightly in the dark and, when seen together, show us a full picture, like a magical map of who we are, that we too may shine on.

Note: I use both terms, suffragist and suffragette in the book because Jessie mostly referred to herself and the women she worked with as "suffragettes". The term "suffragette" was first used in 1906 as a term of derision by the journalist Charles E. Hands in the *London Daily Mail* to describe activists in the movement for women's suffrage. Before that the word Suffragist was widely used. Suffragist can refer to men or women. Some think the word "suffragist" refers to the more gentle, parliamentarian manner and "suffragette" to the more militaristic methods.

A woman is like a tea bag;
you never know how strong it is
until it's in hot water.

- Eleanor Roosevelt

MRS. HUGH BUTLER (Jessie Butler), Teacher of Effective
Public Speaking. Among her pupils are Business and Pro-
fessional men and women, wives of members of Congress
and Embassy Diplomats, members of the Junior League,
American Red Cross, Girl Scouts, General Federation of
Women's Clubs, government employees and others.

CHAPTER 1

In the Beginning: Pueblo, Colorado

Jessie Haver Butler as a baby

I was the first child in our family, born in 1886, with no one there but my father to help my mother with the process. In that valley of the Arkansas River, near Pueblo, Colorado, the farm area where my father started his ranch, there wasn't a single family whose mother brought up her own children to maturity. The mothers all died early, including mine.

There were no doctors, there were no sinks in the kitchens, there were no bathrooms.

My later inspiration to help women and speak out for their rights must have come from my brave mother, Clara.

Clara Rehwoldt was raised in Nebraska by her father, a German immigrant, who trained as a Lutheran minister at Berlin University and founded a great many churches and Lutheran schools still in existence in Iowa and Nebraska. Clara received a good education, taught school, and read every book she could get her hands on.

Before she and my father, Edwin B. Haver, were married, they read a book by Edward Bellamy, *Looking Backward*, about an imaginary society where everyone lives in comfort provided for by an all-wise state. Both Father and Mother were greatly impressed by it.

Many years later, in the 1920s, after my own marriage, I sat at a table at the Fabian Summer School near London when someone told me it was this same book that turned my new acquaintance, George Bernard Shaw, into a socialist. At that very moment, Shaw sat down next to me at the dining table, and we struck up a friendship. How unexpected life can be!

The summer before she married, my mother went home from Pueblo to visit her German relatives in Nebraska. She tacked a notice on the door of her father's church, to the effect that Clara Rehwoldt would deliver a free talk on socialism. You can imagine what they thought in that traditional German farm community, where the girls were supposed to be housewives for life. What a shock it must have been to see a young woman lecturing on socialism. Everybody showed up to hear her, but disapproved thoroughly, as I later learned. I stopped there once on my way home from Smith College. My mother's younger sister told me this story with great reluctance, saying, "You know, your mother was quite peculiar. We never quite understood her."

Years later, I remember with vivid clarity when the campaign for women's suffrage circled throughout Colorado, how my mother climbed into the spring wagon. Clara toured that valley to urge the men to vote for women's rights. And that wasn't something that a good little housewife, even in Colorado, in those days was supposed to do. She proved to be a staunch feminist way back then. Of course, it was the same time when the great women's suffrage leader, Susan B. Anthony, spoke all over the state for months. Clara helped women secure the victory for voting rights in 1893. The western women were "wild with joy" when Colorado became the first state to enfranchise women through popular referendum, and it happened over a quarter of a century before the achievement of national women's suffrage in 1920.

Jessie's mother, Clara, with hair cut short

My mother possessed an exceptionally good mind. She must have longed for intellectual stimulation. But she soon found herself overwhelmed with the demanding round of household duties, along with the near-constant cycle of pregnancy and childbirth.

With four children to care for, my mother cropped her hair short to her head to make life easier and to keep it out of the way. Much to my dismay, and with many tears, she cut short my beautiful head of hair at the same time. Mother carried on her heavy work without complaint, but I often found her in despair.

She used to tell me, in veiled terms, that she feared she'd not be with us many more years. One Christmas, she gave me a large, beautiful doll with yellow hair and blue eyes.[1] "You must keep her always," she told me. "You must remember what I gave to you the last Christmas of my life." Her remarks gave me a cold chill, but I didn't tell anyone what she said. I never liked that doll or any other doll. Mother must have been exhausted most of the time, but she never stopped working. How could she? Too much depended upon her.

Like most housewives, Clara did the cooking, baking, and churning; washing and ironing; sewing and darning. She scrubbed floors, cared for four young children, and fed six hired hands—all in a house lighted by kerosene lamps, heated by stoves, and without running water. Every drop of water had to be pumped from the well or carried in from the irrigation ditch. In addition to all this, she raised chickens and sold eggs to earn spending money for the house.

She must have been very lonely for the companionship of women her own age. There were no cars, no telephones, and no radios to break the monotony of those long days. Mother made me her confidante. I know now that she must have felt trapped, with the ever-present threat of pregnancy and the never-ending workload.

But the real trap became psychological in nature. Her frustration caused by her inability to continue her intellectual interests fueled the bitterness she felt and explained her almost fanatical determination that I should be spared "her fate," as she called it. She planned for me to have an education, which would fit me for something "better than the kitchen of some man's house." As I grew older, she used to talk to me about this more and more.

---

1   I still have the beautiful china doll with yellow hair and blue eyes that Clara gave to her daughter Jessie, my grandmother, that fateful Christmas.

Jessie (left) with siblings, Emily and Fred

My brother Fred, my sister Emily, and I went to Carlisle School, an excellent school, on the edge of Pueblo. We lived three miles from the school, out of the valley, up over the hills, and across the prairie. As we got older, our father bought us a Shetland pony and cart to drive to school. That little pony and cart created a sensation at the Carlisle School.

It was a regular public school with a principal who was a very strong, domineering woman and an excellent teacher. But I never liked Miss Chase; she complained that her life was very difficult because she never could get Jessie Haver to stop talking, in class or out. I also had a gifted teacher of rhetoric in the fourth grade—her teaching has stayed with me all my life. She was a homely little woman with a hunchback, but a great teacher. I loved English rhetoric even at that age.

In the fourth grade, I invited all the girls in my class to come out to our ranch one Saturday in the summer for a picnic.

I planned the entire day down to the smallest detail. We were to spend the morning in the barn. After lunch, each girl would have a ride on the pony, and after that we would go to the river. My brother,

Fred, was furious and hurt because we excluded him from all the fun and food. I insisted upon an all-feminine day on the theory that we would have more fun that way. Afterward I felt ashamed for being so selfish with my brother, whom I really loved for we were pals. Fred and I often snuck out at night to raid the neighbor's fields for extra food.

The girls were thrilled with the ropes in the barn, flying through the air as though they were on a trapeze. Each had to wait her turn in order to be fair to all. With much giggling and laughing, every girl took a ride on the pony, sedately walking up and down the lane. But soon this became too tame, so we took the pony to the orchard to see if we could ride bareback. We dropped down onto his back from the limb of an overhanging apple tree and stood barefoot on his rump. Only one girl had sufficient poise to remain standing as we led him gently out of the orchard. The rest of us promptly fell off.

I saved the trump card for last. I knew that wading in the river would give them an experience they would never forget. As it turned out, I was right. The choicest spot on the riverbank was on a stretch of warm sand backed by a grove of willow trees. Cut off from prying eyes, like those of my brother for example, the sheltered spot proved a blessing for as we waded in the bright, warm sunshine, first one petticoat, then another, dipped down into the water.

"Take it off and hang it on a bush," was my sage advice to a girl frightened of what her mother would say. Soon the willow trees were decorated with an array of white petticoats drying in the sun.

Then came my next spontaneous inspiration. "Let's take off everything! Then we can go in where it's deep and really have fun." With that, I began to strip.

Everyone giggled gleefully at the idea, but at first, only one or two followed my example.

"What are you waiting for?" I called out. "The boys go in naked, so why can't we?"

My conservative cousin, Edna, continued to wade, fully clothed, trying not to look shocked. Soon the willow trees were covered with a rainbow of dresses and petticoats.

I can still see our twelve white bodies falling recklessly in and out of the water. I can hear the gleeful screams as we ducked and threw water onto each other with abandon.

Suddenly it dawned on my guests what a dreadful thing they had been persuaded to do. They began to dress instantly. All of them looked ashamed except me. They gathered their belongings, along with their lunch baskets, and made for home with hardly a thank you to me or my mother.

The following Monday, I found myself treated with noticeable stiffness by all my girl classmates, who had no doubt told their mothers what had happened. Their mothers, I suspected, told them I could not be a very nice little girl. Of course, the ostracism that followed really hurt.

Finally I related the incident to my mother. She smiled to herself but pointed out that I had taken a serious risk. The river was full of quicksand and deep water holes, into which one of us might have fallen and been sucked under. Then she confessed that she and my uncle had anxiously hunted for us up and down the river that afternoon. Evidently, the grove of willows had concealed us.

Thus, I suffered early in life for trying to "free" the members of my sex. Yet there lingered more a feeling of satisfaction having dared them to do something against their upbringing. Somehow I knew I had given them an experience they would never forget.

Jessie, age ten

Home on the prairie, three miles outside Pueblo, Colorado

CHAPTER 2

Tragedies Strike

First, my little sister Frances drowned in the irrigation ditch. I got the fantastic idea that she wasn't dead, only asleep. I wanted them to open the coffin and let her out. At the graveside, my ten-year-old self became hysterical, screaming that they were burying her alive.

Frances was buried on a Wednesday. My mother followed her to the grave the next Saturday.

How could I know that the situation was not of my making? What is there in the soul of a child that makes one so ready to take on the unbearable burden of guilt? For me the burden became particularly heavy because I'd had no time to recover from the shock of the first tragic death before the second occurred . . . and all within a single week. The whole world crashed in on me.

The Colorado Chieftain (Pueblo, Colorado)
Thursday, May 13, 1897

FUNERAL OF MRS. HAVER.

Services at the Family Home Conducted by Rev. A. A. Tanner.

A long line of carriages filled with bereaved friends followed the hearse that conveyed the remains of Mrs. Clara Haver yesterday afternoon to their last resting place in Mountain View cemetery. Short services were held at the house, three miles west of the city, and they were conducted by Rev. Allen A. Tanner. There were many beautiful floral tributes.

When I came to, I found Miss Finch and her mother installed as our housekeepers. My mother always told my father that if anything ever happened to her, he was to get Miss Finch to take care of the children. Her skill with children became apparent at once in the way she handled me. She told me to get on my pony, Robin, and ride as much as I liked. So, for many days I left home early in the morning and again right after our noon meal.

I rode by myself for hours across the prairie, which swept up to the base of the Rocky Mountains off in the distance. Over in the north, Pikes Peak, towered over us, still capped with glistening white snow. Gradually, I gained some feeling of stability.

School became my heaven. There, through books and learning, lay paths to adventures, security, and the outside world. My mother told me so, and I felt it must be true. I became important there, for I eventually led my classes with a report card filled with A's.

One spring day, our teacher told us to put away our books, explaining that we were to have a treat that morning. A very famous man was coming to our town—a candidate for the presidency of the United States.

William Jennings Bryan (1860-1925)
United States Secretary of State

He had a massive brow. His eyes were large and gentle. Then he began to speak in a powerful voice with great depth and beauty such as I had never heard before. There, before my eyes, stood the Great Commoner, the Silver-Tongued Orator of America, William Jennings Bryan.

I never forgot hearing that noble man speak. For weeks after I could hear his resonant voice ring through my ears. As I looked up into his face, I made a great decision: someday I am going into public life.

Eventually my father married Miss Finch, and a year later little Bobby was born. Past forty years old when the baby arrived, Miss Finch nearly died giving birth. Our stepmother never fully regained her strength and couldn't keep up with the demands of our cattle ranch.

Father now employed a considerable number of men who had to be fed three times a day. They ate in our dining room before we did. Then the table had to be cleared and reset and another meal served to our family. Cooking went on constantly during the long, hot summer days. My little sister Emily and I became the official dishwashers. I washed, Emily dried and put away, and we chattered like magpies all the while. Our new mother saw to it that we did our work promptly and well. How I hated it! My back ached night and day.

One evening, I rode out across the prairie at twilight seeking refuge from the incessant drudgery of our kitchen. The sky, painted in brilliant hues of gold, yellow, and rust changed before my eyes into deep pinks and reds as the colors splashed across the drifting clouds. Underneath it all was the deep sapphire blue of the mountains.

Off in the distance, a transcontinental train passed by. The lights were on in the diner and the shades were up. I saw men and women seated at supper. My heart ached to be with them. "There goes the world while I waste my life out here on the prairie," I thought.

Emily reacted differently. A sweet, loveable girl, my sister occupied herself with many little activities, and she seemed more satisfied than I with our life on the ranch.

My brother Fred loved playing jokes on us—mostly on me because the madder I got, the more fun he had.

For example, one April Fool's Day, he covered some squares of laundry soap with chocolate. Always eager to eat candy, I fell upon one with vigor. Fred rolled on the floor with laughter as I raged and gagged.

A series of catastrophes on the ranch made Father give up cattle farming. First, he sent all his cattle by train to Oklahoma to sell. When they arrived, the cattle barons said they could no longer pay what they had promised. The price proved less than Father had paid to raise and transport them. He had no choice but to accept the offer—it wasn't possible to ship all the cattle back to Colorado. The year after that, almost the entire herd got caught in quicksand and perished.

Father sold the ranch, moved us into town, and began selling real estate. So, my second year in high school found us living in a two-story white clapboard house with running water, a real bathroom, electric lights, and a telephone.

By this time, my stepmother started going through the menopause. This change, combined with the aftereffects of pregnancy after forty and a difficult confinement, began to affect her mental health. Of course, neither my father nor we children realized it at the time. Until then, she had handled us wisely, but we were puzzled by the fits of temper and sullenness to which she commenced to give way. Often she would refuse to do any housework at all. She and Bobby remained in her room upstairs for days at a time, emerging only at mealtimes and returning as soon as the meal was over. This left Emily and me with all her work, in addition to our usual dishwashing and cleaning.

Many mornings found me, during the first hour of classes, trembling so hard over some incident or scene at home that it would take two hours to calm down enough to be able to concentrate on studies. But eventually the order of the classroom won out, transporting me into the realm of intellect and harmony.

CHAPTER 3

A Heroine Enters My Life

School became a real haven for me. I loved every second I spent there. Lucky for me, I lived in a state that had one of the finest public school systems in the West. The school buildings were old and needed paint, but within those walls I was free and happy. Compared to housework, studying was fun!

It mattered little to me that I was badly dressed and without friends. I went about alone, though deep down inside I longed, in every cell of my body, to be one of the crowd. I wanted to laugh, romp, and play as the others did. But I seemed to have forgotten how.

Then a teacher came into my life who had a profound influence upon me during the rest of my high school days and for years afterward. I fell deeply in love with her on first sight, but this affection was of minor importance compared to the exciting discovery I made in my effort to attract her attention.

A handsome woman, nearly six feet tall, she moved with a stately carriage. Her clothes were smart and stylish, giving her an air of mystery and sophistication, unusual at a high school in those days. The second she entered the room I knew she was going to change my life in some way, but little did I suspect how. For alas, it seemed utterly hopeless to expect that she would ever notice the pale, self-conscious, forlorn, round-shouldered girl I had become. My only chance to attract her attention was to do well in my studies, and yet, up to that date, mathematics proved to be my most difficult subject.

At first I managed to get along fairly well, for Miss Munford was an excellent teacher who knew how to explain the problems on the blackboard. But I was stumped by the homework, which consisted of an original mathematical problem, which had to be solved on the basis of the lesson learned that day in class. Soon I noticed that when Miss Munford asked each morning how many pupils had succeeded in solving the homework problem, few if any reported success. If I could just find the correct solution every time, then she might notice me.

So, night after night, as soon as Emily and I had finished the dishes, I would sit down at the kitchen table where I did my homework and try desperately to find the answer to the math problem given us that day. But it was no use.

My will was strong enough, but my body was tired after strenuous hours at school, as well as the round of household duties before and after school. I often went to bed with the answer still evading me.

Finally, on one particular night, I stumbled off to bed still puzzling over the problem of the day. What in the world could be the solution? There must be a way to solve it. Soon I sunk into a deep sleep. Sleep had always been one of my greatest comforts.

That night I had a dream. In the dream I saw myself at the blackboard. There on the board was a drawing of the geometric figure and under it was the equation that gave me the solution.

Still in my dream, I found myself explaining the problem with the help of a pointer, and Miss Munford looked at me with an expression of surprise, as if she were seeing me for the first time. There was the answer! Still asleep, I told myself to memorize it. I repeated it to my sleeping self over and over again to make sure I would not forget.

At four the next morning, before the rest of the family awoke, I slipped out of bed and down to the kitchen. It was September, and though the days were warm, the mountain air grew cold during the night. I shivered as I hastily built a fire in the kitchen stove, but soon the room was warm and cozy. I pulled the kitchen table in front of the fire. With intense excitement, I wrote out the problem on a fresh piece of paper with my mind as clear as crystal.

Jessie and siblings with Grandfather
— Herman Rehwoldt

The solution proved itself. Mentally I danced with joy. I had the answer! I had it! Now Miss Munford would notice me. She would like me! I had won!

That morning as I climbed onto my bicycle, I felt like
a conquering hero. Now at last I could meet her without
embarrassment and look her straight in the eyes. What did it matter
that I had ill-fitting dresses and bent shoulders? I had found a mind
within myself! My heart was beating fast, the blood rushed to my
face. My hands were cold as the moment arrived for reports on the
mathematical problem.

"Who has the solution to the homework problem?" the teacher
asked. Not another hand was raised as mine shot into the air.
Surprised, Miss Munford turned to me. "Why, Jessie, do you have
the answer?"

I gleefully wrote out the solution on the board, exactly as in the
dream, and in a loud, boastful voice I explained the solution, after
which I walked proudly back to my seat. I have a hunch that my
boastful attitude did not add much to the scant popularity that I
then enjoyed from my classmates.

Popularity—much as I would have liked to have it—was of
much less importance to me than the goal for which I strived. I had
other fish to fry!

Homework became easy for me during the rest of the year.
For one thing, I now knew that I could do it. At eight thirty every
evening, I sat down in the bare little kitchen and tackled the other
subjects, leaving geometry to the last.

Then I laid out the homework problem for the next morning
and copied it down on a fresh piece of paper to memorize and
dream about.

I showed up to school with the solution to the mathematical
problem every day for several weeks when Miss Munford called me
to her desk after the other pupils left.

She turned to me. "Jessie, I want you to tell me something. You
have been solving the homework problem now for some time. At
first you seemed to find geometry difficult, then suddenly you started
coming in with the correct solution every day. I wish you would tell
me who is helping you."

*Jessie's family moved to 1052 Veta Avenue in Pueblo, Colorado
— a home with running water*

I pulled myself up to my full height and, looking her squarely in the eyes, said, "Miss Munford, I would not dream of having someone else solve my mathematical problems for me."

I did not tell her how I managed to reach the correct solutions. Wild horses could not have dragged that secret out of me. I feared that if I told Miss Munford that I dreamed the correct answers, she would laugh at me or refuse to believe it.

Jessie's father, Edwin B. Haver

Jessie, age 12, sitting sidesaddle on her pony, Robin

CHAPTER 4

Three Miracles and Another Tragedy

Our principal resembled Abraham Lincoln—tall and lanky with big staring eyes. The day I went up to his office to tell him I wanted to go East after graduation, Mr. Barrett put many more stars into my firmament. When I indicated that I preferred a women's college, he suggested Smith. He said it was one of the most democratic of the women's colleges and gave me the address to write for an application.

Shivers ran down my back that night as I wrote to the registrar of Smith College for a catalogue. Some manipulation was required to procure the ten dollars enrollment fee, but I eventually triumphed. Then, in due time—unbeknownst to my family—I received notice that my application was on file at Northampton, Massachusetts.

My stepmother had days and weeks when she carried on her household duties quite normally. Then there were days when she and Bobby remained in her room. I became afraid of her and her threats to set fire to the house, threats that were being repeated more and more often. So, I obeyed her commands out of downright fear.

School life carried along happily enough throughout my senior year, although my stepmother interfered with homework by finding extra chores for me to do. Soon, I sensed that she wanted to keep me from going away to college.

Mr. Barrett selected me to appear on the commencement program because of my outstanding scholastic record; I earned almost all A's that year. He asked me to read *The Lost Word* by Henry Van Dyke.

One bright Saturday morning, I raced through the breakfast dishes in order to get off to town. I had an appointment to have my commencement dress fitted. But my stepmother, in one of her bad moods, announced that I could not leave until I cleaned the entire house.

The dressmaker didn't have a telephone, and I would lose the appointment. The dress might not be finished in time. So I protested. Whereupon she said, "If you go out that door, you need never return again."

I stopped dead in my tracks. What an idea! She had opened the door for me. All I had to do was step out! This I did, although I could hardly walk, I trembled so.

I kept my appointment and afterwards found a room to rent in a school friend's home, Lorena Underhill—a sweet, clean room, which I could have until after graduation. Next, I went on to Father's office and announced to him that I had left home. He looked at me stunned. But what could he do?

What a relief from tension! My old friend Sleep, who had deserted me of late, came back. Twelve hours a night in restful slumber. There were no more household duties to perform.

My father, brothers, sister, and stepmother came to the commencement exercises, but no one seemed impressed by my performance of *The Lost Word*. My father did admit that I was the only speaker on the platform except the principal who could be heard.

By now, my father realized I remained determined to go east for my education. He would have preferred to send me to the state university at Boulder, not far away and certainly less expensive than Smith.

Just three weeks before I was to leave for Northampton, Father came to the Underhills', late one afternoon, to take me home. That morning our stepmother had committed suicide.

The minister who officiated at her funeral visited us in due course. When he learned that I planned to go east to college, he pointed out that my duty lay at home with my family.

The next day, my guardian-angel schoolteacher, Miss Munford, returned from her vacation in Ohio. When she learned of our tragedy, she called at once on my father.

"I hope Jessie is carrying on with her plans to go to Smith College," she said.

"But what will I do without her?" my father asked.

"That's your problem, not hers. If you don't send her out of here at once, she will be dead in a year," Miss Munford answered. "She can't endure any more crises. She's been pushed to her limits already."

A second angel came to call on my father. I had spent many weekends with my close friend from school, Mary Thornton, on her family's beautiful ranch. They had accepted me into their family as if I were one of their own. Mary's father, Cholmondeley Thornton, an aristocratic Englishman, pointed out to my father the precarious state of my health. Without a change in environment, Mr. Thornton said, my father would soon be arranging another funeral. He went on to say it was a miracle that I'd carried on as well as I had all these years under so much strain.

Then the third miracle took place. A letter arrived from Emily Bonham, my father's second cousin, asking to come for a visit. Several days later, we met her at the Union Depot in Pueblo. There stepped off the train, into the glowing Colorado twilight, one of the prettiest women I have ever seen with velvet brown eyes and a gay smile.

The next day, when I returned home late in the afternoon, what a sight greeted my eyes as I entered the kitchen. Amid fragrant smells of a dinner cooking, the linoleum shone, the coal and wood stoves gleamed with fresh blacking, and a spotless white tablecloth showcased freshly polished silver.

All was settled by the next morning. Cousin Emily, who evidently enjoyed cooking and cleaning, would stay as our housekeeper and homemaker. I could leave for college without a qualm. She helped me pack my few clothes for the long journey across the continent. I stopped every now and then to gaze in awe at the fascinating long, green railroad ticket in my purse—my passport to freedom.

PUEBLO, COLO., FRIDAY, SEPTEMBER 1, 1905.

BODIES OF MOTHER AND SON FOUND IN BESSEMER DITCH

*Actual headline from the Pueblo Chieftain Newspaper
of Jessie's stepmother's death*

Jessie's high school graduating class with Mr. Barrett
(Mr. Barrett standing in back row, far left)

Chapter 5

Off to Smith College

Finally, the day for departure arrived. Cholmondeley Thornton rushed down from his ranch to join Miss Munford and my family at the railroad station, as the train for Colorado Springs pulled in shrouded by a cloud of dust and a rattle of brakes.

And then I was off without a backward glance. It was September 1906, I was almost twenty years old, as I settled myself into a Pullman seat on a train headed for Chicago. Finally, I found myself one of the passengers. In my pocketbook, I carried a check large enough to pay tuition and board for half a year, with plenty left over to open a checking account. At last there was nothing to do but think, sleep, and eat. Eating was no problem for I could feast on the bountiful supply of fresh chicken sandwiches, dainty cakes, and fruit, prepared and carefully packed by Emily Bonham.

I watched the landscape of my life thus far roll away: the parched, dry earth; the scattered, emaciated farms where human beings struggled to make a living against almost impossible odds; the tumbleweeds, which in the spring danced across the prairies in billows of dust as high as the horizon. I suppose the stark scenery symbolized the starved existence I left behind.

By the time the train pulled into the station in Chicago, I felt unbelievably rested and refreshed. There was a two-hour wait in Chicago where my reservation had been made for the New York Central train carrying a Smith College car. How very important I felt to be going to a college that rated a special train car all its own!

As I sat with my bags around me, quietly drinking in the fascination of a city railroad station, I noticed several groups of people gathered around young girls who obviously were going to be on my car. How beautiful they were! So gay and happy with their loving, attractive parents and friends to see them off! The air was filled with laughter and anticipation. I had never seen such fashionable, clever-looking people.

The mothers intrigued me the most. Such fine-looking, well-dressed women they were! What must it be like to have such a mother? I could not imagine. But at the same time, I felt that I was not so badly off. I was having the fun of running my own life from now on with no one to tell me what to do.

That evening on the train, I ventured into the diner, my food box having been exhausted. I went early so that no one would see what an amateur I was at ordering a meal. The headwaiter placed a lovely girl opposite me. She was short with the bluest of eyes and curly, fair hair. I figured she was an upperclassman, for I had noticed her greeting old friends earlier.

She was very courteous and sure of herself, but a bit condescending and obviously uninterested. We ate in silence with little conversation, except that I told her I was a freshman and she in turn told me that this was her last year.

This experience should have warned me that my road ahead might not be too easy, but what did that matter? Nothing really mattered except that I was on my way to Smith College!

I awakened at nine the next morning and rolled up the blind to a vista of unbelievably verdant countryside. Rows of the greenest trees I had ever seen bordered the fields (such a contrast to the faded cottonwoods of the river valley in Colorado).

Our car was now filled with laughing girls, most of them upperclassmen, welcoming friends as they were picked up along the way. Snatches of talk about the lazy summer at the seashore or the lakes floated my way. The girls groaned because vacation was over, and they must return to college and the dreary business of books.

Most of them seemed quite sophisticated to me. They wore their handsome clothes with such ease. They were so sure of themselves! Was it possible that I could ever look and behave like them? It seemed hard to believe.

Just as we pulled into Northampton, the sun celebrated my arrival by popping out of the clouds with the brilliant radiance of an early fall afternoon. I found myself on the station platform amid crowds of shouting, laughing girls and trunks piled as high as the station roof.

I stuffed myself into a crowded taxi with three others. The taxi lumbered up the cobblestones of the broad, curving main street of Northampton, lined with gaily decorated shop windows on both sides, until we reached the wide gates that led onto the campus. Through these gates we drove down a straight concrete road bordered by green, well-kept lawns, past the dark red-brick dormitories set at varying angles and covered with ivy.

It was the first ivy I had ever seen. From each tiny leaf and blade of grass clung a glistening drop of rainwater, sparkling like a jewel in the soft rays of the sun. There was magic in the air for me. There was magic in the thought that I too was now part of this beautiful landscape.

My room was not large; it was furnished with two cot beds, two dressers, two battered desks, and a clothes closet. The furniture was made of yellow pine, nicked and dinged with hard use. I began at once to unpack and make myself at home.

I had not been there long before my roommate arrived, accompanied by a very elegant mother and a porter carrying an armful of bags. Mabel was short, dark, and very pretty. The mother gave the room one look and me a second look, then before you could say "Jack Robinson," she snatched Mabel out of there and deposited her in a large corner room on the second floor, alone.

But later in the evening she came up to see me. She said she was sorry that she was not going to room with me.

"I can see your mother's point, Mabel," I tried to reassure her.

"I've just come all the way from Colorado alone because my mother is dead. I had no one to help me with my clothes, and I know they are not right. You just wait a bit. I'll get better ones."

The next morning, Mabel offered to go downtown with me to buy new clothes. Her closet bulged with beautiful new dresses, which she seemed to accept as a matter of course, but she jumped at the idea of helping me shop.

The shops were filled with beautiful dresses suitable for college girls. In no time we found a dress for school and an evening dress for the freshman party that was in the offing. Then Mabel took me to her room to show me a new way to arrange my hair.

Soon a soft, fresh glow bloomed in my cheeks and my eyes grew bright with excitement. Some of the girls grumbled incessantly about the food, but not a word of complaint came from me. I ate every morsel, grateful that I did not have to prepare it. I couldn't get enough.

Two days later, as I plowed through the mob of chattering students at the first school party, someone rushed up, grabbed me by the arm, and all but swept me off my feet. Lo and behold, there stood my former table companion on the train, the haughty senior, Gail Tritch.

She looked at me in wonder. Could I be the same repressed, sickly-looking girl she had dined with a few days ago? She couldn't believe her eyes, she told me afterward. She had made up her mind that I would last about two weeks. Well, she didn't know me! I was there to stay. So, she took me in hand, introduced me to dozens of her friends, and later became one of my best friends.

And so my new life at the college began under the best of auspices. My dream was now a reality.

Jessie as a Freshman at Smith College

Smith College, 1906

ANNA PENFIELD HARWOOD
515 Meade St.
Appleton, Wis.

EDITH HODGEN HATCH
Hotel Beardsley
Champaign, Ill.

MARGUERITE SOUTHMAYD HATCH
Norwalk, Conn.

MARGARET HATFIELD
108 Cherry St.
West Newton, Mass.

JESSIE REHWOLDT HAVER
1052 Veta Ave.
Pueblo, Col.

LOUISE CATHARINE HAY
26 Front St.
Bellows Falls, Vt.

ALMA ESTELLE HAYDOCK
173 Orange Road
Montclair, N. J.

ELIZABETH HAYS
14 Washington Terrace
St. Louis, Mo.

GRACE ADELAIDE HAZELTINE
Warren, Pa.

Jessie in Smith College yearbook with classmates

CHAPTER 6

A New England Education

S ophia Smith, founder of Smith College, could hardly have found a more lovely setting for a women's college than that provided in Northampton in the heart of New England. Also, I doubt if any student ever came to that campus who enjoyed the beautiful setting more than I did.

The fall flowers were everywhere—in formal beds around the dormitories and classrooms, near the greenhouse surrounded by perennial shrubs, and down by Paradise Lake at one side of the campus. They grew wild—all without irrigation!

Early in October, as I raced across campus to morning Chapel, I looked toward the familiar maple tree near Paradise Lake. Only it was not familiar that morning. During the night, someone had taken a brush and painted every leaf a bright golden yellow.

As the nights grew sharp with cold, other trees changed their appearances in different colors, all brilliant and varied. Some were bright rust, some a flat red, some kept their soft green but with yellow tinges at the tips of the leaves. Gradually the ivy on the dormitory changed into shades of yellow and deep rust.

Later, when the leaves began to drop to the ground, they resembled an oriental carpet, which I liked to walk upon as I took shortcuts across campus. The leaves made a swishing sound as I walked. The entire campus was aglow that autumn with color showcasing different effects as the sun rose and set.

On most Saturday afternoons, I joined a group of students who, armed with hastily purchased food, set out for the country to Mount

Tom or some distant spot in the north.

I needed all the breathers of this sort I could get, for soon I began to worry about studies. The college authorities made things as difficult as possible the first three months to test out new students. Rumor had it that every year a certain number of students were sure to be dropped and sent home. The very thought of being sent home was enough to keep me awake most nights!

Since book learning had never been easy for me, I developed a rigid routine of study, something the early mornings before the kitchen stove in Pueblo had taught. It was difficult to study in my room with all the chattering around and girls dropping in at all hours of the day and night.

So, I took myself to the college library, and there, hidden in an alcove alone, I struggled with Latin, Greek, and mathematics. I had to go over and over each lesson, but I was more than willing to do so because I had to stay in college. I knew that if ever I were to be sent home because I had failed in my studies, it would be the end of me!

During my four years at Smith, I read all of H. G. Wells, Bernard Shaw's plays and prefaces, and many other authors of the day, as well as most of the current magazines.

From the beginning of my freshman year, continuous arguments took place in our room. We discussed religion, marriage, men, and politics for hours on end. My bed sagged from the weight of students crowding on top of it.

Before we knew it, Thanksgiving was upon us. It hardly seemed possible to me that the months had passed, for it was only yesterday that I had caught my first glimpse of the campus. Now I felt as if I had lived there all my life.

Mabel invited me to her home in Newburyport for Thanksgiving weekend. I can still feel the thrill of excitement as our train rattled over the roadbed of the Boston and Albany Railroad, crowded with happy girls escaping the pressure of study and college life.

I soon saw why Mabel came escorted to college by both parents. Her home was a beautiful palace, and she was an over-protected princess. Her father and mother treated her as if she were still a child, yet they gratified her every whim. I felt deeply jealous of her. I would have given anything for just one month of such attention, for a few of the clothes and gifts, which were showered upon her but which she accepted with indifference.

Mabel's father was a successful manufacturer of combs. From the first, he talked to me about his business, as my father had done during my last years at home. Later he told Mabel that I was one of the most interesting friends she had ever brought home because I had so much "common sense."

My first matinee in Boston was a great thrill. The only play I had seen to date was *The Little Minister* starring Maude Adams[2] in the opera house in Pueblo. This time we sat in expensive seats near the front so we would not miss a word, although now I cannot even remember the name of the play!

Mabel thought it dull, but I loved every minute of it, from the moment we entered the beautiful theatre on Tremont Street until the last curtain fell. Then Mabel's father took us to tea at the Hotel Touraine on the corner of Boylston and Tremont Streets.

The soft carpets, the heavy draperies, the quiet tinkling of silver against china, the fragrance of flowers, and the sight of other guests so beautifully dressed and sophisticated in manner created an atmosphere of luxury that took my breath away.

Back in Newburyport, we drove through the town and down to the seashore, where I saw my first glimpse of the Atlantic Ocean. I could not get enough of it.

All too soon, Thanksgiving vacation was over, and we were hurrying back to college. Monday morning, the routine was on again, but I liked the stability of my new life.

It was not long before I understood why New England needed no irrigation, as the rain fell for days on end during that fall. We all had to buy rubber coats, boots, and umbrellas. Later the rain changed into ice and snow, and Paradise Lake turned into a shiny mirror of ice.

---

2   Maude Ewing Adams Kiskadden (1872 –1953), known professionally as Maude Adams, was an American actress who achieved her greatest success as the character Peter Pan on Broadway.

As soon as notices appeared on the bulletin boards announcing safe skating, I bought the best pair of hockey skates that the store could provide. They were fastened to warm skating boots with good leather ankle braces.

I felt guilty about paying the huge sum of eight dollars, but in the end it paid off, for I skated eight hours that first day, cutting all classes. More and more I was taking Miss Munford's advice: "Have fun in college," she had said. "Don't study all the time, but learn to have fun." Well, skating surely fell into that category!

One winter morning, I decided to go for an early morning horseback ride, another of my rare extravagances. The riding stables were located down a side street. On this same street, I passed the factory where high-grade silk stockings were made. On this particular morning, I ran into the motley crowd of young and older women on their way to work.

It was seven thirty in the morning and barely daylight. These workers from another planet looked cold as they hurried along in their shabby clothes. Often in the evenings I noticed them wearily walking on their way home.

That was the era of the ten-hour day for factory workers. Judging by the looks of the workers, mighty low wages were the rule as well. For some reason, I felt bothered by these contrasts to the world in which I now lived.

Northampton is surrounded by towns with many factories. The bare factory walls, with only an occasional window so dirty that no light could possibly enter, looked forbidding and terrified me when I thought of the hundreds of people bottled up inside.

During the winter months, they saw little of the beautiful world around them, except on Sundays, for they went in when it was dark and came out when it was dark again.

I signed up for some writing courses. I did not want to write fiction; I merely wanted to write what I thought about a lot of questions, especially because we had so little opportunity to express ourselves in the classrooms. Original or creative thinking on our part was not encouraged, I soon found out.

McCallum Hosiery Mill near Smith College where Jessie later helped set the minimum wage from $4 a week to $8 when she worked for The Minimum Wage Commission in Boston

I also took one course in public speaking, but here again, the teacher was concerned with voice placement and diction. I still had a voice that could be heard for miles, but what I wanted was to learn how to give expression to my thoughts so I could influence others or share knowledge with them.

Then, almost overnight it seemed, June came and I was on the train for home. I arrived radiantly healthy and tastefully dressed. I had seen the world! What a contrast I must have been to the sickly, pale, uncertain eighteen-year-old who departed Union Station in Pueblo just nine months ago. It is a miracle how quickly youth can heal!

It soon became evident that there was not room in the one house for two women. Emily Bonham and I got along fairly well, but of course I resented being delegated back to the kitchen to do the dishwashing when I had been in charge of myself for such a long time. And so I spent many weekends at the Thornton Ranch, where there was always good talk and something to do.

One day Mr. Thornton asked, "Jessie, what are you going to do when you finish college?"

"Oh, teach I suppose," I said casually.

"You would make a damned poor teacher," he told me. "I'll tell you what you might do. I believe you have inherited good business judgment from your father. Why don't you study shorthand and typing during your summer vacations? There are many executives today who need educated women secretaries. I believe you would find unlimited opportunities for employment if you added shorthand and typing to your college education."

"A Smith College graduate a stenographer or clerk? Hardly," I said to myself, feeling a bit snobbish. However, when I returned to Colorado at the end of my sophomore year, I decided to investigate the possibilities of a secretarial course at the local business college. Anything was preferable to the housework, which father said I ought to be willing to do during the summer vacations.

In due course, I enrolled in the Pueblo Business College, conducted by Mr. and Mrs. Clarke. There I discovered that shorthand and typing required concentration and study of a high order. Also, I found out that I was a poor speller.

I found it so difficult, in fact, that I devoted full time to the study during two summer vacations. This, of course, also solved the difficulty of family living in our home, for I was at school five days a week.

I used to smile to myself when I heard my Smith classmates tell of their happy summers at the seashore, in contrast to my summers bent over a typewriter.

I never told them what I was doing, knowing full well how they would ridicule the idea of a college girl being a stenographer! Such a humble ambition was unheard of!

In my junior year, I received an infrequent letter from my father, though I was very faithful and regular with my letters home. Father wrote that he loved Emily Bonham and would like to marry her. What did I think of this plan?

Frankly, I greeted the announcement with intense relief. This would let me out of any obligations to my father's household.

And soon after that, they were married. Father was obviously very happy in his new marriage and so was Emily. She worshipped my father, hung on his every word.

She was perfectly satisfied to devote every moment of her time to making an attractive home for him. It was never hard for me to call her "Mother."

Father blossomed under the warmth of her love, which was, I fancy, the first deep affection ever lavished upon him in his long life. He used to sing while he dressed in the morning and while he worked around the yard.

When I was a college junior, I signed up for a course in psychology, conducted by Professor Pierce. Forthwith, psychology became my major and philosophy my minor, along with ethics and aesthetics.

Professor Pierce was a brilliant teacher, a pioneer in the field of psychology. I became fascinated by the subject at once and by the writings of the great British authority Havelock Ellis[3] and the American G. Stanley Hall,[4] both of whom were required reading.

In this same time period, my dear friend, Mary Thornton, married the young man she met at Yale. She invited me to be one of her bridesmaids.

The two plays I remember participating in were *She Stoops to Conquer* by Oliver Goldsmith and *A Midsummer Night's Dream*, chosen as our graduation production.

Father, afraid to leave the dry climate of Colorado since his move there so many years ago for his asthma, did not come east to see me graduate. I doubt whether he would have done so anyway, for it would have taken too much time and money from his busy office, where he was now one of the most successful real estate

---

3   Henry Havelock Ellis (1859 –1939) was an English physician, writer, progressive intellectual, and social reformer who studied human sexuality.

4   Granville Stanley Hall (February 1, 1846 –April 24, 1924) was a pioneering American psychologist and educator. His interests focused on childhood development and evolutionary theory. Hall was the first president of the American Psychological Association.

Picture of Mary Thornton's Wedding —
Jessie is the bridesmaid *(in front of the bride)*

Jessie *(far right)* **in Smith College play — She Stoops to Conquer**

operators in Pueblo. Hence, no one from home came to see me walk up that platform and receive the precious diploma, except for my high-school friend Mary Thornton and her new husband, now a professor at Yale University.

I became known as the only member of my class who didn't want to graduate! I suppose I hated to see the four happy, carefree years end. I wanted them to go on forever. One thing was certain: I had been completely successful in my studies.

**Summer spent at home
— riding with current boyfriend**

Jessie as career woman

CHAPTER 7

Career Woman in the Making

I so dreaded returning to Pueblo after my graduation in 1909 that I spent most of the summer visiting friends in the East. I didn't return home until late August. Adjustment to life in the family home is hard for any girl just out of college. The congenial companionship always available on campus, the stimulation gained from teachers and from books, the conversation and peaceful routine of college—all of these were past, and I missed them terribly. Soon it was arranged that I should work as a secretary in my father's office, learning the real estate business while perfecting shorthand and typing.

A class reunion at Northampton gave me an excuse for leaving Pueblo, this time for good. Off I went again without any fanfare of trumpets.

Our reunion was filled with reports of engagements, weddings, and babies. I pretended to be bored with all this—in fact, I persuaded myself that I honestly preferred a career to marriage. I knew that I could support myself, and I learned that I would have to do just that, sooner than I had anticipated.

That same day, I learned that Dr. Elizabeth Kemper Adams, a faculty member, had organized an employment bureau for Smith graduates, so I went to see her in College Hall. She was a bright little person, bubbling over with enthusiasm and imagination, as shown by the fact that a woman with a college education was something new in the business world, and that she needed guidance.

Her face lit up when I told her that I was a trained and experienced legal secretary, prepared to take a position in a business office.

"You are the first Smith graduate to enter this office trained to be a secretary. I've been urging students to study shorthand and typewriting for a long time. They seem to think that there is something inferior about office work. Now at last my dream has come true and here you are! I could give you eighty jobs this very minute. What a thrill!"

The most attractive opening was a position as assistant to the head of the college textbook department of the Macmillan Publishing Company on Fifth Avenue in New York City. During the interview with the head of the department, I found he wanted me to supervise the work of two stenographers and two file clerks. The catalogues of all colleges and universities needed to be searched to locate courses in which new textbooks published by Macmillan might be used.

The pay for this work proved very disappointing—only fifteen dollars a week! I did not quite see how I could conquer the world on that salary, but my boss assured me that if I made good, I would get a raise by Christmas.

So, I joined the Women's University Club on Madison Avenue and found a rooming house just around the corner, where I could use the club dining room, library, and reception rooms during the evening period.

There are no words to describe a hall bedroom in a cheap New York rooming house in the business section in those days. For one thing, the house smelled—of kerosene, mustiness, and lifelessness. The bedding was dingy and soiled; the poor excuse for a rug was threadbare; the iron bedstead, with spots of rust showing through cracked paint, creaked with every move. Why do landladies, managing this type of house, so often wear wigs? Mine did. It was a faded red wig, which did not fit her.

My new work started on September 1. At the start, I loved everything about it. I found it exciting to walk down Fifth Avenue to my very first job in the big city. The offices were airy and clean. I liked the smell of paste on the new books and the sight of stacks and stacks of books all about.

It was something of a shock to punch a timeclock upon entering and leaving, along with file clerks, salesmen, and office boys, but everyone was friendly, especially Miss Waldeck who was in charge of files.

She had worked ten years in this department. Primly dressed and much too thin, she bore the stamp of a girl who'd become the breadwinner of her family before she had time to fully grow up. But her blue eyes were always merry. She told me that my predecessor, who lasted one year, left to accept a position as editor on a women's magazine at a salary of one hundred dollars a month. So I thought that, in no time at all, I too would be making real money. Why not? Was not a college graduate something special in the business world?

Curiously enough, although my employer expected me to know shorthand and typing to secure the position, I never used either. He gave me two secretaries.

Neither in high school nor in college had such a mundane subject as letter writing received any attention. I found that I could not compose the simplest letter properly. I spent a good part of nineteen years and a large sum of money procuring the best education America could offer and still was not able to write a good business letter. It seemed to me an indictment of our educational system.

Within my first month at Macmillan's, I learned via the office grapevine that wages here tended to remain the same over the years. A legend circulated that it was such an honor to work for so distinguished a firm that people felt lucky even to be there.

The legend accomplished its purpose. I found faithful and competent employees who had been with the company for years and were still getting wages that barely kept them alive. The longer they stayed, the more they feared to leave. The company seemed to take full advantage of their fears.

The wages paid to women were the lowest of all. Miss Waldeck, who practically ran our department, had not received a raise

in over five years. They paid her twelve dollars a week, and she
was the main support of her mother. She believed her future to
be secure because she worked a steady job, but there remained
little hope in the way of advancement. She dreamed of meeting
a millionaire on a streetcar one day who would carry her off to a
palace on Fifth Avenue and a life of leisure!

The pressure of my work became terrific. From 8:30 a.m.
to 5:30 p.m. I hardly looked up from the great piles of letters
and memos heaped on my desk. I used to stagger out of Childs
Restaurant[5] on Fourteenth Street, the only place where I could
afford a full dinner, feeling every drop of vitality drained from
my body.

At Christmas time, I found an extra dollar bill in my weekly pay
envelope. The "raise by Christmas," which I had been promised,
was one dollar a week? At once, I asked for an interview with my
boss. He looked up pleasantly as I entered his office. A nice-looking
young man, but with a sarcastic twist to his smile.

"I have just received my pay envelope with an extra dollar bill.
Is that the increase you mentioned when I accepted this position . . .
the increase at Christmas time?"

"Yes, that's what I had in mind."

"How do you think I can continue to live in New York City on
sixteen dollars a week?" I asked.

"Lots of people live on much less than that," he replied,
sounding a bit irritated.

"Yes, I am sure they do, but they haven't just invested a lot of
money on a college education," I retorted.

By now, my boss was beginning to look worried, for
immediately after Christmas he planned to take a long trip to
the West Coast and counted on me to be there to manage his
department while he was gone.

---

5   Childs Restaurants was one of the first national dining chains in
the United States and Canada, having peaked in the 1920s and 1930s with
about 125 locations.

"You must admit that you are getting a fine business experience here," he said. "Any employer to whom you would apply for work when you leave the Macmillan Company will be impressed by the fact that you have worked for us. Experience here guarantees you a position anywhere. But you must leave with a good recommendation."

Now he really applied the pressure! Right then, I decided not to be roped and tied by that sort of talk, so I walked out of his office to consider my future.

John William Cunliffe

CHAPTER 8

I Help Put Together
the Pulitzer School of Journalism

I remained so scared that I could hardly think for the rest of the day. What a dreadful thing I had done—walking into his office like that and challenging him! How like me! When would I learn to be a lady, pleasant and easy-going? Why couldn't I stop this habit of kicking against circumstances and just be feminine and sweet? If I kept on this way, I would never earn a living.

So, I quieted down. But within a few days, on my work break, I found myself at the Associated Women's Colleges, which had just opened an employment office in New York City. I went to see the woman in charge of placements. She agreed with me that it was wise to make a change at once, and shortly afterward she offered me a position as a secretary to the director of the new Pulitzer School of Journalism being established at Columbia University.[6] When I told her my experience at Macmillan, she said, "We thought that was going on there."

My salary increased to eighty-three dollars a month, or one thousand a year. I could live in Whittier Hall, one of the university residences, where room and board would cost something like forty dollars a month. I received a real jump in salary—from $68 to $83.33 a month—with lower living expenses, no bus fare, and life on a college campus. Thus in no time, I had materially improved my status.

---

6   The Columbia University Graduate School of Journalism, founded by Joseph Pulitzer in 1912, is located in Pulitzer Hall in New York City. It is the only journalism school in the Ivy League and one of the oldest in the world.

I left the Macmillan Company without a backward look. The experience proved to be a bitter disappointment to me, but I know now that it was valuable. I learned business methods in a large organization. I learned many interesting facts about books and how they are produced. Most important of all, I made the adjustment from the status of a protected girl at home and at college to that of a woman standing on her own feet and paying her own way. I also found out how easy it is to exploit women in business as well as in the home.

My new boss, Professor Cunliffe,[7] was a pleasant man to work for. I liked his methodical, deliberate, easy manner with no strain or hurry. Organizing the School of Journalism was a task for which he was well suited.

He seemed to enjoy his dip into administrative duties. He exercised a quiet way of getting things worked out as he wanted them, without agitation or tension. My desk was at one end of his office, so I liked to listen to the many interesting daily conferences he held with all sorts of people.

I found it fascinating, over the next year, to help a new school being built from the ground up and fitted into a great university system. The adaptation of the newspaper business from downtown New York into the slow-moving, deliberate machinery of academic life proved full of surprises but also produced many sources of friction.

There was Arthur Brisbane[8] from the Hearst papers and Franklin Mathews from *The New York Times* ("Boss" Mathews the students called him.) There is a plaque in his memory at the entrance to the newsroom today, which reads as follows:

---

7   John William Cunliffe (1865–1946) was a scholar and author. He was a professor and English department chairman at Columbia University and also directed the school's journalism department.

8   Arthur Brisbane (1864 –1936) was one of the best-known American newspaper editors of the twentieth century.

Franklin Mathews

1858–1917

Associate Professor of Journalism in Columbia University
Serene, kindly, tolerant, he won the affection
and regard of all who knew him.

Presented by alumni who cherish his memory.

My private life brought me into contact with all kinds of interesting people. I was introduced to Greenwich Village life. I went through the usual round of wild parties, long discussions of everything on earth, and thrilling meetings with "geniuses" and "near-geniuses," writers, poets, politicians, lawyers, musicians, and actors—most of them young and dreaming of future fame.

We met at restaurants in all sorts of unexpected places—in basements and down dark side streets, where our friends knew good food was to be had, as New Yorkers have always known.

Sometimes we would spend half the night going from one eating place to another.

I decided from the beginning to stay away from alcoholic beverages, not because of moral suasion but because I thought I didn't possess the self-control to drink in moderation. What I did, I did with vigor, and drinking might fall into that same category. My party friends were amused at this firm decision, but they ordered pink grenadine as they explained to bored waiters that I was from Pueblo, Colorado, and couldn't help my eccentricities. A teetotaler was a novelty in New York and New Yorkers like novelties, so I was always a welcome addition to our gay sorties into New York's nightlife.

Talcott Williams,[9] the new director of the Pulitzer School of Journalism, did not appear on the scene until a year later in September, just before the opening of the school. A stark contrast to Professor Cunliffe, he was a former editor of a large Philadelphia paper with a nationwide reputation as a newspaperman. He exhibited many of the bad habits of his profession: a desk piled high with letters and newspapers from all over the world; a penchant for dictating wordy letters of little consequence; endless telephone calls on all sorts of questions, none related to the business at hand; and a complete lack of understanding of academic routine.

His mop of unruly graying hair topped a massive high forehead, from under which there peered dark, penetrating eyes that fastened themselves upon one and all with a distinctly suspicious look.

Many an evening I found myself still taking dictation at 8:30 p.m., without a bite to eat. By that time, the Whittier dining hall was closed, so I had to buy a meal wherever I could get it. The instability of this man and his office soon began to tell on my health.

I decided to talk it out with the new director, though it took several days for me to gather up sufficient courage. I explained to Dr. Williams that I had come to Columbia for the shorter hours of work, that I wanted to have some life of my own outside of the job.

All night long, during a restless sleep, the following refrain ran through my mind, beating away like a drum: "Will you never learn to adapt yourself to situations as they are? Now you'll be fired. You'll have to hunt for another job, and with no recommendation to go with you." I woke up in utter despair with myself.

The next day and thereafter, Dr. Williams came hustling in promptly at one o'clock, having gone through his mail that morning. In ten minutes, I found myself taking dictation at his desk. On the dot of five o'clock, with an air of great generosity, he would say, "It's five now and time for you to go home." And off I went.

---

9   Talcott Williams (1849–1928) was an American journalist and educator. In 1912, he became director of the new School of Journalism at Columbia University after it was established by J. W. Cunliffe.

Again, a very bad employment situation from the feminist point of view. I didn't know I was a feminist in those days, but I knew what was endurable and I didn't intend to die on the job. All in all, I stayed two years.

Later on, I heard that in his long tenure as editor, Dr. Williams never kept any secretary for more than six months at a time. I suppose I made something of a record by lasting a year with him and by refusing to allow myself to be imposed upon. I find this very important for the sake of the other women who were to follow me, and very important for my own integrity as well.

I hurried down to the college employment office in search of a new job, grateful to these women for the way they were opening doors for the college women of the future.

A new chapter opened in my career. I gave up secretarial work altogether to enter a comparatively new profession for women, that of social work, a field just beginning to develop and one that initiated my long experience in public service.

MINIMUM WAGE DECREES ESTABLISHED IN MASSA-CHUSETTS UP TO JAN. 1, 1917

BRUSH DECREE.

The Minimum Wage Commission of the Commonwealth of Massachusetts, having before it the report of the Brush Makers' Wage Board, after public hearing thereupon held June 29, 1914, and for the reasons set forth in its opinion of even date, in accordance with St. 1912, c. 706, par. 6, makes the following decree: –

1. The lowest time wage paid to any experienced female employee in the brush industry shall be $15^1/_2$ cents an hour.
2. The rate for learners and apprentices shall be 65 per cent. of the minimum, and the period of apprenticeship shall not be more than one year.
3. These findings shall apply also to all minors.
4. If in any case a piece rate yields less than the minimum time rate, persons employed under such rate shall be paid at least $15^1/_2$ cents an hour.
5. This decree shall take effect on Aug. 15, 1914, and shall remain in effect until altered by the Commission.

By the order of

MINIMUM WAGE COMMISSION
OF THE COMMONWEALTH OF MASSACHUSETTS.

H. LARUE BROWN, *Chairman.*
MABEL GILLESPIE.
ARTHUR N. HOLCOMBE.

Attest:
   AMY HEWES,
      Secretary.

CHAPTER 9

Minimum Wage for Women

When I went again to the employment office on Fifth Avenue, they found me a job in Boston as a statistician and investigator for the Massachusetts Minimum Wage Commission at a salary of $1,300 a year. Amy Hewes, executive secretary of the commission, gave the interview and then invited me to come to Boston the next month. I was hired to help bring about a minimum wage for working women.

This was the era when women were beginning to work outside the home. They were earning around four dollars a week in candy factories, in laundries, and in five-and-dime stores. The Massachusetts Consumer's League had secured passage of a law that allowed employees of the Minimum Wage Commission to copy payrolls. The Commission sent us out to big factories and industries to copy payrolls, and they taught me how to put them into statistical tables. I received a comprehensive education and training.

I wanted, more than anything else, to help women. I became dedicated, in a way, to the woman's world and the needs of women. That dedication was born from the tragedy of my own family life and my mother's death when I was ten.

The Commission sent me to Northampton, Massachusetts, to copy payrolls at the McCallum Hosiery Mill, the very factory I used to walk by on the way to the riding school in my college years.

I often glanced out the windows, as I sat in the office of the mill copying the tedious payrolls, to watch the college girls going by. The carefree life of Smith College now seemed to belong to another world. It didn't seem quite right somehow.

During my second year in Boston, I joined the Boston Fabian Society, modeled on the British group of that name. George Grover Mills, formerly a Unitarian minister, was founder of the Boston group. We met every other week where we enjoyed a buffet supper, followed by a lecture from a prominent person on some political subject of the day.

I left Boston after four years to become an employee of the U.S. Bureau of Labor Statistics. World War I was on, and I heard they were looking for statisticians to do a survey of the cost of living in Washington, D.C.

Mill workers circa 1908

By the time I left Boston, the minimum wage became an accepted fact. It doubled from four dollars a week to eight. When Edward Filene built the most beautiful women's store in Boston, all this shouting about a minimum wage had reached his ear. From the beginning, he offered the highest minimum wage ever paid, eight dollars a week, and so the finest saleswomen came to his store, which thrived.

Young mill workers labored long hours for very low wages in unsafe conditions

***Jessie Haver joined the Suffrage Movement
in Washington, D.C.***

CHAPTER 10

Moving to Washington, D.C.
and Joining the Suffrage Struggle

Immediately upon arrival to Washington, D.C., in 1916, I became involved in the women's suffrage movement, which at that time was working to get a resolution through the U.S. Senate. In Boston I had attended a lot of meetings on suffrage and birth control. Margaret Sanger often came up to Boston and lectured because they had a very bad law in Massachusetts and no information on birth control. I also went several times to hear Mrs. Pankhurst lecture when she came from England. I attended all the big suffrage meetings.

I began going to Alice Paul's place. She and I were born in the same year—1886. Alice had a PhD from the London School of Economics, where she learned her militant methods. The leader of the National Woman's Party, she had been given a lot of money by Mrs. O. H. P. Belmont[10] and organized a lovely house as her headquarters right on the edge of Lafayette Park, across from the White House. There was a big dining room, and I took a great many of my luncheons there, even while I was working in the U.S. Bureau of Labor Statistics, and that's where I met all those women. They were my intimate friends. One of the leading pickets, Mrs. Harvey Wiley, later became one of the women who attended my first class in public speaking when I returned to Washington after eight years in London.

---

10   Alva Belmont (1853 –1933), known as Alva Vanderbilt from 1875 to 1896, was a prominent multimillionaire American socialite and a major figure in the American women's suffrage movement.

Then there was Mrs. Kent, the wife of William Kent, who would later give me the money to travel cross-country, speaking with Carrie Chapman Catt. They all went to prison for picketing the White House, when they made newspaper headlines for going on a hunger strike and, as a consequence, having food pushed down their throats with a hose so they wouldn't become martyrs.

Carrie Chapman Catt worked many years with Susan B. Anthony and founded the League of Women Voters in 1920

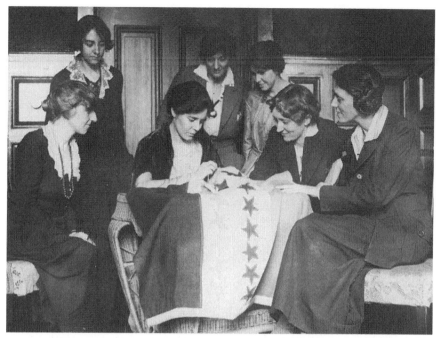

Alice Paul sewing a star on a flag for each state ratified

I was very close to all the action. Often, when I went to luncheon or tea, Alice Paul's group worked hard to line me up with their more radical methods, but I couldn't be converted. For one thing, I soon became a lobbyist at the Capitol for the Consumers League.

And I wasn't inclined to go in for as rugged a program as they followed. I liked Mrs. Catt's legislative system better, but I believe we'd never have achieved women's suffrage if we had depended only on Mrs. Catt! Handed the baton by her mentor, Susan B. Anthony, she spent twenty years working for women's rights and remained very much a statistician and a parliamentarian.

Alice Paul, much younger—my age—and a Quaker from a prominent family in Mount Laurel, New Jersey, had been taught by Mrs. Pankhurst in England when she received her doctorate in London. Alice Paul followed Mrs. Pankhurst's militant way of fighting. This Mrs. Catt vehemently disagreed with, and that's why they separated.

There is another explanation for the fierce antagonism between these two women reformers. Their birthdays were within two days of each other: Alice Paul was born January 11, 1886, and Mrs. Catt on January 9, 1859. To have two Capricorns latched together in a violent historical struggle could hardly be more trying. Each stood for the truth as she saw it, and each in her own way brought about lasting freedom and equality for women.

When I first arrived, Washington, D.C., was bathed in warm sunlight. A soft, balmy breeze floated on the air that morning in early April as I walked down 17th Street from my rooming house on Eye Street, past the side entrance of the War and Navy Building, into the Labor Department on F Street, across from Pearlman's bookstore.

The magnolias were bursting into bloom. Their fat white petals, faced with pink, shone in the sunlight. Yellow forsythia and trailing bridal-wreath were in flower everywhere, giving vivid color to gardens and parks along the way. The flower shops down 17th Street were filled with vases of spring daffodils, tulips, and narcissus. Everyone moved along in leisurely fashion as though there were no special hurry.

Soon, I joined sixteen women investigators in the offices of Royal Meeker,[11] chief of the U.S. Bureau of Labor Statistics, in the Labor Department. We were given maps of the city and a questionnaire to follow in our interviews. Each investigator was assigned to certain sections of the city and, forthwith, we became doorbell ringers. Seldom did anyone slam a door in our faces when it was revealed that we came from the government on a mission of helpfulness.

We tramped along streets of row houses in the north and southeast, where government civil servants of the lower grades lived; sometimes we caught a glimpse of the "poverty alleys," for which Washington became so notorious.

---

11   President Wilson appointed Meeker Commissioner of Labor Statistics in 1913. As the commissioner of the Bureau of Labor Statistics, Meeker managed special economic studies during World War I and began its regular publication, the *Monthly Labor Review*, in 1915.

In Boston we copied exact figures on weekly wages; here we had
the figures on monthly or bimonthly wages to jot down, then we
had to find out where the money went. We struggled with people's
inaccurate recollections. Few of them either budgeted their income
or kept written accounts of their expenditures. Housewives had
to estimate the amount they habitually spent for meat, groceries,
clothing, recreation, et cetera, in any given month.

Irene Graham from Buffalo was my roommate. We heard
that there were canoes to be hired on the outskirts of Washington.
So, one beautiful Sunday morning, we took the streetcar out
Pennsylvania Avenue to Dempsey's boathouse on the Potomac River.

The Chesapeake and Ohio Canal, built by George Washington
to bring coal from the Allegheny Mountains via boats drawn by
mules, followed the banks of the Potomac for 150 miles to Harper's
Ferry in West Virginia.

Canoeing on the Charles River when I lived in Massachusetts
had been just about perfect, but as we glided up the winding
canal with the broad Potomac River on the left and the high bluffs
of Maryland on the right, all covered with verdant shrubs and
flowering trees, it seemed that I had never seen such scenery or
heard such a chorus of birds.

After that first foray on the Potomac, Irene and I organized
Sunday canoe trips with our fellow workers. These jaunts rapidly
developed into all-day affairs, with food and swimming thrown in.
By late spring, we owned a canoe jointly—a sleek gray number,
seventeen and a half feet long and very tippy, but swift and easy to
paddle. Then we heard of a large summer boarding house on the
Washington side of Cabin John Bridge. By July we had moved our
belongings, plus canoe, to this unique spot.

Just below Cabin John Bridge, a swimming pool beamed,
surrounded by rocks and fed by a cool, swift-flowing stream.
There, in the evenings before dinner, we could splash in the cool
water and shake off the heat and dust of the humid, Washington
summer. On weekends we took long canoe trips to the upper
reaches of the canal.

After some practice, we ventured into the rapids of the Potomac, spending many days exploring the little islands dotted up and down the river. We could never understand why this rare scenic spot had not been set aside as a park that all might enjoy its beauties.

By the end of summer, we had assembled at our boarding house a long table of friends and co-workers.

The cost-of-living investigation lasted for a year. First, the figures on family expenditures were gathered in the field. This process we called "doorbell work" when we returned to the office to tabulate the data.

This investigation provided the basic cost-of-living index, upon which all subsequent cost-of-living figures rest. Although much of our work was mechanical, the many wives and mothers we met were always in our minds, as they patiently explained their difficulties in feeding and caring for their children in wartime (World War I) Washington.

One day, someone told me of the Consumers League of the District of Columbia, a privately supported organization with headquarters in New York City. Mrs. Florence Kelley,[12] a well-known social worker and reformer, was the executive secretary of the national organization with many branches of the League throughout the country.

I knew the organization, founded on the theory that responsibility for bad industrial conditions affecting women and minors rested largely upon the "consuming public," wanted to bring about better, decent working conditions. This meant clean, well-lighted, safe buildings and wages sufficient to maintain decent standards of living for the workers and their families.

---

12   Florence Kelley (1859 –1932) was a social and political reformer and the pioneer of the term wage abolitionism. Her work against sweatshops and for the minimum wage, eight-hour workdays, and children's rights is widely regarded today. From its founding in 1899, Kelley served as the first general secretary of the National Consumers League. In 1909, Kelley helped to create the National Association for the Advancement of Colored People (NAACP).

***Florence Kelley worked tirelessly for the
rights of workers***

At this time, they were about to present a bill to Congress that would provide a minimum wage for women workers in the District of Columbia. It was common knowledge that women employed in stores and laundries in Washington were exploited even more than in New England.

When I heard that Mrs. Szold was soon resigning to have a baby, I told her my experience with Massachusetts Minimum Wage Commission and the U.S. Bureau of Labor Statistics and applied for her position. The executive committee of the League offered me the position, which I promptly accepted.

My duty to promote the League's program, acting as its representative whenever questions arose affecting the welfare of women in industry, also meant raising funds for the budget, which included my own salary.

Josephine Goldmark

I am very proud of the three projects carried through during the next three years. Two of these undertakings—the Saturday closing of department stores in Washington during the summer months and the passing of the Minimum Wage Law for the District of Columbia—were generated in New York City by that dynamic leader, Florence Kelley, and her two assistants, Pauline and Josephine Goldmark.[13] I found myself responsible for the third, advancing the interest of women in the investigation of the meat-packing industry for the United States government.

Mrs. Kelley had devoted her life to the cause of social justice. She raised her voice (it was resonant and not easily forgotten) continuously in private, in the press, and on public platforms to persuade men and women to share responsibility for the welfare of their brothers and sisters in industry.

---

13   Pauline and Josephine Goldmark's work as reformers in the Progressive Era did much to redesign the American social contract. Between 1903 and 1930, they shaped laws regulating child labor, the legal length of the working day, and minimum wage. They worked with executive director of the NCL, Florence Kelley.

To sell a social conscience proved more difficult than to sell goods, I realized as I heard Mrs. Kelley speak. But she succeeded in making her audiences understand that if they helped obtain social justice for others, they also obtained something for themselves.

Her first project was to persuade the retail stores of Washington to close their shops on Saturdays during the hot summer months so that their employees could have a long weekend. Under Mrs. Kelley's expert guidance and that of my executive committee, I visited the leading proprietors. If I could persuade them to head the procession, in theory, the other stores would follow their example.

That summer, for the first time, all Washington department stores closed on Saturdays during July and August, thanks to the District Consumers League. Word of this development spread throughout the country via retail trade journals so that it was not long before many other department stores in other cities began to follow the lead of Washington stores, to the benefit of all concerned. It was a good project on which to cut one's teeth.

Powerful voices were, by this time, being heard around the world—on the one side urging America to enter the World War,

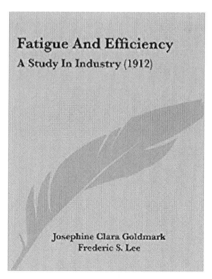

Fatigue And Efficiency *by Josephine Goldmark,*
is still in print today

and on the other advocating continued isolation. President Wilson[14] was no isolationist, but he understood and hated the sorrow and wastefulness of war. He was strongly opposed to the use of force as a means of settling disputes.

Eventually, neutrality was no longer possible. The ruthless sinking of the Lusitania[15] by Germany precipitated the president's decision. On the night of April 2, 1917, we stood in a hushed crowd outside the Capitol, waiting while President Wilson delivered his historic speech asking Congress to declare war on Germany.

There were no loudspeakers in those days, so we had to wait until the newspaper extras appeared on the street to give us the exact words the president had used.

It was as though life stood still that night! We knew that we were experiencing the birth of a new day in American and world history—an acknowledgment that what concerned the rest of the world concerned America as well.

We just stood there quietly trying to think what it all meant. Soon the papers spread onto the streets, and we read the president's speech, word by word, spelled out under the huge headlines.[16]

---

14   Thomas Woodrow Wilson (1856 –1924) was an American statesman and academic who served as the twenty-eighth president of the United States from 1913 to 1921. A Democrat, Wilson served as president of Princeton, from 1902 to 1910, and as governor of new Jersey from 1911 to 1913.

15   The RMS Lusitania was the world's largest passenger ship. On May 7, 1915, less than a year after World War I (1914–1918) erupted across Europe, a German U-boat torpedoed and sank the British ocean liner en route from New York to Liverpool, England, and sent her to the seabed in eighteen minutes, with the deaths of 1,198 passengers and crew.

16   On February 3, 1917, President Wilson addressed Congress to announce that diplomatic relations with Germany were severed. In a Special Session of Congress held on April 2, 1917, President Wilson delivered this "War Message." Four days later, Congress overwhelmingly passed the War Resolution, which brought the United States into the Great War.

President Woodrow Wilson

PRESIDENT'S SPEECH

It is a war against all nations. American ships have been sunk, American lives taken, in ways, which it has stirred us very deeply to learn of, but the ships and people of other neutral and friendly nations have been sunk and overwhelmed in the waters in the same way. There has been no discrimination. The challenge is to all mankind. Each nation must decide for itself how it will meet it. The choice we make for ourselves must be made with a moderation of counsel and a temperateness of judgment befitting our character and our motives as a nation. We must put excited feeling away. Our motive will not be revenge or the victorious assertion of the physical might of the nation, but only the vindication of right, of human right, of which we are only a single champion.

Hugh Dewitt Butler

CHAPTER 11

He Walks into My Life and
We Start a New Kind of Household

Almost at once, Washington became an uncomfortable place to live. Prices skyrocketed. Living quarters were scarce and the leisurely, easy-going atmosphere of this Southern city changed under the pressure of world events. Government buildings were swarming with young men and women in search of employment. Soldiers and sailors thronged the streets. All amusement parks, such as Glen Echo Park, out on the Cabin John car line, were crowded with merrymakers.

My friends and I remained comfortably isolated in our boarding house near Cabin John Bridge. Few found the upper reaches of the Potomac River, which had now become our weekly haunt. In the fall, we all moved back again into the P Street boarding house.

There, one evening, I met Hugh Butler.

Sidney Evans brought him over to dinner. I remember sitting next to Hugh and wondering what to talk about. I found he was in Washington to do war work for a private company that sold and installed electric searchlights on army and navy airfields. There were two such fields in Washington then, as the use of airplanes in the war effort was just beginning.

Hugh stood at a medium height, slight of build, with light curly hair already growing thin on top. His high forehead framed his deep-set blue eyes, which were shaded and cautious. There was not so much force in his manner, but in the quiet way he talked, one sensed his conviction. He had many interesting things to say and great personal charm as he said them. I liked the enthusiastic way he danced, but all too soon he seemed to tire and went off with Sidney.

He came often for dinner, but he did not show a special interest in any of us until one night when we started to talk about Cabin John and canoeing on the Potomac River during the summer. Then his face lit up.

"Take me out to see that place?" he asked.

"All right. Let's go next Sunday."

On the following Sunday, we packed a lunch and set forth. The late March rains had just ceased, and the yellow soil, as we got off the car at the end of the line, was muddy and sticky, as only Maryland and Virginia soil can be.

We climbed to a hilltop at right of the streetcar tracks, overlooking the Bannockburn Golf Club on the Maryland side, the river and the Virginia shore on the other side. Never did I see a drearier sight. Mud flats stretched out of the river to the shores on both sides.

The islands, dotted about in the river, were covered with dark gray mud, out of which rose bare sticks that, in summer, would turn into trees. A sharp, cold wind was blowing over the bleak landscape. Hugh gazed on the scene with real interest. "I can see that when spring comes, the river must be beautiful. Of course, I'll come out to live here this summer! It looks wonderful to me."

I could have hugged him I was so grateful. Here stood a man with some imagination and vision. What a treat!

That summer, Hugh, Sherwood Trask,[17] and Sidney Evans joined our crew. Mrs. Decker, our landlady, put sixteen of us at the same long table. Hugh sat at one end and I at the other.

We all shared many common interests: canoeing, swimming, and talking. We were keenly interested in national and international affairs, so our dinners were lively with discussions of all sorts of opinions and questions. By this time, many of us owned our own canoes. When we set off, two miles up the river and across to the little camp, which we had rented during the summer for weekending, a whole fleet of canoes paddled along.

17   Sherwood Trask (1890–1973), American educator, poet, and author.

74

That fall we hated to part. A jovial, congenial group, our recreational hours were stimulating, both physically and mentally. The prospect of separating and returning to Washington to live in isolated rooms seemed unattractive and boring.

Washington became a dreary city to the new army of young men and women who lived scattered about in single rooms and ate solitary meals at drugstore counters and cafeterias.

The government supplied recreation for the armed forces, but the civilian personnel were without any sort of social life, except what they could find in churches, in Young Men's and Women's Christian Associations, and in some of the boarding houses.

Hugh and I proposed to take over a large furnished house and run it cooperatively so that we and our friends could have a home together. The idea met with instant success. Marion and Sherwood Trask agreed to live with us as chaperons.

And so it came about in September that we all moved to Kenyon Street. What a time we had! We engaged a maid to clean the place once a week; everyone had his or her own shelf in the pantry for breakfast supplies; dinners were cooked jointly when we ate at home, but we planned to take this meal out most of the time.

Hugh and I signed the lease, so we took personal responsibility for the scheme. We more or less decided who the occupants would be.

The fame of our establishment spread. Within a couple of months, another cooperative coed household sprang into being, sponsored by Stuart[18] and Margaret Chase,[19] who I had known at the Fabian Society in Boston.

---

18   Stuart Chase (1888 –1985) was an American economist, social theorist, and writer.
19   Margaret Madeline Chase Smith (1897 –1995) was a U.S. politician in the Republican Party. She served as a U.S. representative (1940–1949) and senator (1949–1973) from Maine. She was the first woman to serve in both houses of the U.S. Congress. A moderate Republican, she was among the first to criticize the tactics of McCarthyism in her 1950 speech, "Declaration of Conscience."

Stuart was becoming a writer of note, working for the government. Margaret began producing babies and working for the U.S. Forestry Service, responsible for mapping out the Appalachian Trail from Maine to Georgia.

Benton MacKaye,[20] with his wife, Betty, used to come out to Cabin John armed with *The Adventures of Huckleberry Finn* to read aloud to the crowd, gathered around an open fire after a picnic supper in the woods. You have never really read that story or fully enjoyed the flavor of its humor unless you have heard Benton MacKaye read it aloud! Thus our social life had now become rich, varied, and satisfying. I knew Betty from luncheons at Alice Paul's place. She had recently been hunger striking with the militant suffragists and just let out of prison.

Why is it that the beauty of nature must be spoiled by Man?

Man, though the highest of beings, is, in one [sense], the lowest, never contented until he has spoiled all the beauty of nature in his power by cutting down vegetation, killing animals, and even cutting down hills when he has the power to do so ...

How much more beautiful the surrounding would be, in every way, if men were not such fools.

- Benton MacKaye

---

20   Benton MacKaye (1879 –1975) was an American forester and conservationist, as well as the planner and creator of the Appalachian Trail in the Eastern United States, extending between Springer Mountain in Georgia and Mount Katahdin in Maine. The trail is about 2,200 miles (3,500 kilometers) long, though the exact length changes over time as parts are modified or rerouted. The Appalachian Trail is the longest hiking trail in the world. More than two million people are said to take a hike on part of the trail at least once a year.

Benton MacKaye

Jessie and Hugh with summer adventure friends —
Benton MacKaye, standing center to the left of Hugh

CHAPTER 12

My First Speech

I was asked to address the Girl Scout leaders of Washington on the work and progress of the Consumers League. Mrs. Kelley was now deep in her latest project to protect from exploitation women workers in factories making war uniforms. This program was beginning to be very successful.

She used the plea that happy, healthy workers contributed more to employers than ill, tired workers could, pointing out that it was in the interests of the employers and their firms to bring about decent working conditions for all employees, men as well as women.

At the scout leaders' meeting, I learned that I was to be preceded on the program by Ruth Hanna McCormick,[21] the daughter of Mark Hanna, a Republican senator from Ohio. Ruth was now the wife of the senator from Illinois and a nationally known speaker on women's suffrage.

The Evening Star, *Tuesday, March 26, 1918*

> The war service committee of the Anthony League will meet Wednesday from 4 to 6, at the home of the president, Mrs. Anna E. Hendley, 2007 Columbia Road. Mrs. Medill McCormick, commissioner of the Girl Scout Association of the District of Columbia and Miss Jessie R. Haver, secretary of the Consumers' League, will be the speakers. Mme. Sterne of New York will give piano selections, and Miss Stahl of Minnesota will sing.

---

21   Ruth McCormick Simms (née Hanna) (1880 –1944) was a U.S. representative from Illinois and active in the women's suffrage movement.

My heart sank. This was the first speech of my life and with such a competitor! Luckily for me, Mrs. McCormick spoke first and left, but as I listened to her fluency and noted her poise and self-confidence, I thought I would sink through the floor right then and there.

The postmortem I held after my feeble attempt was even worse. All the things I should have said and didn't raced through my troubled brain. Then I began to blame my education at Smith College for my failure. How could anyone be considered well educated who did not know how to deliver a good speech or write a decent letter? Of course, I realized that, up to this time, comparatively few women had spoken in public, and women who wrote well were few and far between.

For myself, I did not aspire to become an orator or a famous writer. I merely wanted to speak and write well enough to further the causes in which I believed. Obviously, a degree did not automatically fit one to be a public speaker, yet a woman without a college degree, like Ruth Hanna McCormick for example, could become an outstanding speaker. If colleges did not equip their students with the necessary techniques for platform speaking, where could such training be obtained?

Subsequently, I made two basic decisions to add to my collection. First, I would track down and acquire the techniques needed to become an effective public speaker if it took the rest of my life. It followed that someone, somewhere, would know how to teach me to speak with the poise and self-confidence shown by Mrs. McCormick. She didn't even use notes!

Second, I determined that someday I would urge schools and colleges to offer courses in public speaking and creative writing, which would have equal status with courses in the sciences and liberal arts. What was the use of being well informed on any subject if one could not share that information with others effectively enough to influence their thinking?

All too soon, I would be plunged into work where platform speaking was not incidental but of major importance to the success of the whole project. And this was not the only new skill I needed to acquire; I would soon have to learn how to develop working relationships with high officials in Congress and with the general public. In other words, I would be entering the field of public relations in a big way.

During this period of busy work and companion living, I noticed that Hugh insisted upon spending considerable time alone in his room. He was vague about what he was doing there, but I finally discovered that he was a dedicated member of the Christian Science Church. In fact, I learned that he had been a moderator and healer in the church at the age of sixteen, working with his mother in Chicago.

One of the first Christian Science healers in River Forest where they lived, his mother helped build the first Christian Science Church there, with Hugh as their organist. Considered a child prodigy, Hugh had trained on the organ from the age of six when his mother bought him a pipe organ.[22] So, one day I asked him to let me study with him. I pointed out that I had always been interested in religion but could not find one that was right for me.

We began to read the daily lessons together. I found it very soothing and inspiring to read those lovely, planned lessons with quotations from the Bible, which I did not know well, and Mary Baker Eddy's book, *Science and Health*. Hugh was pleased for me to show so much interest, and soon we were reading and studying regularly together.

We were just platonic friends, thoroughly enjoying our home, our family, our companionship, without it being at all personal.

It took me a long time to realize that our relationship began to change, for I was radiant with joy over the exciting work I did, work that had been a long time developing in a world not very kind to women.

---

22   My grandfather, Hugh, would treat me to hour-long performances on various grand pianos. He made up the music on the spot, all very developed and multilayered as if it had been composed on sheet music. He had the keys to the chapel with the giant pipe organ at one of the Claremont College campuses in Pomona, California, and would take me there for private concerts.

With the enthusiastic support of the board members of the District Consumers League, I found myself in a situation with a tremendous amount of creativity unfolding.

May 10, 1920

TO WHOM IT MAY CONCERN:

Miss Jessie R. Haver has acted as Legislative Agent of the National Consumers' League since June, 1918. During the first part of this period, Miss Haver was Executive Secretary of the Consumers' League of the District of Columbia, identified thus with both the local and the national organizations.

Miss Haver's service has been valuable because of her energy, initiative, capacity for quick decisions, and her dignified and persuasive method of presenting to Senators, Representatives and officials of the Government, the case for the legislation advocated by the National Consumers' League.

As a speaker, also, Miss Haver's work is valuable. She presents her subject-matter clearly, convincingly, and can be heard unusually well.

Miss Haver leaves the National Consumers' League of her own initiative, to accept a similar position with the League of Women Voters.

Florence Kelley
General Secretary

Letter of Recommendation for Jessie Haver from Florence Kelley

CHAPTER 13

I Become a Lobbyist

Lobbying at the Capitol had always been in the hands of men until, one day, the tap, tap of women's heels on marble floors began to be heard in the long corridors of the Senate and House office buildings. Women went up and down and in and out, urging senators to vote for the women's suffrage amendment, which had been closeted safely in the Senate committee for years.

These women were considered a disturbing element in the Senate office building by some gentlemen. But once the women discovered that they had as much right to be there as the representatives of other interests, they came and stayed.

Lobbying became almost as much a part of government as Congress itself. All possessed one purpose: to keep the legislatures informed on particular interests and to persuade them to support these issues.

In a way, lobbyists can be of immense help to a legislator.

Big business engaged skilled men, usually highly paid lawyers, to do this work. These men were often suspected of using unfair pressures to accomplish their ends. But it was difficult to prove improper practices, so for the most part, lobbyists operated without interference.

They were often successful in obtaining legislation desired by their employers and in preventing the passage of bills their employers did not want. At the same time, legislation in the public interest remained too often neglected because there was no one with sufficient money or time to provide effective representation for urgent needs of people.

However, as women entered the picture, lobbying in public interest became a factor to be taken seriously by Congress. Women as a group were concerned with issues affecting the public welfare. They had already won the right to vote in certain states and were practically certain to get universal suffrage within a short time. They were beginning to represent a political power to be reckoned with.

Therefore, it was a strategic moment for the National Consumers League to introduce a minimum-wage bill for the District of Columbia with teeth in it. We hoped this would be a model for the rest of the country.

The National Consumers League appointed me as their legislative secretary so I could lobby for the bill. This meant

The Capitol, Washington D.C. 1918

keeping an eye on its progress and trying to win support for it from influential members of Congress. It was my responsibility to report its progress from time to time to the District League and the parent organization in New York.

They commissioned me to study the United States Congress and contact the men who would be interested enough in our bill to work for it. To me, there was nothing dull about Congress. The legislators there came from all sections of America. Even the elevator men and the guards at the doors, humble and folksy, were interesting to me.

No one ever seemed in a hurry on Capitol Hill. To all appearances, everything up there was out in the open. As a matter of fact, compared to legislative assemblies in almost every other country in the world, the Congress of the United States is remarkably easy to access.

Anyone can go to committee hearings, unless for some special reason they are "executive" and closed to the public. Almost anyone can speak at such hearings.

Mr. and Mrs. Citizen are welcome on Capitol Hill as nowhere else in the country. They are welcome in the offices of their representatives. They are welcome at hearings and in the galleries of both houses.

Finally, a model Minimum Wage Bill for the District (providing mandatory penalties for offenders) was introduced and referred to the District committees of both the Senate and the House.

The chairman of the District Committee of the House, Congressman Ben Johnson of Kentucky,[23] was known to be a stubborn old gentleman where women were concerned. He used to badger the women lobbying for suffrage by shouting to them to go back to their homes where they belonged.

---

23   Ben Johnson (May 20, 1858–June 4, 1950) was an American lawyer and a Democrat representative for Kentucky in Congress from 1907 to 1927.

He remained the bane of the citizens of Washington, for he seemed to delight in killing anything new or progressive or humane. If he opposed some legislation, it was as good as dead.

"What are you going to do about Ben Johnson?" Josephine Goldmark asked one day. "You know he has to be seen. In his position, he can easily kill the bill. He will be delighted to do just that because the bill would help women who work in laundries and stores to get a decent living wage. He thinks they should all be at home taking care of their families!"

"I don't know what to do about him," I answered. "I'll have to think about it. But I know there must be a way. Surely there's always a way if you have a bill that is fair. We're out to aid other women to help themselves."

I relied on implicit faith that Congress would help us once I pointed out the need.

Finally, the day arrived when Congressman Johnson had to be interviewed. The day came, hot and sultry, when I arrived at his office, clad in a bright red-and-white checked gingham dress, freshly starched with a frilled ruffle down the front.

No one occupied the outer office, but the door to the inner office stood wide open. So, in I sailed, with chills rippling down my back in spite of the heat. There he sat at his desk looking like an old bear as he glanced up and scowled at me.

"Good morning, Congressman," I said in a sweet and respectful voice.

"What do you want?" he roared.

A powerfully built gentleman, he stood six feet, two inches in height, with a handsome large head and a great mane of graying curly hair.

Prior to this visit, I had spent hours in the gallery of the House watching him in action. A man of force and character, who, when he believed in a bill, he could fight for it with such oratorical skill and wire-pulling as few men possessed.

Timidly I replied, "I just came to see you about the Minimum

Wage Bill for the District, which has been referred to your committee." I shook, scared to death.

"What are you doing here?" he bellowed at me. "Why aren't you home having babies, where you belong?"

A heavy silence permeated the room. The fate of our bill hung on my reply. That I knew.

"Well, you see, Congressman, it's very awkward," I heard myself saying as if I were someone else talking. "It is customary to have a husband to have babies."

"Well, why don't you get a husband?" he asked.

"All the best men are married! What am I to do?"

At that he threw back his head and roared with laughter.

"That's tough," he said. "I'll have to help you. Now what is it you want me to do?"

Taking a deep breath, I began to speak: "We need you to set a date for a public hearing on this Minimum Wage Bill so that women in laundries and stores can receive a decent living wage. The District Consumers League wants you to help us get this bill through Congress."

I told him that Mr. Filene,[24] who would speak at the hearing, had won glory for Massachusetts by being the first store owner to pay his employees a minimum wage of eight dollars a week instead of four.

"There will be a lot of front-page publicity for you too, if you'll help us on this bill. There is a great deal of interest in this subject among employers of women in the District." I hurried on to get in all the important points while I had his ear.

"Who's against it?"

"No one so far. If Mr. Filene speaks, I doubt if there will be any opposition because he has such a high standing among employers.

He founded the National and International Chambers of Commerce too, so businessmen respect him and his ideas."

---

24   Edward Albert Filene (1860 –1937) was an American businessman and philanthropist. He is best known for building the Filene's department store chain and was a pioneer in employee relations. He instituted a profit-sharing program, a minimum wage for women, a forty-hour workweek, health clinics, and paid vacations.

"What do you do to have fun?" he asked suddenly.

Here was another moment weighted with heavy potential for my cause!

"I go swimming and canoeing all the time I can get," I replied.

His eyes lit up with pleasure. Then he proceeded to spend nearly thirty minutes telling me of his swimming experiences in his home state when he was a boy. He proved human after all and seemed glad to turn from the complicated problems, which must have weighed heavily on his mind. He stopped his reminiscing and asked, "When do you want the hearing on this bill?"

I suggested a date, which he put on his calendar. Then I departed, after thanking him for his interest and cooperation. I could hardly wait to return to my office in the Munsey Building to report the good news to Mrs. Kelley and Miss Goldmark.

On the day of the hearing, the local press came in full regalia, well represented because they had been informed that Mr. Filene would testify for the bill. Anything Mr. Filene had to say became news, especially as his remarks related to local department stores, which were their greatest advertisers. Most of the local department stores sent representatives to the hearing.

I can still see Mr. Filene as he stood before the Committee. He explained, in simple, halting words, how paying decent living wages to women workers became profitable in the long run.

Mr. Filene explained that he, "just a storekeeper," had come to see that increased living wages caused increased demand for goods. Increased demand for goods caused increased production. Increased production put more money in the pockets of workers, as well as employers.

Congressman Ben Johnson conducted the hearing with outstanding skill. The event garnered front-page publicity in Washington papers, carrying the full speeches of the most important witnesses in direct quotes.

The bill passed the House in less than six months, with little opposition. The next day, I ran into Congressman Johnson in the hall and thanked him personally for what he had done.

"That's all right," he said. "It was a real pleasure to work for the Minimum Wage Bill. Just call on me any time you want something done. You know, I have a lot of influence around here."

"Oh, I know that, Congressman," I hastily replied. "That's why we came to you in the first place."

Whenever I hear people today rail against our Congress, I think of Ben Johnson of Kentucky, long since gone. He worked stubbornly for the right, as he saw it, yet his mind did not close to new ideas once you got his ear.

He spent many years in conscientious efforts to bring about wise legislation. Undeniably honest, the congressman never supported a measure in which he did not believe.

Dates States Granted Women the Right to Vote

**States granting women the vote
prior to the 19th Amendment:**

Wyoming 1890

Colorado 1893

Utah 1896

Idaho 1896

Washington 1910

California 1911

Arizona 1912

Kansas 1912

Oregon 1912

Territory of Alaska 1913

Montana 1914

Nevada 1914

New York 1917

Michigan 1918

Oklahoma 1918

South Dakota 1918

"The vote is the emblem of your equality . . ."
~ Carrie Chapman Catt

CHAPTER 14

1918: Women Almost Get the Vote

As I remember, there were no women in the U.S. Congress. I found that the leaders in both houses were willing to listen when approached in the right way, especially when convinced that there was no serious opposition. Personal acquaintance with the men on "The Hill," however slight, was a real asset and well worth cultivation.

During this time, the women representing the National American Woman Suffrage Association and the members of the Woman's Party were thronging the corridors of the Capitol, giving legislators as little chance as possible to forget their cause. They bombarded President Wilson with demands that he speak to the Senate in person to urge passage of the federal amendment that would give all women the vote.

The methods followed by the two suffrage organizations differed widely. The militants of the Woman's Party (led by Alice Paul) picketed the White House throughout the war, carrying banners pointing out that the president should give women the vote if he believed in democracy, as he professed.

They burned President Wilson's speeches in public and finally burned him in effigy in the park in front of the White House. When arrested for "disturbing the peace," they refused to pay fines and were taken to jail, where, as the militants had done in England, they went on a hunger strike until they had to be released.

Mrs. Carrie Chapman Catt and her organization decried these methods and opposed the use of force. They were staunch supporters of the slow democratic process of education as a means of bringing about social change.

Finally, in 1918, the president succumbed, and he delivered his fifteen-minute historic speech to the United States Senate asking for the vote in favor of the federal amendment. I think it was the first time a president had ever gone to the Congress to ask for legislation.

Colonel Harry Kramer, who was close to the administration, gave Hugh two coveted tickets to the Senate gallery to hear the president speak. He asked me to go with him.

Together we heard Woodrow Wilson plead for the enfranchisement of women, first as a war measure and then as "essential to the right solution of the problems which we must settle."

He went on to say, "I, for one, believe that our safety in these questioning days, as well as our comprehension of matters that touch society to the quick, will depend upon the direct and authoritative participation of women in our councils. Without their counsellings, we shall be only half wise."

But when the Senate voted the next day, the suffrage amendment lost by two votes. The amendment was not passed until June 4, 1919. Then Mrs. Catt, the chosen leader to follow Susan B. Anthony, totaled up the price of the women's suffrage amendment as follows:

---

52 years of campaigning. . .

56 State referenda campaigns. . .

480 drives to get state legislatures to submit amendments to voters. . .

317 campaigns to get state and national party conventions to include woman suffrage planks. . .

19 campaigns for the 19th amendment with **19** Congresses.

As Mrs. Catt later told her followers, "The vote has been costly. Prize it!"

CHAPTER 15

Dangerous Waters:
Canoeing Down the Potomac

Our cooperative household weathered the first winter together. Once summer arrived and our legislative program was over, we were all back at Mrs. Decker's boarding house again at Cabin John Bridge. Pauline Goldmark, sister to Josephine, now with the Railroad Administration, joined us.

At my suggestion, Helen Hill from the Minimum Wage Commission of Boston came down to assist Miss Goldmark. Almost at once she became our treasurer. I can see her now running around with notebook in hand, collecting nickels and dimes from delinquents.

In the early spring, Saturdays and Sundays were spent in the yard. We sandpapered and painted the canoes to prepare for summer tours. The second summer, Dorothy Pope, who worked for the council of National Defense, joined our group. She was a tall, austere-looking Wellesley graduate, with a strict New England mother and an Irish father, so that she was really gay and full of fun once she unbent.

Dorothy was one of the most skilled canoeists among us. Late that summer, she and I shipped my canoe and our duffle bags, bedding, and food by canal boat to Harpers Ferry. We went there by train so as to paddle back 150 miles down the Potomac. Rumor had it that few canoes had ever come down through the difficult rapids, and those few had been piloted by men. But we were in search of adventure, as well as an inexpensive holiday, so this seemed an ideal way to combine pleasure with a new experience.

Dorothy secured a contour map from the Department of the Interior to help us spot the fish dams, which had to be forded or bypassed via the canal. There were also several large dams built by the District of Columbia to back up the water for its reservoirs. These also had to be bypassed. This necessitated carrying our canoe and supplies from the river to the canal, and later back to the river, often as far as half a mile. At first we staggered under the weight of the heavy canoe. But within two days, we could hoist it to our shoulders without the slightest difficulty.

Jessie ready to canoe up the Potomac River

If we were looking for adventure, we surely found it. The swift passage of the canoe down the rushing waters of the river, studded with huge boulders on top and under the surface of the water, provided plenty of opportunity for thrills. A hidden jagged rock could easily have ripped our canoe asunder, spilling us and our gear into the swirling stream.

We camped out on islands along the way, where we built stone fireplaces for cooking. We swam au naturel in the cool, early dawn. We took long siestas at midday, while the heat was on. On all that long journey, hardly a human face or habitation was seen, except at the locks where lock keepers let us down into a lower level. All around us loomed the lush, dense vegetation of trees, grasses, and flowers so characteristic of Virginia. Every turn of the stream presented ever new and fascinating vistas of sky, water, and clouds. We had, in very truth, come back to nature.

The last night of our trip, just before we turned over in our blankets to go to sleep, Dorothy began to talk about Hugh. She waited for the dark before she could muster courage to bring up the subject. "You know, Jessie, you should marry Hugh!"

"Whatever for? We're good friends, that's all. He doesn't want to marry. Neither do I." By now, I was very drowsy with sleep.

"You're in love with each other and don't know it. You're driving us all crazy. We're afraid you won't find out in time," she burst forth. "When are you going to wake up?"

"Dorothy, you're silly! How could anybody be in love with someone and not know it? Let's close the subject," I snapped. And with that, we went to sleep.

The last day of our journey was the most terrifying of all. Everyone had warned us that the falls just preceding the calm stretch of the river were the most dangerous part of the trip. However, we decided to try it, in spite of the fact that most men on the river carried their canoes to the canal to dodge this dangerous section.

There was plenty of water, but huge rocks stuck their necks out all over the place. Since I was steering the canoe, it was my job to avoid those vicious rocks that lurched up before us without notice.

As we started through the falls, we saw two men standing on the left bank of the river watching us with some concern. However, in almost no time, we came dashing through safely, pulling up to the shore where they were standing.

They seemed terribly relived that they didn't have to rush into the river to save us. They said, "We never heard of a man coming through those falls safely. We are very much impressed with your daring!"

In the late afternoon, Dorothy and I paddled safely down the canal to where Hugh, on the bank, waited for us to turn up.

He did not attempt to conceal his relief for our safe return. He knew that an accident in the upper reaches of the Potomac would have been difficult to trace. He was right! Anything could have happened, but we made it safe and sound. We arrived back home deeply tanned from the sun, looking much more like barbarians than dignified women in positions of responsibility. I could not remember being more thoroughly relaxed and without tension.

We also came back with a plan to find some far-sighted legislator to persuade the government to set aside the area from Harpers Ferry to Washington as a national park. A dam at Great Falls would back the water up for miles, forming a great lake for fishing, swimming, and boating. Decades later, much of the area won designation as Harpers Ferry National Park.

Campsites and inexpensive summer cabins, built on models now popular in some of the western national parks, would provide Washington families with places to take their children at low cost for brief retreats from the oppressive heat of the long summer days.

That year, most of our summer crowd became interested in Christian Science through Hugh. We often read the Christian Science lessons together after dinner. Lengthy, heated discussions on metaphysics were added to those on politics and government.

The end of August found us taxiing gaily back to Washington and back to work. In no time at all, the blissful summer days faded away as though a beautiful dream had come and gone. The dream was soon drowned out by a rush of impending events, into which we were all to be plunged.

CHAPTER 16

Another Legislative Job
and I Reveal a Crime

One day as I was scouting around the corridors of the House office building, the open door of a hearing room came to my attention. Inside, at a long table, sat several members of a committee of the House; to the right of the chairman, a man testified. One or two newspapermen and a woman reporter were off to one side, and the committee stenographer sat on the other, recording the testimony.

Committee hearings, unless executive, were open to the public. I considered myself a member of the public, and so, always curious, I drifted in to see what was going on. I soon found out. The committee was investigating a government report brought out by the Federal Trade Commission to the effect that the five large meatpacking companies of Chicago were in collusion, fixing prices of cattle on the markets of Kansas City, St. Louis, Chicago, and other cities. They were charged with throttling competition and restricting trade.

From then on, I became a regular attendant at the meatpacker hearings, sensing the social significance of the unfolding scandal. At this point, my experience with the Pulitzer School of Journalism came in handy.

It came to my attention that none of the news of these proceedings reached the public, despite the presence of the press at the hearings. But every day, the local papers carried full-page advertisements about the wonderful meatpackers in Chicago and how they processed every vital part of the animal, almost down to the pig's squeal.

So, I wrote down the whole startling story as it was presented, and I then hurried down to the office of *The Christian Science Monitor*, where my good friend and woman reporter was on duty. I knew *The Monitor* was not carrying the meatpackers' full-page ads, so they were free to print any essential news that was worth reporting. I knew that all newspaper editors watched *The Monitor's* stories, making this a good place to break loose the news of the hearings.

My reporter friend fell on the story with delight. Don't forget, I knew the background of this meatpacker scandal from personal experience. Never could I forget the years on the cattle ranch in Colorado. I recalled the time my father's load of cattle had been shipped to Kansas, only to be met with a fixed sales price that proved fatally unprofitable for him. It had been set by the five big meatpackers before the cattle arrived in Kansas City. Of course, once the cattle were there, father had to accept the deal. They could not be held there for a higher price except at terrible cost to him. Nor could they be shipped back to Colorado.

It was a keen example of killing the goose that laid the golden egg, a repetition of what had been going on in the cattle business for many years. That year, my father left the cattle business, knowing he could not cope with the unjust monopoly in the market.

So, after that first day at the hearing in Washington, with the consent of the District Consumers League, for which I was still working, I attended the meatpacker hearings every day. I took careful reports of what went on and wrote them up in the perfect professional style taught at Columbia University.

Not only did I share my reports with my friend at *The Christian Science Monitor*, but also with a United Press reporter that I knew well. He came under such pressure during those war years that he seldom had time to attend the meatpacker hearings, so he also took my reports and used them as his own.

The meatpacker hearings finally found their way into the national press. No one ever found out who was responsible for the reporting. I might have been in terrible danger if anyone knew.

The Washington Times

March 28, 1919

D. C. WOMAN TELLS OF "PACKER TRUST"

St. Louis, March 28—With business of the convention virtually completed, the National Woman Suffrage Association today simmered down to a program of addresses and discussions.

Miss Jessie R. Haver, legislative representative of the National Consumers League, and national secretary of the Consumers; League of the District of Columbia, was scheduled to tell the convention of the "packers' trust."

Miss Haver attended recent sessions of the Federal Trade Commission in Washington, and will detail revelations of packers' workings presented them.

Suffrage leaders attending the convention were still jubilant today over the reported action of the peace conference in recognizing women.

"It is the most glorious and democratic thing that has yet been done in hastening the day when real democracy shall prevail in all countries of the world," Dr. Anna Howard Shaw, honorary president, declared.

On the day I first entered the room where the hearings were happening, I was the only visitor because no one else in Washington knew anything about them. The very next day, ten nice women board members of the District Consumers League arrived, pencils in hand, and did they create a sensation! Not only were the congressmen on the committee astonished at their presence, but the brilliant corporate lawyer, Henry Veeder, stood stunned as the ladies took their seats close by so they could hear every word spoken.

It became a classic example of how much can be accomplished with little when the truth is involved. I enjoyed myself those many days as news of the meatpacker hearings broke loose throughout the United States.

I found great personal delight when I noticed how much weight, even in those early days, the presence of women carried. Why do we women hesitate to use our command more often?

With the reports, President Woodrow Wilson, became alarmed. Soon he wrote to the Federal Trade Commission, requesting that they draw up suitable legislation for him to present to Congress, which would put an end forever to further monopolies of this type in our country.

That legislation was passed. President Wilson issued a proclamation on October 8, 1917.

I went on to follow the progress and to report any changes and developments.

CHAPTER 17

Hugh Will Never Marry

Mrs. Butler – Hugh's Mother from Chicago

About this time, Hugh's mother visited us. We were very curious to meet Mrs. Butler because of our new interest in Christian Science and because she sounded like such an unusual woman. Hugh told us that she had been a Christian Science practitioner for thirty years—one of the first in Illinois.

Brought up on a farm in Wisconsin, one of seven girls and two boys, she taught school, as my mother had. A tomboy as a girl, Mrs. Butler's nickname was "Dick."

She became the first woman member of the school board in her town and one of the founders of the Woman's Club. Evidently, she turned into a pioneer for women, as well as an unorthodox religious thinker.

Imagine our surprise and delight to be presented to an unusually beautiful, elegantly dressed, feminine woman with the most erect carriage I ever saw. Her snow-white hair was piled stylishly high upon her head. But what I admired most about her was her complete self-confidence and poise—too often lacking in me—and the aura of charm about everything she said and did.

Glamorous, she presented herself as a grand lady. No wonder Hugh adored and admired his mother, for she glistened as a truly bright character, obviously with courage and vision as well.

Mrs. Butler seemed to thoroughly enjoy our flock of young people, who sat at her feet in adoration from the beginning. Evenings after dinner, we eagerly joined her and Hugh as they read the Christian Science lessons together and explained them to us.

One evening, I joined Mrs. Butler before dinner as she sat in the swing in the yard. Suddenly she said, "You realize that Hugh isn't ever going to marry, don't you?"

I nearly fell out of the swing. Handsome, charming Hugh, the darling of the ladies wherever he went, not going to marry? What a fantastic idea!

"Why isn't he going to marry?" I asked breathlessly.

"He's going to devote his life to religious work. It's his only real interest."

I knew that Hugh was an organist, though I had never heard him play. He had already told me of the six years when he was the organist of a large church in Chicago. His mother wanted him to make music his life work. Hugh had been thought a child prodigy, compared to Mozart from the age of four. He loved music, but not that much, he explained. He found that he did not have the temperament to isolate himself sufficiently from real life to become a full-time musician.

He wanted to do something more human, possibly in public service. The idea that he might dedicate himself to the life of a Christian Science practitioner seemed to me to be even more unlike Hugh. Something just didn't seem to fit.

"How do you know that he will never marry?" I asked, greatly puzzled. Hugh and I had been living in the same house, eating together and playing together, now for three years. He never told me of any such decision.

"Because it has been decided that way," she said evasively.

"Who made that decision?" I asked, even more bemused, for I had been deeply impressed by the beauty and wisdom of this woman, but now I felt suspicious. Then I sensed that she did not like my subtle criticism.

"Anyway," I said, "we think we have solved the marriage problem here in our cooperative household. We have the companionship of both men and women without having to complicate it with marriage. For myself, I have a career to which I am dedicated. I have no intention of ever marrying. So you see, Hugh and I are both in the same boat, Mrs. Butler."

She must have felt some relief at this statement, for in a short time she returned to Chicago, giving our way of life her blessing.

I could hardly wait to report this interesting conversation to the crowd waiting in the next room for the dinner bell.

"What do you think is the latest? Hugh's mother says that Hugh will never marry!"

They greeted the news with shrieks of laughter. "What," they said, "the handsome Hugh never to marry? What a joke!"

"Remember, hands off! Hugh is never to marry!" We jibed at all hours of the day after that.

***Jessie preparing to canoe up the Potomac River
in stylish bathing suit***

CHAPTER 18

Two Suffragists Speak Across the West

I learned that Mrs. Carrie Chapman Catt planned to take a trip through the Far West to urge state legislatures to ratify the women's suffrage amendment, that it might become an amendment to the Constitution. I decided to call on Mrs. Catt at her hotel in Washington. I told her of the hearings in the meatpacking industry, pointing out the significance of this issue being made known to women voters. Women, after all, did most of the food buying in our country.

"I wish someone would go with you on your trip west, Mrs. Catt, to tell the story to the women who will soon have a chance to vote."

This was my first personal interview with Mrs. Catt, though I had often heard her speak. I can see her now, sitting at her desk in her spacious headquarters on Rhode Island Avenue, as she listened to my story.

A heavy woman, with snow-white wavy hair parted in the middle and knotted on the nape of her neck, she had a sweet, tender smile and blue eyes with drooping lids. An expression inhabited her face that indicated a capacity for infinite patience, and for sorrow too. She wore a gown, as always, in a lovely shade of deep blue.

She listened to my story with a marked ability to concentrate. After a thoughtful silence, she said, "We have no money to finance this added expense. Have you any idea how to fund it?"

"Yes, I think I know where I can get the money. If I do find it, and if the National Consumers League is willing to sponsor it, will you permit me to go with you to speak on this subject? Such a speech might highlight an issue on which women will want to vote in the future," I added.

"You may go with us if you can pay your own way," she said.

This was a real concession on her part, for up until now, she had steadily resisted all attempts to go on record about any subject of current importance until the vote was actually won. She was not a crusader for unpopular causes.

She was a woman with only one cause: women's suffrage. Now that the Senate was about to pass the amendment, I found her willing to take this risk, though she still lacked the endorsement of thirty-six state legislatures needed to amend the Constitution. Mrs. Kelley gave her consent to the trip, with the same provision as to securing the funds to finance my travel expenses.

That very day, I secured an interview with Mr. William Kent of the U.S. Tariff Commission. His wife, Mrs. Kent, had recently returned from a hunger strike in the District of Columbia jail for the cause of women's suffrage.

Thus, Mr. Kent was well informed on the woman's angle and its possible connection with his effort of many years to clean up the meatpacking industry.

I found him at his office late in the afternoon where I proceeded to describe the opportunity I would have to tell the story of the hearings before large western audiences.

Those audiences were always attracted by Mrs. Catt. Each meeting was followed by long columns of publicity. All I needed was sufficient cash to pay my travel expenses.

Without a moment's hesitation, Mr. Kent reached into his desk drawer, drew out his checkbook, and presented me with a check for five hundred dollars.

Mrs. Catt and Mrs. Kelley were astonished, then alarmed, when I told them I had procured the money. What if I made a slip in my presentation of the facts and thus brought a libel suit against them? Such a suit would be disastrous, for they had little money or time to fight an expensive lawsuit instigated by the country's powerful and wealthy meatpackers.

So, I prepared a careful speech to reassure them, summarizing the facts which had been presented to the congressional committee, checking and rechecking each point with the public records. I found plenty of safe material to report and sufficient facts to support every statement.

One night, as I was working late in my little office in the Munsey Building, Hugh dropped in, as he often did, to go with me to dinner. These evening meals had by now become almost routine.

I found it immensely helpful to discuss the day's events with Hugh. He possessed the gift of putting his finger on the important points.

I read my speech to Hugh before dinner. He liked it but thought the title weak and the opening sentence trite. He suggested a more arresting opening sentence, and he wrote in "The Government and the Market Basket" as the title. Then he went carefully over the manuscript, crossing out words here, changing sentences around there, and adding some light touches of humor every now and then.

As a result, my speech changed from a dull essay to a timely, compelling story. My, my! I was really impressed as I noted his skill with words and remembered that he didn't have a college education. What a fellow!

I thought it cozy to have Hugh see me off and wish me well at the modern new railroad station in Washington. I was armed with "The Government and the Market Basket" tucked safely away in my bags. Fellow travelers probably thought we were brother and sister, so impersonal and matter of fact our parting.

What an adventure! I got to travel in the company of one of the greatest women of our age. Her wise counsel, sympathetic guidance, and understanding of the philosophy of democratic government were destined to stay with me for the rest of my life.

I wrote to my father to let him know I traveled west.

My father and stepmother came to Denver to hear my maiden speech. They were polite in their praise, but not effusive. They could not understand how I had arrived there.

"There was tremendous publicity—Mrs. Catt received tremendous publicity. An interesting thing, too, was the smooth way in which she ran her organization.
People couldn't do enough for her. They were eager to help and there was this great victorious enthusiasm.
At every station where we stopped to go and speak, there were huge crowds there to greet Mrs. Catt. You never saw such adoration and such admiration and faithfulness that the women gave to that great seasoned leader.

I think possibly that Mrs. Catt had the most influence with women and had the greatest effect in joining women to a great cause than any other woman that I've ever heard of. They were all back of her; they were all sacrificing for her."

-Jessie Haver Butler

From the Sherna Berger Gluck interview with
Jessie Haver Butler for the book, From Parlor to Prison

Providence, Rhode Island
October 25, 1918, 5 p.m.

Mr. Edwin B. Haver
119 Central Block
Pueblo, Colorado
*En route on western trip with Carrie
Chapman Catt*

Dear Father,

      Leaving tonight for the state of
Washington after a 2 week speaking session
in this old New England town—the back bone
of conservatism. Think I have stirred the
ladies up to some degree for the Housewives
League yesterday passed a resolution
backing the F.T.C. and urging legislation
for packers. Spoke to 100 girls at Smith
College last week. Have to be in Denver
Nov. 12th so expect to leave Wash. D.C.
Nov. 5th and reach home the 8th. I wonder if
Mrs. Ball and mother don't want to get up a
meeting in Pueblo for me and I will talk on
the mother's food. Can't you and mother go
to Calif. with us? The women are very eager
for straight information on food and we are
simply giving it to them. I spoke five times
yesterday. So glad I'm coming home.

Lots of love,
Jessie

Frankly, I felt rather confused myself on that point. Neither did the audience seem particularly impressed. No doubt the startling facts I presented were so unexpected coming from the suffrage platform that they did not know how to take them.

Mrs. Catt's publicity, on the other hand, was front-page news because of her efforts to obtain ratification of the Nineteenth Amendment. The prospect of seventeen million new women voters was rapidly becoming headline news.

As I sat behind Mrs. Catt on the platform that first day, I wondered how she could deliver a long and impressive address without looking at a note. Her hands, too, were clasped behind her as she spoke. She developed her theme, step by step, drawing heavily on a profound understanding and knowledge of the history and development of the United States. But I noticed that as her speech grew in intensity and power, she began to wring her hands behind her.

"Why do you wring your hands behind you as you speak?" I asked her later.

"Because I suffer so when I speak," she answered with a wry smile. "If I hold my hands behind me where the audience cannot see them, then it doesn't matter what I do with them."

Her speech was not just a speech, it was an oration. I found it difficult to understand why, after her many years of speaking experience, her delivery was accompanied with such emotional tension.

"How did it happen," I asked, "that you chose a career that required public speaking when you found speaking so difficult?"

"I did not choose my cause," she replied sadly, "it chose me and would not let me go." As she spoke, I realized that this great crusader was at heart timid and shy, but that she had been driven relentlessly by an idea, by something she had had to do.

"Have you any suggestions for my speech?" I then asked.

"Yes, you must learn how to deliver your speeches without notes. I've found that written speeches do not go over well."

"How do you learn to speak without notes and yet be sure of your facts?" I asked.

"If you say your speeches over and over, either alone or before an audience, you learn to think out loud after a while. But first you must know your subject thoroughly."

Thus, I received my first lesson in public speaking from a woman who turned out to be, without doubt, one of the greatest orators of our time. Had she been a man, she probably would have been a president or prime minister somewhere. Yet she had no formal training in platform speaking. She learned the hard way—by doing.

It became obvious that I must look for a shortcut to learn public speaking quickly. Meanwhile, I decided to watch and listen to every speech she spoke, to try to understand what made them so profound.

And they were profound. Her large audiences sat enraptured, drinking in every word. One felt that what they heard would remain with them for days, for years, forever. For she demonstrated great wisdom as a teacher, leader, philosopher, historian, and inspired orator, all wrapped up in one person.

The other event was an address Mrs. Catt gave at Reno High School. We drove out to a brand-new school building on the outskirts of town, with the distant blue mountains gleaming in the morning sunlight and the clear, crisp air filling our nostrils. What possibilities for the future lay with the fine boys and girls gathered in the school auditorium that bright fall morning! I felt a certain pride and joy to be addressing these hundreds of young people, gathered in this large, imposing public building. Surely they were a unique American product!

Mrs. Catt must have felt something of this too, for her speech that morning was especially inspired and moving—one I have never forgotten.

"We women have spent the last fifty years working for a cause to see that you girls have the right to vote when you are twenty-one and have more freedom. Yours will be the most difficult of all . . . to make wise use of these great privileges."

Throngs of excited women—members of the National American Woman Suffrage Association, which is organized on a nationwide basis—greeted us at railroad stations and hotels where we were entertained, eager to be the first to welcome their leader.

Programs for our short stays consisted of long hours speaking for high school and college audiences, luncheons, afternoon teas, dinners, and evening meetings.

I tried to understand the secret of Mrs. Catt's personal discipline, which kept her so calm, sweet, patient, and appreciative of all they did for her. At the same time, she quietly made plans to accomplish her purpose of teaching local leaders how to persuade their state legislatures to ratify the amendment as soon as it was passed by the U.S. Senate.

Her capacity for patience resulted in the difficult situation caused by the disagreement between the members of her own organization and those of the Congressional Union, later known as the Woman's Party, organized by Alice Paul when she broke away from the parent organization a few years before.

Mrs. Catt always opposed militancy. She favored the slow, more democratic method of education, followed by pressure for legislation by an informed electorate.

I used to wonder how she could remain so patient when I recalled the many years she had traveled up and down and back and forth across the United States, in all kinds of weather, on all sorts of trains, often speaking before small or indifferent or hostile audiences, driven only by her devotion to the cause of women's suffrage.

That spring, the National American Woman Suffrage Association held its convention in St. Louis. I persuaded Mrs. Florence Kelley to send me as a delegate from the National Consumers League to deliver my speech on "The Government and the Market Basket."

By this time, the leaders in the meatpacking industry were thoroughly alarmed at the attention given by women to the congressional investigation. Mrs. Shopper, with her market basket on her arm, might become much too interested in the way packers ran their business!

So, their handyman in Washington, a soft-spoken economist who had justified their system before the congressional committees with great effectiveness, came to the convention with several of his assistants.

When they discovered that I reported only facts, which were printed on pages of the public records, my speech could not be challenged. Though I heard later that the economist had asked Mrs. Catt for a place on the program to explain their side of the investigation, an opportunity that was never granted.

Mrs. Catt later showed her statesmanship at the St. Louis Convention as never before when she created the National League of Women Voters to carry on and expand the education of women for citizenship already begun by the Suffrage Association. Mrs. Catt wrote me while touring once again.

Congress had not yet voted to submit the proposed Nineteenth Amendment to the state legislatures for ratification. But victory was in sight, and when it came, the original purpose of the National American Woman Suffrage Association would be achieved. It was expected that their next convention, to be held in Chicago in 1920, would be its last. Mrs. Catt hoped that by that time the League of Women Voters would be prepared to set up a permanent organization. Until then, she suggested that the League function as a branch of the Association.

These recommendations were enthusiastically received by the Convention and promptly put into effect. The new National League of Women Voters was organized, and I was asked by their executive committee to be their legislative representative (lobbyist) in Washington, D.C.

NATIONAL AMERICAN WOMAN SUFFRAGE ASSOCIATION

BRANCH OF INTERNATIONAL WOMAN SUFFRAGE ALLIANCE AND OF NATIONAL COUNCIL OF WOMEN

MRS. CARRIE CHAPMAN CATT, *President*

NATIONAL HEADQUARTERS, 171 MADISON AVENUE
TELEPHONE, 4818 MURRAY HILL
NEW YORK

1ST VICE-PRESIDENT
MRS. STANLEY McCORMICK, MASS.

2ND VICE-PRESIDENT
MISS MARY GARRETT HAY, NEW YORK

3RD VICE-PRESIDENT
MRS. GUILFORD DUDLEY, TENN.

4TH VICE-PRESIDENT
MRS. RAYMOND BROWN, NEW YORK

5TH VICE-PRESIDENT
MRS. HELEN GARDENER, WASHINGTON, D. C.

NATIONAL WOMAN SUFFRAGE
PUBLISHING COMPANY, Inc.
MISS ESTHER G. OGDEN, *President*
171 Madison Ave., New York

LEAGUE OF WOMEN VOTERS

CHAIRMAN
MRS. CHARLES H. BROOKS
WICHITA, KANSAS

SECRETARY
MISS KATHERINE PIERCE
112 N. BROADWAY
OKLAHOMA CITY, OKLAHOMA

PRESS DEPARTMENT
MISS ROSE YOUNG, *Director*
171 Madison Ave., New York

TREASURER
MRS. HENRY WADE ROGERS, CONN.

CORRESPONDING SECRETARY
MRS. FRANK J. SHULER, NEW YORK

RECORDING SECRETARY
MRS. HALSEY W. WILSON, NEW YORK

DIRECTORS
MRS. CHARLES H. BROOKS, Kansas
MRS. J. C. CANTRILL, Kentucky
MRS. RICHARD E. EDWARDS, Indiana
MRS. GEORGE GELLHORN, Missouri
MRS. BEN HOOPER, Wisconsin
MRS. ARTHUR LIVERMORE, New York
MISS ESTHER G. OGDEN, New York
MRS. GEORGE A. PIERSOL, Pennsylvania

February 4, 1920.

Miss Jessie H. Haver,
824 Mills Building Annex,
Washington, D. C.

My dear Miss Haver:

This is just an acknowledgement of your letter and its enclosure. I will see that it reaches Mrs. Pennybacker.

I am terribly sorry that you cannot be in Chicago, for I think that we will have a grand and rousing time, and probably we will not have things all our own way.

I shall surely not have returned by the date you mention, but hope nevertheless to see you ere many months roll by, for you have a warm place in my heart. Blessings on you!

Carrie Chapman Catt

Letter from Carrie Chapman Catt to Jessie Butler

National American Woman Suffrage Association

Mrs. Carrie Chapman Catt, President
National Headquarters
171 Madison Avenue
Murray Hill, New York

Telephone 4818

February 4, 1920

[Author's note: seven months before women get the vote on August 18]

Miss Jessie R. Haver
824 Mills Building Annex
Washington, D.C.

My dear Miss Haver:

This is just an acknowledgement of your letter and its enclosure. I will see that it reaches Mrs. Penny Backer.

I am terribly sorry that you cannot be in Chicago, for I think that we will have a grand and rousing time, and probably we will not have things all our own way.

I shall surely not have returned by the date you mention, but hope nevertheless to see you ere many months roll by, for you have a warm place in my heart. Blessing on you:

Carrie Chapman Catt

Image of the letter above is on the previous page.

NATIONAL AMERICAN WOMAN SUFFRAGE ASSOCIATION

BRANCH OF INTERNATIONAL WOMAN SUFFRAGE ALLIANCE AND OF NATIONAL COUNCIL OF WOMEN

MRS. CARRIE CHAPMAN CATT, *President*

NATIONAL HEADQUARTERS, 171 MADISON AVENUE

TELEPHONE, 4818 MURRAY HILL

NEW YORK

1ST VICE-PRESIDENT
MRS. STANLEY McCORMICK, MASS.
2ND VICE-PRESIDENT
MISS MARY GARRETT HAY, NEW YORK
3RD VICE-PRESIDENT
MRS. GUILFORD DUDLEY, TENNESSEE
4TH VICE-PRESIDENT
MRS. RAYMOND BROWN, NEW YORK
5TH VICE-PRESIDENT
MRS. HELEN GARDENER, WASHINGTON, D. C.

TREASURER
MRS. HENRY WADE ROGERS, CONNECTICUT
CORRESPONDING SECRETARY
MRS. FRANK J. SHULER, NEW YORK
RECORDING SECRETARY
MRS. HALSEY W. WILSON, NEW YORK

PRESS DEPARTMENT
MISS ROSE YOUNG, *Director*
171 Madison Ave., New York

DIRECTORS
MRS. CHARLES H. BROOKS,
Kansas
MRS. J. C. CANTRILL,
Kentucky
MRS. RICHARD E. EDWARDS,
Indiana
MRS. GEORGE GELLHORN,
Missouri
MRS. BEN HOOPER,
Wisconsin
MRS. ARTHUR LIVERMORE,
New York
MISS ESTHER G. OGDEN,
New York
MRS. GEORGE A. PIERSOL,
Pennsylvania

May 13, 1920.

Miss Jessie Haver,
913 Munsey Building,
Washington, D. C.

My dear Miss Haver:

      I was very glad to get your spirited letter. You are the one person in the entire United States of whom I have heard lately, who has not felt the tide of reaction setting in. You almost make me feel some people may escape it. I certainly hope so and I am glad you are to be Legislative Worker for the League of Women Voters. And this is to say that while I have not time to write you a proper letter, since I have only one more day in the office before sailing away, I am glad you are at the helm. May God be with you and all the good undertakings which the League of Women Voters has sponsored!

           Most cordially yours,

           Carrie C. Catt

           President

Letter from Carrie Chapman Catt to Jessie Butler

National American Woman Suffrage Association

Mrs. Carrie Chapman Catt, President
National Headquarters
171 Madison Avenue
Murray Hill, New York

Telephone 4818

May 13, 1920

[Author's note: three months before women get the vote on August 18]

Miss Jessie Haver
918 Munsey Building
Washington, D.C.

My dear Miss Haver:
    I was very glad to get your spirited
letter. You are the one person in the entire
United States of whom I have heard lately, who
has not felt the tide of reaction settling in.
You almost make me feel some people may escape
it. I certainly hope so and I am glad you are
to be Legislative Worker for the League of
Women Voters. And this is to say that while I
have not time to write you a proper letter,
since I only have one more day in the office
before sailing away, I am glad you are at the
helm. May God be with you and all the good
undertakings, which the League of Women Voters
have sponsored.

Most cordially yours,

Carrie C. Catt
President

Image of the letter above is on the previous page

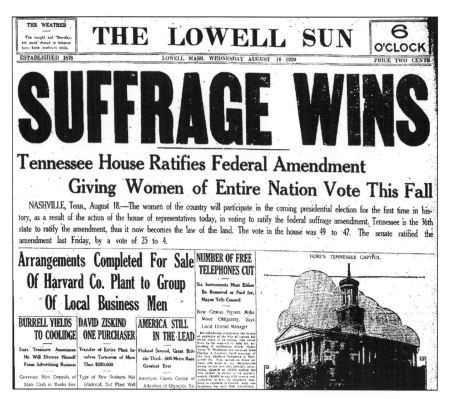

The Lowell Sun, *August 18, 1920*

CHAPTER 19

Women Get the Vote!
Put the "Rat" in Ratification!

A fter all our efforts, state after state ratified the suffrage amendment until the total reached thirty-five. We needed only one more state endorsement in favor of ratification. The governor of Tennessee was finally persuaded to call a special session of the state legislature to take action for or against the amendment.

All eyes were now focused upon Nashville. Representatives of many special interests promptly descended in force upon that Southern city: lobbyists for the liquor industry, the meatpackers, the railroads, and others who feared the women's vote; delegates from the Woman's Party, whose militant tactics were considered "unladylike" by many Southerners; anti-suffragists, wearing bright red roses; a few former friends of suffrage who opposed the amendment on the ground that it violated states' rights; spokesmen for the Democratic and Republican National Committees; and, of course, Mrs. Catt and her cohorts. All were there when the legislature convened on August 9, 1920.

The methods used by the opponents of the amendment showed old-time politics at its worst. Corn liquor flowed freely—it was alleged that many of the legislators were drunk most of the time, and this in a state practicing prohibition!

Scurrilous handbills circulated attacking Mrs. Catt and her followers. Children booed her as she walked along the streets, and even spat at her. The opposition tapped her telephone and opened her mail.

Then came the dramatic conclusion of the struggle. I love the story of the mountain woman whose letter to her son brought victory for the cause of suffrage. It happened this way: Young Harry Burn, a member of the Tennessee legislature, who everyone expected to vote against ratification, gave the deciding vote.

After some days of debate, an effort was made by opponents of suffrage to delay action by introducing a motion to table the resolution calling for ratification. A tie vote resulted, and the motion lost. Now the vote on ratification could no longer be postponed. As they called the roll, Burn voted for ratification.

Men rushed up to him, pounded his back, told him he had made a mistake, insisted that he change his vote before the roll call ended. But he shook his head, maintaining that his vote remained final and that he wanted it to stand. When the roll call reached the last name, by a majority of one vote, seventeen million women were finally admitted to the franchise.

Sensing a story behind Burn's change of heart, newspapermen from the press associations rushed to question him. Whereupon he pulled out of his pocket a letter from his mother, which had arrived that morning:

```
Dear Son:

Hurrah and vote for suffrage! Don't keep
them in doubt. I notice some of the
speeches against. They were bitter. I
have been watching to see how you stood,
but have not noticed anything yet. Don't
forget to be a good boy and help Mrs. Catt
put the "rat" in ratification.
Your Mother.
```

The reporters, skeptical of the letter's authenticity, hired cars and set out to see the woman who had written it. They found her, in the late afternoon, carrying in pails of fresh milk. After she invited them to sit down on stools at the kitchen table, they asked, "How did you happen to write this note to your son?"

"You see," she explained, "in the winter, we like to read Shakespeare out loud. Shakespeare is always 'funning' with words. So, I thought I would write my son to help Mrs. Catt, and then I thought about Shakespeare and how he liked to 'fun' with words, so I thought I would try it too. That's all."

At last the long struggle was over, settled in the end through the influence of a farm woman, named Phoebe Ensminger Burn, in the mountains of Tennessee. Fifty years of hard work had ended, giving seventeen million women the vote. Never in a thousand years had the suffragettes expected such an ending. Democracy in action had triumphed.

Then I had a big idea. Why not ask Mrs. Catt to stop on her way north to New York to tell Washington the inside story of the final fight?

Mrs. Catt agreed to speak. Poli's Theatre at 15th Street and Pennsylvania Avenue was secured free of charge, thanks to a kind manager. The local florists sent beautiful potted plants to decorate the stage. Everyone wanted to share in the great victory for women and the dawn of a new era.

Boxes in the theatre were reserved for leaders in other fields, some of them grown old and weather-beaten in the long struggle for human rights. But all were eager to come and help the women celebrate.

Mrs. Catt told the inside story of what had transpired in Tennessee. Although weary after her hard experience, Mrs. Catt held the audience spellbound as always. In measured, thoughtful words interspersed with many pauses, indicating a great awareness, she recounted detail by detail the hard struggle she had just endured. She received a grand ovation at the close of her remarks.

There was one sad note in Washington that day. The day before, I had eaten, as I frequently did, at the headquarters of the Woman's Party on Jackson Place. The militants were feeling very much left out of the picture, for although they had devoted their energies for years to the struggle for suffrage in the way that seemed best to them, the press and country as a whole now took little notice of them. They received scant credit for the successful culmination of the long crusade.

On the day of the presentation, I called on Mrs. Catt.

"Mrs. Catt, it would be a most gracious gesture, now that the fight is over, if you were to invite representatives of the Woman's Party to sit on the platform with you tonight and perhaps even to ask Alice Paul or one of her assistants to speak with you. Such an invitation would show the men and the world that women can disagree and then afterward be friends again."

Mrs. Catt gazed at me sadly and wearily, but shook her head. "You're right. An invitation should be given to the Woman's Party to join with us, but I can't do it. I simply can't do it."

"Oh, please, Mrs. Catt. Please think twice before you say no. It would be such a magnificent gesture . . . to unite the entire women's movement in celebration. The good feeling generated would heal the bitterness of the past. It would restore harmony, at least for one evening, and would help us to attack the new problems that await us together. Please, please, try hard to forgive and forget as the men do daily in the Senate. It would be wonderful of you, if only you could." Tears flowed as I pleaded with her.

"It's hard to be a good Christian in this world, Jessie," she stated, and then no more was said on it. But she remained adamant.

Only she knew the whole story behind the split in the women's suffrage movement, when Alice Paul, a brilliant young agitator and political propagandist, had become impatient with the conservatism and slowness of the old organization and withdrew, taking with her a large following of the younger women.

Maybe their differences were merely those often present between two generations, the one slow and deliberate and the other impatient to try new ideas.

Or perhaps it resembled the age-old mother-daughter conflict in another guise!

I felt terribly disappointed and depressed as I left Mrs. Catt, for I believed that she failed to rise to a great opportunity. But then, who was I to judge?

Mrs. Catt *(front row, right)* **and some of the women
who worked with her. Maud Wood Park** *(front row, left)*

Maud Wood Park's first-person account
(Suffragist and first President of
the League of Women Voters)

*That evening we had a jubilee meeting at Poli's Theatre, where every
seat was taken and standing space was crowded to the last limit
permitted by the fire regulations. The greetings and congratulations of
the President were presented by the Secretary of State. Mrs. Harriet
Taylor Upton and Miss Charl Ormond Williams, who had had
important roles in the campaign in Tennessee, told about the "ways
that were dark and the tricks that were vain" on the part of the
opponents there, and then Mrs. Catt made one of her greatest speeches.*

On the night of the event, Poli's Theatre was packed to the doors and gay with flowers and floating banners. The great and near-great of the government and Congress were in attendance.[25]

Prominent members of the Woman's Party were to be seen here and there in the audience, grimly watching the proceedings, but taking no official part in the celebration.

Late that night, Alice Paul and her group held a meeting at their headquarters, outlining a new program for the future. They dedicated themselves and their organization to sponsoring another amendment to the Constitution, to be known as the Equal Rights Amendment, which wasn't passed until 1972.

Thus, out of victory, there came both the promise of great good and the seeds of another struggle. Only this time, the conflict was to be mostly between opposing groups of women—those who opposed the Equal Rights Amendment and those who favored it—and not between women on one side and men on the other as before.

Never again was my life to be so uncomplicated, so exhilarating, so stimulating as in those weeks, months, and years, during which I followed an undeviating course from the simple background of a Colorado ranch to one of the highest paid and most important positions held by a woman in Washington.

---

25   *Maud Wood Park (1871 – 1955) was an American suffragist and women's rights activist.*

CHAPTER 20

We Are Invaded

A letter from Hugh reached me in Chicago, where I was speaking, explaining that his parents were finding their life together more and more difficult since his two sisters had left for college. The tension between them had increased to a point where something had to be done about it.

The situation in his home that Christmas lined up with previous statements made by Hugh to the effect that it was he who had for years kept his family together. I sensed that he must have often used his diplomatic skill to mediate the differences between these two very strong-minded individuals.

So, the letter continued, he had persuaded his father to retire from his business of thirty years, sell their family home and furnishings, and move himself and Mrs. Butler to Washington to live in our cooperative household! Hugh had himself been so happy there that he wanted to share his enlightened environment with his parents.

I sat stunned by this sudden turn of events. Hugh and I always conferred before admitting new members to our household, agreeing about whether or not they would fit in. Now, to precipitously inject his own family into the picture, and an unhappy family at that, created something quite different.

The worst part of the arrangement—it was too late to be undone. By the time I returned to Washington, Hugh's parents had already moved in. And along with them came the tense, strained atmosphere, which I remembered from visiting their home in

Chicago. The household no longer belonged to us. It became theirs; we were transformed into lodgers to help pay the rent.

I received a second jolt. For over three years, Hugh and I had been together constantly. Our companionship had become an important part of our lives. We talked everything over together— our work and our interests in national and international affairs.

Best of all, we played together, and most important, we read our daily Christian Science lessons together. Other members of the household sometimes joined us for the evening meal in a Chinese restaurant or a favorite cafeteria, but more often than not, he came to my office at dinner time and we dined alone. Afterward, we walked; on winter weekends we skated and in the summer we canoed and swam together. Our relationship had become as natural and easy as breathing.

But Hugh no longer called on me to go to dinner. He ate with his family at the house, where his mother prepared excellent meals. Apparently, it never occurred to him to do otherwise.

One day I ran into him in the corridor of our office building. "I need your advice on something," I said. "How about dinner together?"

"Sorry, but I have to eat with my family." He said it as though he had a secret date with another woman.

Suddenly I woke up. Almost without my knowing it, I had allowed Hugh to become important and even necessary to me. His sympathetic interest and his understanding of me and my work had become essential. Now he retreated, back to his family and their problems.

Could I no longer live without him? I certainly didn't want to make any such admission, even to myself. But I did admit to my naiveté in allowing myself to carry on such a close relationship for four years with a casual friend!

Sometimes in the evening, Mrs. Butler invited me to join her and Hugh while they read and discussed Christian Science lessons together, which they read in unison. Hugh's father remained downstairs, apparently absorbed in current magazines.

Mr. Butler, a prolific reader and very well informed, often brought to the dinner table or our evening gatherings clever bits of prose or verse or articles he read aloud. I had a suspicion that he made a deliberate effort to bring outside reading to his family in order to keep their minds open. That fine old man, sweet and loving, was caught in a trap, being torn to pieces before my eyes. Hugh and his mother were blind to his suffering. Hugh was caught too, but didn't seem to know it.

One evening I went for a long walk. I decided right then to move out of that household just as soon as spring came and the boarding house at Cabin John opened. I wanted to get out right away—that very night! I sensed danger, and I wanted to leave at once.

Then, without warning, I began to cry. The gay, carefree companionship I'd enjoyed with Hugh had disappeared. As for me, I was getting out just as soon as possible.

I hurried up to Hugh after returning from my walk and asked him to join me outdoors. Then I told him of my decision.

"You can't do that. What's going to happen to me?" he asked in genuine consternation.

"You have your family, Hugh. You brought them here on your own. They have ruined our cooperative household. It isn't ours anymore. So, I'm leaving."

"You can't do that. You can't leave us. But if you do, I'm going to leave with you."

"You can't leave them, Hugh," I replied.

Weekend Potomac
River hideout

CHAPTER 21

Tug of War: Career Versus Marriage

May of 1920 was just as beautiful on the Potomac as all the previous Mays had been . . . but there was no longer any sparkle to life. The trees were just as green, the flowers as profuse as ever, but they no longer seemed to matter.

The river lost its charm; our old haunts looked bedraggled and messy. What could be wrong? My heart felt heavy. I could not shake off the persistent depression, nor a premonition that something terrible waited around the corner. Even my new work with the National League of Women Voters, the most challenging and exciting position I had ever had, failed to lift my spirits. All of a sudden life had become dull and monotonous. What could be wrong?

On the second Sunday outing on the Potomac, as we were getting our canoes ready, we heard the crunch of car wheels on the drive. There was Hugh, all smiles, looking as pleased as punch to be with us again.

"Here I am," he announced gaily. "I've come for the day."

All at once, everything seemed right again: the sun shone, the air became fresh and clear, and the flowers glowed in the bright sunlight. We carried on as of old and gathered our duffels together for a trip on the river.

Hugh insisted that we spend the day at our hideout two miles up the river on the Virginia shore. From the top of Eagle Rock, one could look north to Great Falls, some ten miles up the river, where the water roared through a large rock-filled gorge to Stubblefield Falls close by, whose rippling sound filled the air just below. Only rarely were we bold enough to paddle through Stubblefield Falls into the rapids of Great Falls, where many fatal accidents occurred.

Looking south from Eagle Rock, the wide river stretched in the setting sun like a golden band toward the Washington Monument, whose monolithic shaft pointed skyward. Every changing light reflected on its pencil-like face, which in turn reflected on the surface of the river as the shaft of dying sunlight shot toward Washington. Hugh taught me to take time to drink in such scenes of nature, for he loved and appreciated beauty wherever he found it.

On this particular Sunday, we left our crowd to read the Christian Science lesson together on Eagle Rock. From this prominence, somehow the beautiful quotations from the Bible and from Mrs. Eddy always seemed to have more meaning. Then Hugh said his interest in my causes had opened his eyes to the possibility of employment in the government. I enthusiastically endorsed the idea. Perhaps this would lead to a way out for him, I thought.

We did not see Hugh again until two weeks later. Then, early Sunday morning, there he came—but not alone. His mother sat confidently by his side in the front seat of the car. Our hearts sank.

"Hugh loves it up here so much I thought I would come along and enjoy the day with you. I want to see the river, which he finds so attractive."

Dressed for a Sunday in town—high heels, hat, and veil—quite unlike the casual clothes we wore for our days canoeing. Her very elegance made the rest of us appear very sloppy in contrast. Almost at once things began to go wrong. That week the tide ebbed and left behind a thick yellow mud, which we had to cross to get into the canoes. Ordinarily we would not have minded. We would have just ripped off our shoes and stockings and waded in up to our knees if necessary, washing off the mud when we reached deep water, with legs hanging over the sides of the canoes.

We could not, however, urge this elegant lady to follow our example, so a great to-do ensued as we hunted up boards on which she could cross to a canoe. Alas, on the other side of the river, there were no boards, and the mud was deeper than ever, so Hugh's mother had to wade ashore, carrying her shoes in her hand.

On the opposite bank, even the rocks we had to climb were coated with mud, so that by the time we reached the cabin, we were covered with mud from head to foot, and so was she. Hugh did not seem to mind, casually taking his mother's discomfort in his stride. The day, which ordinarily would have been just another adventure, had fallen flat for all of us.

As Hugh and his mother left for Washington, she politely, but stiffly, tried to assure us that she'd enjoyed the day. But Mrs. Butler, much too dainty a woman to be roughing it in the wilds of the Potomac, did not fool us.

The following Sunday, Hugh came back again, this time alone. No one wanted to go up the river; there was still a bad memory from the week before. So Hugh and I, intrepid canoeists under any conditions, set off alone. We aired out the cabin, hung up the hammock on the porch, and went for a swim. I rested languidly in the hammock as I gazed through the narrow vista between the trees on the surface of the swift-flowing water, once more thoroughly at peace, when Hugh began to talk of his future.

"My plan to go abroad looks very hopeful," he said casually. "But how can I go without you? You're always in the picture somehow."

"You should go alone, Hugh," I replied with deep conviction. "You need time away from your family and your old associations to find yourself. You haven't had a chance, with your folks on your neck, all these years."

Hugh kept insisting that he had become so accustomed to talking over his plans with me that he could not imagine going off to Europe without my being with him.

"But, Hugh, have you forgotten your mother? What would she say to such an idea?" I felt so peaceful at this point that I refused to get excited about anything.

"Oh, she won't mind once she finds out I have decided to go."

"Well, of course, anyone would like to go abroad for a few years. I think it would be fun," I unexpectedly heard myself saying.

"Do you really mean that? You aren't joking?"

"No, I mean it."

It was as simple as that. Right then I knew that the past few weeks apart had not been right. We needed each other. But it took living apart to discover this fact.

So, we began, in quite a practical way, to plan our future, just as we had planned our cooperative household and other living arrangements during the past four years. Hugh could get his foreign assignment for the fall, as he had passed the foreign service examinations.

Already he worked for the United States Department of Commerce, in charge of their foreign commercial service. He could therefore assign himself to the London office, where a vacancy waited.

I would resign my position in the fall to take a trip back home to Pueblo. Hugh could not leave Washington at this critical time, so we planned to be married in the East, just before sailing. It all seemed so easy and natural.

A formal wedding seemed impossible for many reasons. For one thing, neither of us had the money for it. For another, Hugh thought that the quieter the ceremony, the less opposition we would face from his family.

Hugh left early to break the news to his mother, and I retired in a strange, calm state of mind, without any feeling of joy or excitement. We didn't even kiss each other when he left, but instead acted like an old married couple discussing plans for a new house. This lack of emotion between us suited me fine.

Two days later we met for lunch. Hugh looked ashen and strained. "Mother has taken the announcement of our plans very hard," he said in a worried tone. "She thought she was going to Europe with me. She's terribly upset. . . Father is afraid our marriage will kill her. So, I've promised not to see you again for a month until things calm down a bit."

"What is her objection?" I asked, not surprised.

"Oh, she says that if I am to marry anyone, I couldn't find a better wife than you, but her heart is set on my not marrying at all. She bases it all on Mrs. Eddy's teaching."

"I can't find that Mrs. Eddy is against marriage, Hugh."

"Whether she is or not, I'm going to marry you just the same, Jessie. But I'll have to postpone making definite plans for a month, until things clear up at home."

"Your mother is bargaining for time, Hugh. She'll try to find a way to separate us if she has you with her for an entire month. I'm afraid I'll never see you again."

I thought he might even be in physical danger. Without warning, I began to cry again. I was scared for both of us. Now at last I knew the truth. I desperately loved Hugh. I needed his sparkling creativity, his love of beauty, his fresh curiosity always ready to try new experiments. His deliberate ways balanced my exuberant, enthusiastic, impulsive tendencies, which too often led me into trouble. I never intended to fall in love. This romance had crept up on me over a long period, and now it was too late.

His mother's opposition stirred me up. I would let no woman living tell me how to run my life. She made a mistake there. Hugh became adamant. He insisted that this was just a breathing space for us both. We would be able to proceed soon with our plans for the future. I must be patient, he said.

I sought solace and advice with the wise council from a Christian Science practitioner, Mrs. Doolittle. She told me that if I did not marry Hugh, he might never get away from his mother. Certainly, it had been obvious to me for a long time that something ominous lurked in the air around Hugh, of which he seemed unconscious.

I blamed myself for such morbid ideas, so I found comfort when Mrs. Doolittle verified my suspicions.

"I'm not advising you to marry Hugh," she said. "That's something for you to decide. But this I know. If someone is drowning and you can save that person by pushing out a plank from the shore, and you don't, you will spoil your career and your life as well, especially if you are in love with that person." I departed with those fateful words ringing in my ears...

What a predicament! I felt trapped, caught once more in a corner. I took the streetcar to Cabin John, hastily packed up some clothes and food, and set out by canoe for the cottage upriver. My thoughts raced. Did I throw overboard the results of eight hard but happy years of building the perfect career, to marry a man with high qualifications and good prospects for future success, but who was so entangled in his family problems that I wasn't sure whether he could ever get free of them? By the time I reached the cabin, I was crying hysterically.

And then . . . I began to laugh. What a joke on me! I thought I had the world and marriage each by the tail! All this time I had followed the wrong track and didn't know it! I laughed until I cried again. Well, if losing one's life was the solution, I would do that too. I'd try anything. I would resign my job and marry Hugh. He wanted it. Hugh's father even prayed for it.

Mrs. Decker, our landlady, nearly went crazy. She told all our friends, because Hugh and I were in love, and although we didn't know it, everyone else did. A year ago Dorothy had said the same thing. Last but not least, I now knew that I needed Hugh and could not live without him.

"Mrs. Katherine Butler, you had better look out," I shouted to the river. As I paddled back, the whole earth appeared once more alive and beautiful. What did I care if there were new problems to be solved? Glorious new vistas lay ahead of me—ahead of us— Hugh and me, this time. Life had been good to me so far, for no matter the obstacles, something always happened just in time to push me on.

How could I doubt the continuance of this good fortune? This time the two of us would face our difficulties together. We were young, we had idealisms, we had the same interests in public affairs, we liked the same kinds of recreation and the same way of life.

Hadn't we practically lived together for four years? And now we were to start a new adventure in the Old World, in England, cut off completely from the past. What a privilege! I found so much for which to be grateful. Gratitude! Gratitude! Gratitude! sang my heart with each dip of the paddle, as the canoe raced downstream with all the enthusiasm for the future. Somewhere, someone wrote that gratitude was the elixir of life.

CHAPTER 22

Immaculately Conceived

When I pulled up to the shore, Hugh stood waiting for me, his face ashen. He didn't know where I'd disappeared to for two days, and he had been scared.

"When did you say that boat leaves?" He knew the date as well as I, and now he knew I would be with him. We both laughed merrily. Hugh displayed such a delicious sense of humor.

The next day, I found a letter on my desk. Hugh's mother wrote to me with sympathy, since I was not to see Hugh anymore, and offered to help me spiritually "to get over this great disappointment."

We would see who would get over whose disappointment, I thought!

Later, Hugh phoned to ask me to meet him in the park at 14th and Eye Streets, near Mrs. Doolittle's apartment. It turned out he had been visiting her too. Hugh looked distraught and almost ill. He didn't like to fight; he was a peacemaker at heart. Usually able to work things out peaceably, this time he seemed to be failing and he knew it.

I became frightened for him. I feared that he could not stand the strain much longer. Few sons could long resist such a powerful mother. She seemed so sure she was right, so determined to get her own way. Besides he loved and admired her, and it hurt him to oppose her.

"Why don't you go for a holiday, Hugh?" I suggested. "You have it coming to you. You haven't had a holiday in two years.

Get clear away from all of us and think this thing through by yourself. And don't worry about me.

"If you decide not to marry me, I'll be all right. I still have my job. But you look ill. You need a complete rest. You know what the out-of-doors does for you. You'll know what to do after you spend a little time close to nature. You always see things clearly after a trip. Just go clear away and think."

Hugh jumped at the idea. Within two days he had taken off to the Adirondacks, where a friend told him of a place that had canoes to rent.

I didn't hear a word from him for two weeks, but his absence was a relief because I knew he was off on his own where he could make his own decisions.

Then he wrote that he had taken a fresh look at the whole situation and was determined to stick to his original decision to go through with our plans to marry. He suggested that I proceed to carry out my part of the program, as we had outlined it on that last day together up the river.

That afternoon I received a phone call from Hugh's mother, stating that she too received a letter from him. She asked me to come see her that evening. Something told me I'd better go and get it over with once and for all, even if I did fear her. She exhausted all her resources trying to break down Hugh's resistance and failed. Now she tried them on me. She was an experienced fighter, skilled in the use of mental tactics, in which I was a novice.

Many happy memories flooded my mind as I approached our cooperative house where the Butler family still lived. For Hugh's sake, I decided to be courteous, no matter what occurred. After all, she still remained his mother. Mrs. Butler opened the door and I recoiled at her appearance. Always very thin, she looked emaciated. Her glassy eyes stared wildly at me.

She led me to the little bedroom that had been mine and showed me to a chair with the light full on my face. She sat with her back to the light so that her face was in shadow. As I waited in this unfavorable position, my mind recalled a college textbook, which I had been rereading in search of information to pass on to Hugh. The title of the book was Psychotherapy. Its author, Hugo Munsterberg, had been a professor of modern psychology at Harvard. I recently reread the chapter on hypnotism. This chapter came back to mind with the eerie feeling that she would try to hypnotize me.

I felt foolish, letting exaggerated ideas take hold of me. Hugh's mother would never do such a thing, I assured myself. No woman would. Also I reminded myself that no one, according to Hugo Munsterberg, could be hypnotized against his will.

"Jessie, I am going to do the talking here. You are just to listen," she began. Then she told me how she had been praying over this situation between Hugh and me, night and day, hoping to free us from bondage to one another. Then she read quotations from the Bible and from Mrs. Eddy to show me why we must be free. I began to breathe heavily, for who was I to discount the Bible and Mrs. Eddy?

At the end of each quotation, she asked me to agree, which I honestly did. I decided not to argue, for I knew it would be useless. I wanted this unhappy interview to end as soon as possible. Besides, I didn't know enough to argue. My study of these authorities, too recent and too superficial did not qualify me for debate. I felt drowsier and drowsier as I agreed to each quotation, and I began to slump as if my backbone were melting. Then, for one awful moment I felt as if I were about to lose consciousness altogether. All the black horror I had ever known or imagined seemed to descend upon me in concentrated form.

Quickly I jerked my mind back to the present, and I snapped out of the fear of losing consciousness. From then on, I only listened with my ears.

Finally the reading ended. Mrs. Butler's voice lost its power and trailed off weakly. She knew that I had somehow slipped away from her just as she was about to put me to sleep. Had she succeeded, I suppose that when I awoke, I would have promised never to see Hugh again, and neither he nor I would have known what had transpired. There was no longer any doubt in my mind as to what she had intended to do—that moment of horror had been too real to disregard.

My mind reviewed the situation as I saw it. Mrs. Butler, a Christian Science practitioner for over thirty years, may have been a good practitioner when not dealing with her own unresolved problems. Her marriage had evidently been a disappointment to her. And so, this emotional, artistic, frustrated woman, gifted in many ways but living in an age when talented women found few outlets other than family life, turned to Hugh and her religion for satisfaction.

Hugh idolized her, as most sons do when small, so she decided to make their relationship permanent. Their close bond became so vital to her that she used her knowledge of mental science to keep it intact.

I knew that after she became a Christian Scientist, she refused to read any other writer than Mrs. Eddy. "Mrs. Eddy has the answer to everything," she often said. Thus, with the same intensity of her Welsh father, she cut herself off from other sources that might have saved her from extremes.

Mrs. Butler was a fearsome antagonist, much older than I and better versed in mental science. I doubted that anyone had ever successfully defied her before. She appeared now to me a tragic figure, but I did not feel as sorry for her as I did for Hugh. What son could cope with such a warped mother? Sometimes it takes a woman to deal with a woman!

A long pause pierced the quiet while I pulled myself together. I so wanted to do the right thing in this difficult situation.

"Is that all you have to say, Mrs. Butler?" I asked politely.

"Yes, that's all," she answered weakly. Her eyes filled with tears of defeat.

"Now I am going to talk," I said. "If I marry Hugh, it will be the bravest thing I have ever done in my life because I am not ready for marriage. I never intended to marry at all. Hugh is not ready either. Whether he marries or not is his decision to make, so I am speaking for myself now. I've been a long time getting clear from my own family so as to be free to live my own life. I don't intend to have you or anyone else tell me what to do or how to do it.

"As long as I live, I will not allow you to make decisions for me. Neither can you tell me anything about marriage. The sorrow on the face of your noble husband tells the story of your own marriage."

She began to cry. She looked pathetic, sitting there, all the fight in her faded. I rose to leave. She asked if she could walk with me to the streetcar, for she had to meet Hugh's father downtown for supper. We must have made a strange picture, as we walked up the street. Two bitter antagonists at heart and yet fellow women—under the skin, the old and the young, both pioneers and both in love with the same man.

Without warning, she made an astonishing confession. "I think you ought to know that Hugh was immaculately conceived."

"Why, Mrs. Butler! Aren't you getting on shaky ground with such a statement?" I asked. She gave no answer, and until we reached the streetcar, we remained silent.

My body trembled from what she told me. But later on, I heard from other sources that many women believed the same about their sons. The next morning Mr. Butler called on me at my office, as he often did these days. He appeared apprehensive that Hugh and I would not get away! As our strongest ally, he tried to help us in every way he could. From personal experience, he knew how easily we could fail.

"What in the world did you say to her last evening?" he asked. His love for her had never been so evident. He admired everything about her—her beauty, her courage, her dynamic character.

"Why?" I asked.

"She apologized to me for the suffering she had caused me and then she cried. I felt so sorry to see that proud woman crying like a little girl. It broke my heart."

I felt sorry for him. What a generous man he'd turned out to be! They were both fine really—two fine people who found themselves on the wrong track somehow. In spite of their unhappiness, they had stuck it out and kept their home together for the sake of their three children. That gave me food for thought about my own future.

Soon after Hugh got back from his holiday, looking tanned and rested, his mother greeted him with the startling news that his family planned to move to California. Mrs. Butler left at once, with an armful of red roses we gave her in farewell, but his father remained to see us married and off to Europe.

Then I embarked on a hurried visit to Colorado. My father presented me with check for five hundred dollars with which to buy my trousseau. Hugh had used up all his leave by that time, so he could not accompany me.

As Father handed me the check, he said, "And, Jessie, from now on I suggest that you devote yourself to your husband."

When I returned to Washington and showed the check to Hugh, he said, "I wish you would let me go with you to buy your clothes. I like to pick out women's clothes. With two sisters, I'm said to be quite an expert on the subject."

"Well, I should say not! I can still buy my own clothes," I tartly replied. Then it occurred to me that I was fortunate to have a husband who would take the time and show the interest to help me with my clothes shopping. So, we spent our wedding day in New York City at Saks Fifth Avenue, shopping for a complete wardrobe and the wedding ring, which we bought at Tiffany's.

We were married in the late afternoon of December 6, 1920, by the famous Rev. John Haynes Holmes, in his study adjoining the church, with his secretary and another woman as witnesses. Hugh's father joined us two days later to share with us our last week in the United States. Dwight Power, my Smith friend, gave us her apartment near Central Park to live in until we set sail.

Hugh insisted upon keeping our marriage a secret at his office. Like most men, he was anxious to avoid demonstrations of any sort, especially in view of the terrific tussle from which we had so recently emerged. We were, in fact, quite exhausted, but we did stage a farewell party for our New York friends toward the end of the first week. I wore one of my new dresses, which received effusive compliments. Hugh's father, the honored guest, sat at the head of the table.

I suspect that our departure became one of the high moments of Mr. Butler's long life. He couldn't do enough for us. He ate breakfast with us on the last morning and appeared quite happy as we rode down Fifth Avenue to the gay Christmas ship, the Aquitania, where he inspected our stateroom and the entire vessel from bow to stern.

We watched him wave from the dock, the last sight of our family and our homeland, as the little tugboats pushed the great ship away from the pier. He never dreamed that he would see his son appointed a diplomat at the American Embassy in London and watch him depart on a grand British liner married to a Smith graduate.

"When I saw Hugh off, he was a boy. He'll come back a man," he told a friend that day. He did not know he would never see his son ever again. Hugh's father died two years later.

As we walked toward the deck chairs, we watched the last bit of American coast fade into the west. The world we knew disappeared at a rapid rate into the horizon. Only the future lay ahead.

Frank Butler, Hugh's father

"IN NECESSARIIS UNITAS, IN DUBIIS LIBERTAS, IN OMNIBUS CARITAS."

International Woman Suffrage Alliance

President, CARRIE CHAPMAN CATT,
2, West 86th Street, New York, U.S.A.

1st Vice-President, MILLICENT GARRETT FAWCETT, LL.D.,
2, Gower Street, London, England.

2nd Vice-President, ANNIE FURUHJELM,
Helsingfors, Finland.

3rd Vice-President, ANNA LINDEMANN,
Degerloch, Stuttgart, Germany.

4th Vice-President, MME. DE WITT SCHLUMBERGER,
14, Rue Pierre Charron, Paris.

1st Treasurer, ADELA STANTON COIT, 30, Hyde Park Gate, London, England.

1st Cor. Secretary, MRS. STANLEY McCORMICK,
Hotel Plaza, New York.

2nd Cor. Secretary, JANE BRIGODE,
232, Avenue Albert, Brussels, Belgium.

1st Rec. Secretary, CHRYSTAL MACMILLAN,
39, Charlotte Square, Edinburgh, Scotland.

2nd Rec. Secretary, MARIE STRITT,
30, Dürerstrasse 110, Dresden, Germany.

2nd Treasurer, SIGNE BERGMAN,
10a, Arsenalsgatan, Stockholm, Sweden.

Official Organ:
International Woman Suffrage News.
(Jus Suffragii)

Headquarters:
11, Adam Street, Adelphi, London, W. C. 2.

November 15th, 1920.

To Whom It May Concern:—

I have known Mrs. Jessie Haver Butler for a number of years. She is an exceedingly well-informed young woman and especially in regard to all social legislation and problems in this country.

She is an excellent speaker, conveying her message with deep impression upon her audience. She writes well and has had much experience and success in lobby work with members of Congress. She has also had experience training and success in executive work for organizations dealing with legislation.

As an incident to her work, she has taken a hand at the publicity for the organization which she has represented and has done this phase of work remarkably well. In fact there are few young women in this country who have had so varied and extensive an experience in work connected with propaganda and legislation for social problems.

I cheerfully and earnestly recommend her to any British friends of these causes who may desire the aid of one so well equipped.

Very truly yours,

Carrie C Catt

Letter of Recommendation from Mrs. Catt

To Whom It May Concern:

I have known Mrs. Jessie Haver Butler for a number of years. She is an exceedingly well-informed young woman and especially in regard to all social legislation and problems in this country.

She is an excellent speaker, conveying her message with a deep impression upon her audience. She writes well and has had much experience and success in lobby work with members of Congress. She has also had experience training and success in executive work for organisations dealing with legislation.

As an incident to her work, she has taken a hand at the publicity for the organisation which she has represented and has done this phase of work remarkably well. In fact there are few young women in this country who have had so varied and extensive an experience in work connected with propaganda and legislation for social problems.

I cheerfully and earnestly recommend her to any British friends for these causes who may desire the aid of one so well equipped.

Very truly yours,

Carrie C. Catt

Image of the letter above is on the previous page.

Romance of War Ends
Washington Times, Dec. 12, 1920
In Secret Wedding of
Local Woman Lobbyist

Miss Jessie R. Haver, perhaps the most prominent and widely known woman lobbyist in the National Capitol, was secretly married to Hugh D. Butler, a Department of Commerce official, in New York city last Monday evening, according to an announcement made this morning by her Washington friends. The wedding was the culmination of a romance vividly colored with the political and war-time activities of official Washington.

Mis Haver, as Congressional secretary and publicity director of the National League of Women Voters, which position she has just resigned, was personally known to every legislator on "The Hill" through her aggressiveness, her political tact and devoted interest to the cause of women. To her efforts has been attributed the success of many issues coming under Congressional consideration. Her triumphs as a lobbyist frequently aroused the envy of the army of men lobbyists in the Capitol.

CAME FROM COLORADO.

Miss Haver came to Washington five years ago. Her home is Pueblo, Col. She si a graduatae from Smtih College. Upon her arrival here she became executive secretary of the local Consumers' League, and shortly thereafter was named legislative agent of the National Consumers' League.

During the war Miss Haver, with Mrs. Laura C. Williams, organized "The Little Forum," which attracted considerable attention through its freedom of expression. The foremost thinkers of war-time Washington became members of the forum and at the meetings decidedly pronounced views were expressed on current subjects. This forum has since been merged in "The Open Forum," conducted by Dr. L. M. Powers, of the Universalist Church.

Mr. Butler was formerly a bureau chief in the Department of Commerce and was just recently appointed as trade commissioner of the department to be attached to the American embassy in London. Mr. and Mrs. Butler will sail next Tuesday on the Aquitania for a two years' stay in London.

BEGINNING OF ROMANCE.

Miss Haver and Mr. Butler first met through the political and governmental activities of the two. Their friendship developed until later they both took up living quarters under the co-operative household idea advanced by Miss Haver to relieve congested war-time conditions. Under this idea meals and rooms were furnished and rented on a co-operative basis.

The couple were married in the Commodore Hotel in New York city by Dr. John Haynes Holmes, who during the past several years became nationally prominent when he broke away from the Unitarian Church and established a new religious sect under the name of "The Community Church," which immediately attracted a large and influential following.

Jessie and Hugh were married December 6, 1920

CHAPTER 23

Marriage and Moving to London

Four days before Christmas 1920, our ship nosed its way into Southampton Harbor. I suppose we were typical Americans in that we somehow thought England had outgrown the murk and damp of Charles Dickens's tales. We were shocked to find ourselves in the tiny, bone-penetrating chilly railway coach, drawn by a pint-size engine all trimmed up with shining brass, and shivering to our very marrow.

Our first reaction, typically American, was "Imagine the British having such tiny trains. Wouldn't you know it?" But this feeling of superiority did not make up for the cold so far as I could see.

Reluctantly, we noticed the little train could travel at tremendous speed—averaging sixty miles an hour, someone told us later—over a roadbed that did not rock. Soon we were pulling into Waterloo Station.

Only vaguely do I remember catching a glimpse of the Houses of Parliament and Big Ben as we drove through rain over Waterloo Bridge. It's hard to believe that the unaccustomed physical cold robbed us of the glow we should have felt upon the first sight of the "Mother of Parliaments." Yet now, in the back of my mind, I can still see those beautiful, significant buildings, standing on the misty bank of the Thames, as vivid as though it were only yesterday.

At the station, an embassy official informed us that our hotel was one of the few centrally heated accommodations in London. What a disappointment awaited us! As we entered the vast bedroom, we could see our breath in the cold, damp air. No sign of a radiator until finally Hugh shouted from the bathroom that he had found it. A small metal rod, a little larger than one's thumb, upon which the towels hung, was slightly warm to the touch. This was the British idea of central heat! How scornful we felt . . . but only for a moment. We were too cold to feel anything except the necessity of getting warm.

At this point, Hugh began to walk vigorously up and down the room. "I have to keep moving or else my feet will freeze to the floor," he explained. Finally, he decided that the only way to get warm and stop his teeth chattering was to climb into the mighty mahogany bed, five feet wide with high head and footboards.

Even the sheets were damp. So, we rang for a maid to bring dry sheets. Instead she brought a large, heavy hot-water bottle made of pottery and piping hot.

She also brought a little box, about twice the size of a shoebox, which contained two bundles of sticks about eight inches in length, carefully tied together with twine. These she arranged neatly in the small fireplace in a far corner of the room, topping them with a few lumps of coal. Soon a delicate, flickering blaze began to give us some consolation, and in a short time, the temperature of the room changed slightly, although more from the psychological effect of the flames than from any real heat, I suspected.

"Madam," she said, "you and your husband are not properly dressed."

"What's the matter with our clothes?" I asked with some sharpness.

"Madam, you must go out and buy your husband some virgin wool union suits and heavy socks."

At this, Hugh stuck his head out from the heavy bedding and said, "I am not wearing any virgin wool union suits." After twenty days of marriage I now met my first marital struggle in a strange country.

The maid was right.

"Did you sign a promise that you would stay here for two years?" I asked Hugh.

"Yes, I did," he answered.

"Well, are you going to spend the two years in bed?" He said no more as I ventured forth the next day to buy the virgin wool union suits for both of us. So, our first Christmas together was spent in bed. All of London is dead at Christmas time, as the city folk depart for the country. I remember we ate milk toast for dinner because we didn't like the British food.

We were cold, uncomfortable, and homesick. Getting married was bad enough, but to get married and then move to a dreadful climate proved something else again!

We had often read of the famous London fogs, but until such a fog is experienced, it is impossible to imagine its density or its effect, physically and mentally, especially when combined with homesickness. A four-day fog at Christmas time was our initiation. The air was thick with yellow nauseous fumes so blinding that one could scarcely avoid running into people on the street. It was difficult to stay on the sidewalk. All street sounds were hushed as if everyone in London were dead.

Soon the weather took a turn for the better and so did our spirits. The sun shone every day for a week. Not since 1882, *The Times of London* reported, had there been a whole week of sunshine in December and January! The sun took the headlines that week. Gradually we grew bolder as we warmed up and went sightseeing.

The week following our arrival, Hugh reported for duty at the American Embassy. Hugh came home quite disgusted after his first day at the office. "It's about time an American businessman took over in that office! What do you think happened this afternoon at four? Tea was served by the office to all employees. Can you imagine that? Afternoon tea! I'll soon put a stop to that," he added with steam.

"Better wait a bit," I counseled. "You might even learn to like the tea! A hot cup of tea in the late afternoon might be very pleasant in this cold climate with the unheated offices."

"All right, I'll give it a trial, but I have my doubts. It's not very efficient, to my way of thinking."

That evening we attended our first theatre performance in London: Mary Rose by Sir James Barrie. Back in Washington the previous summer, when marriage and London seemed an idle dream, we laughed as we promised ourselves to see this very play. Now here we were, seated in a London theatre, waiting for the curtain to go up. It was incredible!

We had been in such a hurry to get to the theatre as we raced along the Strand, where other people strolled as if they had all the time in the world, that we left the sidewalk to gain speed in the street. We arrived at the box office quite breathless.

As I stopped and panted for breath, I said to Hugh, "Listen, let's stop hurrying. We can't speed up the whole British nation, so why not follow their pace while we are here?"

"Agreed," said Hugh. I suspect that was the first time either of us had jointly and solemnly decided to slow down. Apparently, it took Old England to make us do so.

Some days later we made another basic decision. Up until now, we had been so uncomfortable and so critical of everything—the climate, the food, the dirty streets, the drabness and evident poverty of the people—everything seemed wrong.

But I also noted the cheerfulness and bright faces of the working people we met—maids and porters in hotels, bus drivers and bobbies on street corners, clerks in the stores. All had a bright word of greeting, all seemed gay and contented with their lot, which appeared anything but happy to us. Could it be that some of our unhappiness in London happened to be a result of our own attitudes? Perish the thought!

"You know, Hugh," I ventured one evening, "we're in a bad way. Thus far we have complained about everything. We haven't found much to like. If we keep this up, we will be ill. From now on, let's stop finding fault and agree to make no comments unless they are positive. Let's start looking for something to like. After all, the British people have been here a long time. They seem likely to last a long time yet. Let's see if we can't discover something they have to teach us."

"That's a good idea," Hugh said. "I doubt if we can learn anything from them, but I'm willing to give it a try. Certainly, we can't go on as we have with all this criticism."

From then on things took a turn for the better. I found many fascinating events listed in *The Times*, which I decided to follow up. I attended lectures at the National Gallery during those winter months. What a thrill it was to stand before the very paintings my art professors at Smith had tried to explain on a projection screen!

On Sundays, Hugh went back to the gallery with me, and I repeated the lectures for his benefit. We were surely getting educated fast those first months!

We often went to meetings of the Fabian Society, which were held every two weeks. The original society was founded in London in the winter of 1883 and 1884 by a small group of young people interested in social reform, with the purpose "to reconstruct society in accordance with the highest moral possibilities."

They named themselves "Fabians" after the Roman General Fabius Cunctator (275–203 BC), who attributed his military successes to the policy of proceeding slowly only after careful consideration of all factors involved in any proposed campaign. Thus, the British Fabians preferred to work through political parties already in existence rather than by revolutionary methods, although this course of action took longer.

The Society's publication and the influence of its brilliant leaders—among them Bernard Shaw, H. G. Wells, Sidney and Beatrice Webb,[26] and Graham Wallas—won wide support for the theories they advocated and legislation they backed.

In 1900, the Fabians cooperated with the British Trade Unions in the founding of the British Labor Party, whose first political victory in 1906 made England aware that labor was a factor to be reckoned with. It foreshadowed the part Labor was to take in the British government after the Second World War.

---

26   Martha Beatrice Webb, Baroness Passfield, FBA, was an English sociologist, economist, socialist, labor historian and social reformer. It was Webb who coined the term "collective bargaining." She was among the founders of the London School of Economics and played a crucial role in forming the Fabian Society.

BACK TO METHUSELAH

Inscribed to
Hugh & Jessie Butler
by G. Bernard Shaw.

Priors Field
26th Aug. 1921.

George Bernard Shaw dedicated a copy of his book,
Back to Methuselah, ***to Jessie and Hugh***

CHAPTER 24

George Bernard Shaw

The Fabians and their followers were largely responsible for many of the laws dealing with social welfare in Great Britain, such as statutes on unemployment insurance, workmen's compensation, old age pensions, minimum wages, and health insurance.

The Society encouraged its members to seek posts in the government and to serve on local and national boards and councils.

Bernard Shaw, perhaps the greatest political propagandist in the history of England, spearheaded the program of the Fabian Society, but the powerhouse of the organization was the "firm" of Beatrice and Sidney Webb.

Mr. Webb sat in the chair at the first meeting of the Fabian Society that we attended. A small man, colorless and cold, with dark hair and beard, he remained a typical British civil servant in appearance. As a presiding officer, he seemed to us to lack flexibility and warmth. He looked as if he were bored and slightly contemptuous.

The speaker that evening was a woman, Mrs. Philip Snowden,[27] one of the leading women lecturers in England. Her lecture brought out interesting facts about the League of Nations.[28]

---

27   Ethel Snowden, Viscountess Snowden (1881–1951), was a British socialist, human rights activist, and feminist politician, from a middle-class background.

28   The forerunner of the United Nations was the League of Nations, an organization conceived in similar circumstances during the First World War, and established in 1919 under the Treaty of Versailles "to promote international cooperation and to achieve peace and security."

A beautiful blonde, with clear skin and high coloring, her accent intrigued me. It was neither the famous Oxford accent nor an American accent, just the English language at its best.

Later, when I came to know her personally, she told me that she had visited the United States several times on lecture tours. For years she had given talks there and in England, frequently speaking more than three hundred times in a year, which sounded like a very good job to me.

We often heard Bernard Shaw speak. He proved capable of holding forth for an hour or two without stopping, but I never tired of listening to him. Hugh did not share my enthusiasm for Mr. Shaw, whom he considered cold and over intellectual. To him, any of Shaw's lectures, long or short, ended up an endurance test.

Shaw stood tall and thin, with a long, narrow face topped by a high forehead and a mop of hair, which had once been reddish but now had begun to turn white. He spoke with his head thrown back and every muscle of his face in full play—even his beard vibrated with emotion.

His pale blue eyes sparkled with diabolic glee as he goaded his audience into considering some subject they found unpleasant and best avoided. I suspected that without his rapier-like wit, neither his plays nor his lectures would have penetrated the complacency and indifference of the British people.

George Bernard Shaw, an Irish playwright who wrote 60 plays, political activist, public speaker, vegetarian, teetotaler and a Fabian against vaccinations. Best friends with Lady Astor.

1921- Hugh + Jessie married + living in London.

CHAPTER 25

Dressing Appropriately

Very few of the British people we talked to really knew much about the United States. American history was not taught in the schools, and almost none of our English acquaintances had ever visited our country. A competent reporter, Sir Philip Gibbs, gave a more accurate picture of American culture in a news piece he had written. Hugh wrote from the embassy to tell him so and to thank him for writing the article. Sir Philip replied by inviting us to what he called his "shack" for dinner the following week.

Our first real dinner party in England, and we knew that evening dress was always worn at formal banquets. But Hugh said Sir Philip had mentioned a shack, so maybe he lived in modest circumstances, as most newspapermen in England did, and would be embarrassed if we came in dinner clothes. I wore the afternoon dress that Hugh had helped me select on our wedding day in New York.

To our surprise, the shack turned out to be an imposing Victorian-style residence, set well back in spacious grounds, where we found a distinguished company assembled, all in full evening dress. Lady Gibbs was a tall, distinguished-looking hostess, bred to take visible notice of the inappropriateness of our attire.

We discovered later, however, that the British are never surprised by Americans. To them, we are unpredictable. On the other hand, we had fallen for the British custom of understatement, which we had taken too literally. It proved to be a severe lesson, never to be repeated.

The dinner table, set with beautiful china and silver, not only displayed name cards, but ornate menus, written in French, placed before each guest. A butler and several well-trained maids served one course after another.

During the elaborate meal, conversation dealt almost altogether with social problems of the most alarming nature. The coal miners were on strike. England could not function as an industrial nation without coal, yet no one seemed to know how to settle the dispute, which caused the mines to close.

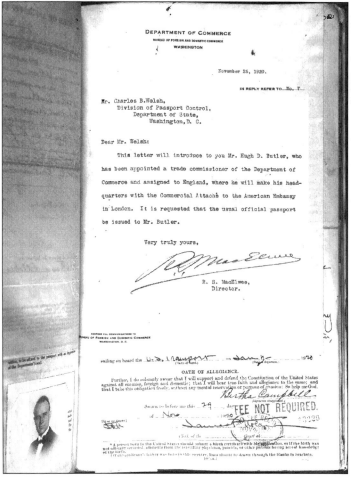

Request for passport for Hugh when he was appointed as a Trade Commissioner to the London Embassy

CHAPTER 26

The Business of Having Babies

There were free child welfare clinics everywhere in England. At the clinics I visited, I found much to admire. The fine-looking mothers with their husky babies would have aroused admiration in the heart of any woman. All mothers, with few exceptions, were nursing their babies. The government encouraged them to do so. Never had I seen such beautiful, contented-looking babies as those brought to the clinics by women whose husbands rarely made more than fifteen or twenty dollars a week.

At the headquarters of the welfare centers, I found that seventy-five percent of the babies born in England were taken to Mothers' Clinics, situated in every town and village in the British Isles. These centers were financed by grants from the central government, which had to be met by grants from local communities. Both infant and maternal death rates had steadily declined in Great Britain since the establishment of these centers.

At last I found something constructive to report at the dinner table. "Could it be that Old England has something to teach America about the baby business?" I asked. "Let's have our family over here, Hugh. Somehow, I would feel safer here than at home. British women seem to take the business of having babies as a matter of course."

Hugh just grunted behind his *London Times*. Up until that day, it didn't feel natural for me to have a baby. I was frightened at the very thought of it—not because I didn't want one, but I couldn't believe that I could produce a baby. It just seemed unreal to me.

I almost wept with joy and relief. I knew that England's child-welfare program included training for midwives. Midwives were trained nurses who spent a year or two after graduation specializing in the care of mothers during confinement and the delivery of babies. After completing this training, they received certificates entitling them to practice midwifery.

Every little town and village in England had its trained midwife. Most of the mothers of England, especially among the working classes, which comprised seventy-five percent of the population, employed midwives. Only in cases of births that were not normal was a doctor called. Prenatal and postnatal care came free of charge at the child welfare centers, which worked closely with midwives and doctors. The standard charge for delivering a baby—a guinea, or one pound, one shilling (about five dollars).

British women were still following the pattern laid down by their mothers, grandmothers, and great-grandmothers. How could I absorb some of their lore fast enough to make it my own?

There was nothing else to do but "make hay while the sun shone." And this I did with the same intensity with which I pushed myself through college and into a career. Without warning, I found a new and fascinating career in an Old World, where we newcomers had much to learn.

I never dreamed I would use my knowledge as an investigator to pry into the technicalities of homemaking and childcare! My destiny brought me into this Old World, so I could pass on to my sisters at home some of the gems I discovered in this field, much larger and broader than that of industry—a field that had to do with civilization itself.

CHAPTER 27

We Go to a New Kind of School:
The Fabian Summer School

The Fabian Summer School meeting in August offered us the first opportunity for a holiday.

The Fabians held summer school at Prior's Field, a country estate occupied by a secondary school for girls during the school year. Since it was only an hour's ride by train from Waterloo Station in London, Hugh commuted part of the time to work and back.

The buildings of the school were situated on high ground, 350 feet above sea level. They commanded a beautiful view of the Hampshire Downs. The grounds covered nineteen acres, which included a formal garden, a fishpond, seven tennis courts, and a cricket ground. There were forty-five single rooms and twelve double rooms, and a fine gymnasium for Swedish calisthenics and folk dancing.

The aim of the summer school was to bring together members of the Fabian Society, and other persons interested in socialism and social reform, to promote the exchange of ideas and to afford opportunity for lectures on sociology, economics, and similar subjects. The first week was devoted to "Socialism and Literature"; the second to "International Affairs"; the third to "Questions Affecting Women"; and the fourth to "Formation of Public Opinion." When Hugh saw the program, he declared a strike.

"You can take in all those lectures on socialism if you wish, but I am going to bicycle instead. I'm not a socialist. I will never be a socialist," he stated firmly.

"If you saw the wretched houses in Strutton Ground and the terrible poverty of some of the parts of London that I have visited, you would be an anarchist," I replied. "Anyway, let's see what they have to say about their problems and how they plan to solve them. And let's sit at the vegetarian table, where I am told Bernard Shaw always eats."

By this time, Hugh had gotten a bit fed up with Bernard Shaw. He decided to sit where he liked, but I found myself eating with Mr. Shaw.

After we registered, the secretary said to me, "One of your great American novelists is here, Mrs. Mary Austin. There she is now, walking in the garden." Sure enough, the woman was strolling up and down the garden paths, deep in thought, just as a novelist should be, I decided. The secretary thought Mrs. Austin was lonesome and suggested I go out and talk to her.

"I'm so glad to meet you, Mrs. Butler," she said. "I need you to help me straighten the British out about our country. It is terrible the way they misunderstand us."

I promised to help, but at the end of the summer's session I could find no evidence that we created much difference in the British attitude toward our countrymen.

Hugh and I, as privileged guests from America, were given two small rooms and a private parlor, costing twelve dollars a week. During that first week we listened to lectures delivered by Cyril E. M. Joad on "The Artist, Author, and Thinker in the Modern State"; J. D. Beresford on "Socialism and the Novelist"; Robert Lynd on "Modern Irish Literature"; Col. G. Schuster on "International Credits"; Mrs. Sidney Webb on "Politics, Science and Religion"; H. W. Nevinson on "Ireland"; Dr. Marion Phillips on "The Place of Women in Public Life"; Dr. Marie C. Stopes on "Women as Mothers"; George Lansbury on "Labor and the Press"; A. Clutton-Brock on "Crowd Psychology as It Affects Politics"; C. Gasquoine Hartley on "Difficulties in Sex Education of Children"; Gerald Gould on "The Influence of the Press"; and Mary Austin on "Social Life and the Community Theatre in America."

The lectures started at ten. Miss Hankinson, known as "Hanky," the Yorkshire woman who ran the school, also taught Swedish calisthenics and folk dancing. The calisthenics were held in the gymnasium, but the folk dancing took place out on the lawn in front of the school. Miss Hankinson brought a long rope, at the end of which was a weight. For one of her exercises, she stood in the center of a circle of people like a ringmaster and swirled the rope around under the feet of her victims, commanding them to jump as it came their turn.

Any great intellectual with heavy feet got tangled in Hanky's rope and thrown out, and as the circle shrank, the rate of jumping increased. I shall never forget seeing Bernard Shaw jump Hanky's rope. He never got caught, though he jumped stiffly like a mechanical man.

Mr. Shaw participated in all the school activities with almost childlike enthusiasm. His hobbies, we learned, were racing through the countryside in a fast car—or at least a car he thought fast, for no one could drive very fast on those winding roads—and modern ballroom dancing.

Sometimes after dinner, we gathered in the gymnasium for modern dancing. Bernard Shaw always participated. Since he was too shy to ask for dances, the younger women used to take him on, for that is what it amounted to. A poor dancer, he hopped like an automaton. He seemed completely devoid of any sense of bodily rhythm.

We heard that Mrs. Shaw regularly provided him with attractive young women dancers, who he took tea dancing at various hotels in London. Incidentally, we also learned from Hanky that Mrs. Shaw never came to the summer school because she could not endure "watching the women go crazy over her husband."

Hanky said Mrs. Shaw devoted her life to her famous husband, providing him with the vegetarian meals he demanded and creating the atmosphere required by a writer. Without Mrs. Bernard Shaw there would never have been a Mr. Bernard Shaw . . . or so Hanky informed us!

I heard it suggested that Bernard might be a sexual ascetic, holding the view that the creative impulse expressed in sex could be transmuted into creativity in a writer. By this very philosophy, he seemed to attract women more than ever. To be near him was to be near a seething, fiery furnace that draws admirers as a bright light attracts moths.

One morning, the scheduled lecturer failed to appear, so they asked me to speak for him, telling the audience about Prohibition in America. Prohibition was new then and a subject that garnered widely differing opinions.

The Fabian meetings were run with precision. After the lecture, which usually lasted forty-five minutes to an hour, there was a fifteen-minute question period, followed by a fifteen-minute discussion period with three minutes allowed each speaker. Then the original speaker was given five minutes to sum up the discussion.

Woe to the audience member who tried to interject a remark into a question period, for he or she was automatically ruled out of order. Woe also to the speaker whose speech did not hold water; his or her premise was afterward punched full of holes by the discriminating audience, whose members took delight in exploding people's speeches.

I had a collection of clippings on Prohibition from *Survey Magazine* and *The Christian Science Monitor*, so I merely explained how Prohibition came about, tracing the development of the saloon and its influence in the early days of our country and describing the growth of state laws controlling the sale of liquor, especially in the Midwest and the East, carefully avoiding taking any personal stand on the question.

Even so, my lecture aroused such controversy that the discussion and question periods continued into two subsequent meetings . . . something quite unheard of.

Next to cricket, heckling was the favorite British sport. Their aim was to heckle the speaker and ruin his or her speech (especially if the speaker was an American), and I remained untouched.

That evening, Hugh told me that they would skin me alive in the last session and he did not want to be there to witness it. He planned to take the train early the next morning to his safe office! And what if this performance ruined his career? (For in that time, the wives of diplomats did not put on such a public appearance.)

In the audience at the third session was a young man who had told me the day before that he had written two books about America.

"When were you in America?"

"Never," he answered. "I do not need to go to that nutty country to know how to write about it!"

I knew this confidant Fabian was lying in wait for me.

The questions proceeded safely until the middle of the period when this bright young man asked a question that trapped me. I knew it related to some very deep British tradition and no matter how I answered, I was caught.

So I stood there, quietly trying to think what to say, when suddenly my lips opened and I heard myself saying something that I did not understand, but the statement startled the questioner and brought down the house. Afterward I met the young man in the corridor. If he'd had a dagger, he would have plunged it into my heart, but instead he turned and left, never to return.

Jessie, in front row with braids, with Fabian Summer Group

I never could remember what I had said or why it proved so vital, but a year later I knew from where the right answer came. Bernard Shaw, sitting to my right on the platform, had provided the answer through ESP, saving my neck.

A teetotaler through and through, he was delighted that America dared to perform this noble experiment of dealing wholesale with the ancient evil of drinking. To him, alcohol was equal to murder and always had been. He invited me to repeat the lecture in the fall for the Fabian course at Essex Hall and several times after.

On all other occasions, Bernard never lost a chance to poke fun at Hugh and me, and Americans in general.

"When are you returning to your country?" he asked me.

"Oh, in a year or two."

"You will never go back to that uncivilized country," he insisted.

One day Hugh came to dinner late. He nodded to me as he passed on to the second table. I sat across from Bernard Shaw.

"Does he belong to you?" he asked.

"No. He belongs to himself," I replied.

"Do you belong to him?"

"No. I don't belong to him either."

"Well then, you mustn't let him give you that proprietary look." Everyone at the table laughed.

A buzz of great excitement encircled the group on the day Beatrice and Sidney Webb arrived. Hugh and I wrote a letter of introduction for them, which I brought to the summer school.

"Let's not be in a hurry to present our letter," my ever-cautious husband warned. "After all, we don't know these people very well, so let's don't rush it." I reluctantly agreed, though my impulse was to thrust our letter into their hands immediately.

Miss Hankinson made a point of placing me beside Sidney Webb at lunch and Hugh across the table from Mrs. Webb. Both of them acknowledged us with cold indifference. Then Sidney Webb pulled out a whiskey flask from his pocket and passed it across to Beatrice.

He said, "Here's to Prohibition and the Statue of Liberty." Whereupon she poured a good measure into her glass and passed it back to him with a smile of approval.

Hugh clutched my skirt. "Don't you try to answer," he warned. "They have the last word and will knife you in the back."

We never presented our letter of introduction to the Webbs!

I can still see Bernard Shaw sitting on the edge of a stone wall after dinner, surrounded by young students peppering him with questions. He once said he attended the Fabian Summer School because if he ever felt tempted to think he knew something, he soon got over it by talking to these young college students.

He became the philosopher of the age personified. I can still hear those young students saying, "Mr. Shaw says so and so. I disagree with Mr. Shaw. . ." and then they blazed away at him with frankness and courage.

Every afternoon the school conducted a bicycle ride along the top of Hindhead or over the Downs, ending in some old inn for tea. We rode our bikes through one of the oldest villages in England, Godalming, its streets lined with ancient thatched houses.

The leading feminist in England attended the school: Mrs. C. Gasquoine Hartley, author of *The Truth About Women*, was a reformer who prompted a much-needed change in the divorce laws and later led in the study of psychoanalysis. We hit it off at once and laid the groundwork for a long personal friendship, during which she later pulled me around a tough corner.

Every Friday night a review took place, or a caricature of the important speakers of the week, just to be sure that the guests did not take the heated discussions too seriously.

They also considered it important for lecturers to learn to laugh at themselves, so that they might not become "hampered by the gushing enthusiasts who mistake their own emotions for public movements," to quote Bernard Shaw.

I remember the actor who appeared in one of the reviews with a cardboard sign on his front that bore the name of Sidney Webb, and another on his back that read "Beatrice Webb." The actor, turning from front to back, spoke in the first-person plural—"we think" and "we have decided. . ."

Another actor came in made up as Bernard Shaw, carrying a large char, on which was a red ink spot labeled "The Blood Spot." The blood spot referred to a lecture in which Bernard Shaw had advocated giving would-be government administrators a blood test to make sure they were fitted for their high office and for leadership.

The British people had a standard treatment for their great ones that we in America might well copy. Even Shaw enjoyed being treated as one of the group, by everyone except me. When I was in college, Bernard Shaw's plays and prefaces were the warp and woof of my thinking. And so I found it difficult to look upon him as just a fellow student at summer school and forget that he was also a great genius.

We had two summer vacations at the Fabian Summer School —1921 and 1922. At the end of the first year, Mr. Shaw gave a copy of his new book, *Back to Methuselah,* to Hugh and I. He signed the following inscription:

Inscribed to
Hugh & Jessie Butler
By G. Bernard Shaw.
Prior's Field
26ᵗʰ Aug 1921.

The excellent lectures, delivered by men and women who were authorities in their fields, followed by the lively question and discussion periods from the audience, helped us to understand England in a way not possible to the casual tourist, or even a resident.

Four weeks at the summer school gave us a more thorough knowledge of that little island than months of traveling from hotel to hotel would have done. Yet, so far as we knew, few Americans had ever taken advantage of this unique institution, which had been operating for many years.

We did not know it then, but the Fabian Summer School at Godalming and the school at Herne Bay, conducted by the Labour Research Department of the Guild Socialists, were laying the groundwork for two Labour governments that were to come to power, one in the 1920s and one after World War II.

We witnessed the birth of a new way of life, destined to destroy some of England's oldest and most cherished traditions and to attack the class system at its roots.

FABIAN · NEWS

Vol. XXXIII., No. 2.   FEBRUARY, 1922.   Price 1d.

Published by THE FABIAN SOCIETY,
25 Tothill Street, Westminster, London, S.W.1.
Telephone:—VICTORIA 1915.

Meetings of the Society.

Lectures during the ensuing months will be held as usual at Essex Hall, Essex Street, Strand, on Fridays, at 8 p.m., and will deal generally with "Current Problems at Home and Abroad."

The following dates, lectures and subjects have been arranged for February :—

Feb. 10.—"Some Effects of Prohibition in America."
By Mrs. JESSIE HAYER BUTLER.

SYLLABUS.

History of Prohibition movement in America. Legislative action resulting on the 18th Amendment to the Constitution. Ratification of the 18th Amendment by State legislatures. States under varying degrees of Prohibition before January, 1920. Evidence from Governors of two of these States. Compensation for abolished business. Facts available as to lessening in consumption, domestic manufacture, arrests for drunkenness, admission of alcoholics to New York hospitals, effects on business, etc. Seven principal causes leading to Prohibition. Testimony of prominent English visitors to America.

Feb. 24.—"The European Situation."
By G. P. GOOCH.

SYLLABUS.

The disintegration of the Grand Alliance. The growing antagonism of Great Britain and France from the armistice till to-day. Eastern Europe: Turkey, the Balkans. Central Europe: The problem of the Rhineland and the British guarantee.

A card of invitation to these two lectures is enclosed to enable members to send to friends. It is hoped that they will be thus used, and that members will make an effort to attend themselves and bring others interested.

Fabian Parliamentary Election Fund.

By direction of the Executive Committee the appeal for a Fabian Parliamentary Election Fund to assist members of the Society standing as Labour candidates at the approaching General Election, was issued to all our members and friends early in January. At that time the election appeared to be imminent, and a good many members responded at once with donations or promises of help. Subsequent events, however, indicated that the election was not likely to take place immediately, and this resulted in a cessation of further contributions to the fund. Consequently, the amount received and promised up to the present is comparatively small and quite insufficient to enable us to give the help that will be needed by many of our members who are standing as candidates. Members are therefore urged to keep the matter in mind and to fill up and return the form as soon as convenient, giving or promising as much help as they can to the fund.

It will be seen from the list of candidates which appears elsewhere in this issue, that already over forty of our members are definitely adopted as Labour candidates. Besides these we have a list of about twenty others willing to stand if suitable constituencies are available. It is obvious that if we are to give any substantial assistance to even a small proportion of them a large fund will be needed. The matter is urgent, as the election, though deferred for the present, is not likely to be long delayed. It is hoped that many more of our members and friends will be able to send us an early and generous response to the appeal.

Fabian Parliamentary Candidates.

The following members of the Society have been adopted as prospective Parliamentary candidates for the constituencies mentioned. The list does not include any

Announcement of Jessie's speech at Essex Hall
and article in London Newspaper

Jessie in London

Article from February 1922:
G. B. S. ON PROHIBITION
PUTTING ALCOHOL IN SAME CATEGORY AS MURDER
(From Our London Staff)
MG FEB 13

Mr. Bernard Shaw, who was a delighted listener to an address given by Mrs. Butler, an American Woman, at the Fabian Society evening on the causes leading to the enforcement of prohibition in the United States and its results, joined in the discussion that followed.

One speaker deprecated the coercing of the minority by a majority. This was not a mere matter of majority and minority, said Mr. Shaw. There were certain questions which, as public morality advanced, were entirely out of the domain of the majority and minority matters. There came a point when society said of certain things: "We are going to put a stop to them, and anyone who objects to the general opinion on this subject will be ruled out as a criminal or lunatic."

At a certain stage in society there was a good deal of private choice and activity in the way of murder, but at the present time, although there were a good many arguments in favour of indiscriminate murders, society did not recognize them. We already had restrictions on the sale of gin, though there was a time when gin was sold almost at cost price and one could get drunk for a penny and dead-drunk for two pence.

The moment one looked at the cocaine or morphia or opium question as it existed in the East, one felt it was such a danger that when an intelligent community had the matter brought before it in the form of overwhelming statistics the thought of majority rule would fade away. The question of prohibiting alcohol would ultimately come up in this way, and it would have to be decided whether, it was not so disastrous that it must be put into the category with murder, theft, and other things that the whole community knew were intolerable.

While at Herne Bay, we spent a day in Canterbury, a quaint, picturesque old town dominated by the Canterbury Cathedral. There we visited the grave of Thomas Becket, one of England's most famous martyrs. All of these old landmarks of England's past kept history alive.

Even in modern England, the feeling permeated the air that history walked side by side with present-day events. Looking backward at heroes and events seemed to give the British people strength and courage to go on. We Americans were not accustomed to looking backward—our eyes were ever turned forward to the future.

Sir Arthur Newsholme,[29] speaking of his two years study of prohibition in America, said there was no doubt about the success of this gigantic experiment. It was spoken of here as an interference with the liberty of the subject, but in many ways England had gone further with compulsory legislation than America had done— sanitary laws, education, income tax, and so on. Prohibition was really an altruistic movement, and people were willing to give up a personal enjoyment, which did not harm them for the sake of those whom it injured.

"I have no doubt," he said, "that if America persists, England— unless she is to be left hopelessly in the rear—will have to follow suit."

Shortly after this, Mr. Shaw gave Hugh and me a signed copy of his recent book *Back to Methuselah*.

---

29   Sir Arthur Newsholme (1857 –1943) was a leading British public health expert during the Victorian era.

CHAPTER 28

I Meet Lady Astor

After a trip to France and Germany, I returned to London with a trunkful of smart dresses and two very stylish French hats, picked up in Paris from a shop whose owner specialized in hats suitable for the woman no longer in her teens. I discovered that, as a morale-booster, nothing can equal new clothes and the right hat!

Hugh met me at the train in London with an invitation to one of Lady Astor's famous receptions. We had been invited because of Hugh's connection with the American Embassy. Already I knew of her ability in bringing together the members of Parliament, leaders of political parties, and organizers interested in social reform, as well as titled and distinguished men and women in court circles. The invitation to Lady Astor's reception came at the right moment for me.

I found it a great thrill, some days later, to approach Lady Astor's beautiful and spacious home on St. James Square, from which streamed the bright lights of the entrance and the long windows of the ballroom.[30]

At the door, we were each given a small name card and told to pin it on so the other guests would know our names.

---

30   Rosina Harrrison, Lady Astor's personal maid for thirty-five years: "Entertaining both at St. James Square (in town) and Cliveden (in the countryside) was done in style and in the grand manner. Immediately after dinner, there was often a reception of up to a thousand people generally held in the ballroom." - From *Rose: My Life in Service to Lady Astor* by Rosina Harrison.

Lady Astor, born and raised in Virginia, became the first woman to sit in British Parliament. She served for 28 years.

Just inside the door of the grand ballroom on the second floor stood Lady Astor. She, a great beauty, gave a warm greeting to every guest.

"Where is your card?" Lady Astor cajoled her recalcitrant British guests, intensely shy and too embarrassed to wear their name cards.

"You must go down the line, introduce yourselves to everyone, and see that everybody has a good time. There are many Americans here that you must meet." Her Virginia accent sounded as fresh as though she had never lived in England.

To Hugh she commented, "I'm so glad you are here from the American Embassy. We need your help to get these people acquainted with one another. Please feel free to talk to anyone." And with that, we were on our way in.

But not before I had time to take in our hostess from head to foot. She was short and slender, with the figure of a schoolgirl, so it was hard to believe that she had given birth to six children (a point of special interest to me at this time).

She looked out from intense blue eyes, her skin delicate yet healthy. Her warm smile testified to her deep interest in people.

"She's glamorous, beautiful, and brainy too!" I commented to myself. "She has everything, and great wealth as well. She's using what she has to help make a better world. She's a superwoman."

A devout Christian Scientist, Lady Astor had recently testified, at a Wednesday night meeting, to the birth of her last child without pain or medical assistance.

A short, slender woman of dignified, modest mien, and especially striking in appearance, followed us into the ballroom. Imagine my surprise to hear Lady Astor saying, "I'm furious with you, Mrs. Pankhurst, for running for Parliament from that district where we already have one of the best Labour leaders. Why in the world didn't you pick a district where we needed a change?"

I thought Mrs. Pankhurst looked rather irritated to be thus accosted in the presence of others. Yet she smiled enigmatically and passed through. So I witnessed how Lady Astor played politics even at a reception.

No wonder she landed in Parliament—the first woman to enter the British Lower House, and an American at that—much to the chagrin of many British people. Known to be a hardy campaigner and a brilliant public speaker, famous for clichés and epigrams, she spoke out as a bitter opponent of the liquor traffic and advocated for women's rights. She favored women and children above party and power. And I found it fascinating that she came from humble beginnings, like myself.

Over in a far corner stood Lord Astor, appearing cold and aloof. He was an American too, but England had done its work on him more effectively than on Lady Astor. He stood over six feet tall, his thick, curly gray hair adding to his height. But his large brown eyes gave him an appearance of quiet poise rather than stiffness.

I could not decide whether England or his own nature made him so difficult to talk to. I gathered that, unless interested, he simply did not take the trouble to converse. Large parties of this type were probably not as popular with him as with Lady Astor.

Farther along the room we recognized Lord Robert Cecil, known as "The Father of the League of Nations." He was well over six feet in height, round shoulders, with a massive head, penetrating brown eyes, and hawk-like nose. He stood quite alone, looking very self-conscious with the name "Cecil" printed on his card.

Hugh and I introduced ourselves. When Lord Cecil learned that we believed in the League of Nations, we were soon deep in conversation. At that time, the United States was persisting in her refusal to join the League. We invited him to sample a soft drink with us, provided by our teetotaling hostess, though she did furnish hard drinks in another room for those who must have them.[31]

---

31   Rosina Harrison: "The Astors' reputation as teetotalers was universally known. Many of the receptions were 'dry,' that is to say, no alcoholic drinks were served, or expected." - From *Rose: My Life in Service to Lady Astor* by Rosina Harrison.

Lord Robert Cecil told us that he seldom attended receptions but that he could not afford to miss Lady Astor's because he met so many worthwhile and interesting people here. Col. Josiah Wedgwood (of the Wedgwood pottery family) and his wife were introduced. During our conversation with the colonel, who was a member of Parliament in the Labour Party, something came up about single tax.

Later we saw him tell Lady Astor, "I like your friend, Mr. Butler. I think he is a single taxer."

As we left, Lady Astor leaned over the bannister and called to Hugh, "Oh, Mr. Butler, isn't it wonderful to be a single taxer?"[32] I never saw a woman who had more fun at her own party than Lady Astor.

I received a letter from Mrs. Carrie Chapman Catt about this time. It demonstrated still further the need for informed public opinion on the other side of the Atlantic:

> *A good deal of water has run under the bridge since you were here and sentiment . . . changes from day to day.*
> *Everybody who comes back from Europe, comes with the same idea of what this country ought to do. They find that the country doesn't know anything about it and . . . is not ready for it.*
> *If the United States takes any action concerning any international things, the initiative will have to come from this side, not from anybody who comes here from any other country.*
> *You have no idea how sensitive people are about the League of Nations. It makes them sick at their stomachs to hear it mentioned. Some fly into a wild passion at the sight of the words.*

---

32   Single taxer: One who advocates the levying of all, or practically all, taxation upon a single object, as land, capital, or consumption; specifically, one who accepts the doctrine of Henry George that all taxes should be levied upon the value of land, exclusive of all improvements due to industry. The measure, if fully carried out, would divert to the government the rent of the land itself.

**The home Jessie and Hugh bought in London
at Golders Green**

CHAPTER 29

Baby Advice: She Arrives and A Crisis

At this time, I hated the life I was leading. And why not? I had been fed on public excitement and external drama outside myself for years. How could I find satisfaction with my new domestic life— in going to market every morning and planning simple meals that our cook prepared? Finally, I got into such an emotional state that I called on Dr. Froberg.

"Doctor, you were so good to tell me that I am an ideal woman, wife, and mother. I have a baby coming, but I don't feel like the kind of woman you see in me. What do you suppose is wrong with me?" Then I told him something of my life before marriage.

"I'm ashamed to admit it, Doctor, but you know when I go to meet Hugh at his office, I'm jealous of him. The atmosphere of his office . . . desks and typewriters, the sort of place I worked in for so long . . . I want to get back there.

"I can't think of having a baby if I am unfit to be a mother. I will do anything you say if only you will tell me how to prepare myself." I buried my face in my hands and sobbed and sobbed.

"Go where you can see babies and talk to mothers about babies," he suggested. "Ask them to let you take care of their babies. Learn from them how to be a mother." For his final instruction, he told me to hunt for a doctor at once to make sure everything was all right.

That night I announced to Hugh that I was going the next day to look for a doctor.

"But, Jessie, surely you are not going back on the Christian Science principles that have meant so much to us!"

"I'm sorry, Hugh, but I'm scared. I want a child, and I am going to do my very best to be ready for our baby, who is on the way."

The next day, I found a woman doctor with offices near Golders Green. She acted very casual. People in England seemed to take childbirth as part of a normal day's work. She told me that her fee for delivering a baby was five pounds (about twenty-five dollars). Most babies were delivered at home.

I must admit that this attitude helped me greatly. The fact that the death rate of British mothers in childbirth remained the second lowest of any country in the world helped too.

Hugh kept reminding me that his mother gave birth to all of her three children without a doctor because she was a Christian Scientist.

I had no morning sickness and appeared well. I carried out Dr. Froberg's suggestion and visited many more baby clinics. Just the sight of those beautiful babies helped me enormously. Their fine, courageous mothers made me feel very humble. They did not know it, but those working-class mothers were my teachers.

Later that winter, I delivered the last speech I would make for a long time, when I repeated the lecture on Prohibition, at a full meeting of the Fabian Society in London.

Afterward, I learned that the lecture had caused dissension among the Fabians. The Webbs did not consider the subject pertinent to the Fabian program, but Bernard Shaw and Dr. Lawson Dodd[33] voted them down. Hugh said I delivered one of the best lectures of my life.

By this time, I didn't care if I ever spoke again in public. I felt sick to death of the whole business. Even the Fabians seemed cold and overly intellectual to me now.

Often, in the afternoon, I walked over to the Golders Green to see the nurses with their beautiful British babies and little children.

They all showed off curly hair and bright rosy cheeks. Then I would sit and cry with hunger for a baby of my own.

---

33   Frederick Lawson Dodd (1868–1962) was a Fabian dentist and author. It was he who first proposed the establishment of the Fabian Summer Schools in 1907.

Late on the night of March 16, 1925, Hugh and I drove across London to the hospital in Blackheath. We had entertained guests for dinner, but I knew when I served the coffee that I would soon be on my way.

By three thirty the next morning—Saint Patrick's Day— Rosemary arrived, more beautiful than any baby I had ever seen. She had sapphire-blue eyes; delicate skin, like a piece of Dresden china; tiny, daintily formed ears; and a perfectly shaped head covered with short, silvery down. She vigorously chewed on her fists in search of food.

As I looked into her face, all the pain and agony of the past nine months melted into nothingness. Only joy and gratitude remained and, to my astonishment, the first really vivid memory of my mother after many, many years.

Jessie holding baby Rosemary

So this is what she went through for me, I thought. And then I knew that I began to understand the meaning of motherhood.

The safe arrival of our baby so filled us with daring that we took another bold step soon after—a step seldom attempted by Foreign Service Officers in London! We bought a home . . . on the installment plan, of course.

We were sick to death of living in other people's houses and moving every six months. So when a house just around the corner from where we had been living appeared on the market, we snapped it up. From then on, until our return to the Untied States four years later, No. 5 Bigwood Road, Golders Green, became our address.

There was a formal paved garden in front and a deep garden in the rear. The one in the rear included a rock garden; rose trees along a winding garden path; ten different varieties of ramblers crowding the fences on either side; a flattened-out pear-tree hedge toward the back; plenty of room to plant annuals, such as snapdragons and lupine; and a bit of lawn.

At the very back of the 150-foot yard was a small grove of birch trees, where later Rosemary kept a swing. Our place was appropriately called "Hidden Birches." We were grateful to our predecessor, who had been an avid gardener and had left behind the results of years of expert digging.

We found a wonderful nanny, Martha Salminen, of Finnish birth, who was motherly and placid in temperament. Mary Jones, a Welsh woman, came in as cook and general housekeeper. It was a blessing that I had this expert help, as I needed all the time I could get when not nursing Rosemary to track down the necessary furniture.

The news had spread at the American Women's Club that the Butlers bought a house. This was news, for few of those who had been in London, even for many years, owned real estate. That's how I met Mrs. Sheldon, an American expert on antiques.

"Please, Mrs. Butler, let me help you. I want you to get some of the right pieces. Then they will live with you for the rest of your married life, and they will always make your home lovely."

So together we haunted auction sales crammed with beautiful old pieces of furniture. After the war, many of England's great estates were being broken up. On one day I remember, I bought six chests of drawers (they had a run on chests that day), after Mrs. Sheldon first approved them, of course. Hugh became so interested in antiques that he too took up the hunt.

When I began to buy household goods—pottery, bone china, Irish linen tablecloths and napkins, and Witney virgin wool blankets—I found myself feeling sorry for American women unable to buy these quality goods in our home markets. Without being an expert on home trade, I couldn't understand who would be hurt if England, now almost bankrupt, were to sell some of these goods in our markets.

On this one point I could speak with authority: the plumbing in our new home was antiquated. The gas stove in the scullery dated back to the Flood. The old Kitchener was so old-fashioned that I doubted if we ever had a stove like it in the United States.

It was costly to run. It was difficult to reach. It sent most of its heat up its smoky chimney. Why not exchange goods? Why not buy what the British made well so that they could buy what we manufactured through our skill in mass production? I simply couldn't understand it.

At the club I soon found I was treading on dangerous ground when I began to make these comparisons. The whole question of protective tariffs was very hot at the moment. Most people agreed that economic ills were the root of the trouble between our two countries.

Despite this, it was wonderful to have the first Christmas of Rosemary's life in our own home before our own fireplace. By this time she was nine months old, very fair, and garnished with a tiny curl on top of her head.

Mrs. S. K. Ratcliffe, who lived nearby, came in to call on that Christmas Day, accompanied by her twenty-year-old son from Oxford.

"I haven't seen such a droll baby in a long time. She makes me laugh just to look at her," she said.

But the young man remarked, "What a pity that such an exquisite baby should grow up with an American accent!"

A year before we would not have realized how much feeling he put into this comment, but now we knew. Some weeks previously we had attended a Wednesday night testimonial meeting at the Christian Science Church when an American spoke. I thought I had never heard such a nasal accent.

Turning to a British friend, I said, "That's a strange accent. What is it?"

"Don't you know? That's the American accent."

"Do I talk like that?" I asked in surprise.

"Oh, yes, only much worse," she replied cheerfully.

At last I knew, or rather heard, what they were hearing. The British are as sensitive to accent as a mark of class distinction as we are to fashion. The moment a British person opens his mouth he is "placed" as to background and breeding.

Mr. Holman had taken me to the studio of Madame D'Esterre (Elsa d'Esterre-Keeling) on the Chelsea Embankment. For thirty years or more, British men and women of high rank had gone there to study public speaking. Why Madame D'Esterre had a French name or was called Madame I never knew. She had never married and was of Irish nationality. She had come to England long ago with that group of Irish writers and speakers, of whom Bernard Shaw was most prominent.

Madame D'Esterre, like many Irish people, wore black. Instead of a dress, she was enveloped in a long robe, gathered on the shoulder then draped about her figure in Grecian style. She wore sandals on her bare feet, winter and summer. Her graying, stringy hair was bobbed; she had a round face and a harelip. Without a doubt, she was as devoid of what we Americans call "charm" as any woman I ever saw. She was an ardent Christian Scientist. She adopted and brought up twelve children.

Madame D'Esterre's studio was as odd as her appearance. As you entered, you found yourself in a large room furnished as though it were a public hall. Over to the right was a platform where stood four high-backed chairs. Other seats were arranged in a semi-circle in front of the platform.

At the far end of the room were her living quarters. She had a tiny anthracite stove, a small gas burner for cooking, a cupboard with a few cooking utensils, and dishes on open shelves. At one side was a narrow cot with a thin mattress.

There, in this strange, bare place, the great and near-great of England came to take lessons in public speaking. Madame D'Esterre had taught nine royal princesses to speak in public.

Every Thursday morning there was a debate put on by four speakers, and members of the audience participated. It cost two shillings to attend. At the side of the front door was a tin box, into which students dropped their shillings. No record was kept. I had a suspicion that many dropped more than the required two shillings, being moreover grateful for what they learned from Madame D'Esterre.

By the end of the first interview, I knew I had met a gifted woman. Her love of the English language and her knowledge of classical literature proved profound. All of this she shared with us. Her criticisms were sharp and cut like a surgeon's knife, but they were also true, sincere, and helpful.

Madame D'Esterre was always most flattering toward me. For the first time in my life I was "teacher's pet." I could do no wrong. But I was heading for a fall!

At the very last lesson, we heard a speech made by a club member from North Carolina, who had the fluency so often found in Southern people. At the conclusion, Madame D'Esterre said, "Her speech was delightful. We find the accent of the people from North Carolina the most pleasing of all the American accents. Her gestures were graceful and helpful to her speech." Then, turning to me with a rather sour expression, she said, "But don't you try to speak like that, Mrs. Butler, because you could never do it."

Turning back to the class, she added casually, "Of course, Mrs. Butler's accent is one of the worst of the American accents."

I collapsed like a large balloon that had been pricked. After class, I approached the teacher, quite deflated. "What's the use, Madame D'Esterre, of my continuing to speak publicly if I have such an offensive accent? I might as well stop right now."

"You should leave your accent alone. Americans are quite accustomed to your way of speaking. Besides, it would take several years of hard study to change it. By that time you would have lost many excellent qualities, which you now have as a speaker. I should not worry about that accent if I were you."

I was mystified by the natural fluency all Madame D'Esterre's pupils seemed to possess. Where did they learn how to use words so easily, to put into words the subtle shades of meaning, the turns of phrase, the subtle humor that often plays through everything the British say or do?

Then one day, I found the explanation for British fluency. One of my classmates explained that from the second year of school on, pupils wrote a composition one day and the next day delivered a spoken composition, standing in front of the class and speaking to the other pupils, not to the teacher. They talked about their interests, holidays, pets, and hobbies. Consequently, speaking was as natural to British students as walking.

Because of our diplomatic status, Hugh and I attended several of these tea dances and were much impressed to find ourselves sipping tea and dancing in this historic setting. Hugh boldly asked Lady Astor and other British women of prominence to dance with him while I sat with Mrs. Philip Snowden, who supplied delectable bits of gossip about the people who came and went.

The summer Rosemary was a year and a half old, the State Department ordered Hugh to return to America for three months travel. This was in accordance with the usual custom of Foreign Service Officers returning every few years to keep in touch with home affairs.

Hugh's expenses were paid but, of course, his family's had to be paid out of his income. We figured that by renting our house and making certain economies, we could afford to have Nanny go too, to help us care for Rosemary, whose regular program schedule must be maintained. So, in due course of time, we were aboard the SS President Harding passenger ship on our way back home.

My sister Emily, who was now married and living in New Jersey with her professor Anton DeHass, met the boat. From then on, our progress across America—to Chicago, Colorado, and on to San Francisco and Oakland, where Hugh's family were now living—was a triumphal procession because of Rosemary, who everyone wanted to see. My daughter was on exhibit to all relations, for she was pretty, gay, and developing rapidly. But she badly needed sunshine, having become slightly rickety in spite of all our efforts to prevent this from happening. These long days of warm sun came at the right moment for her, and us too.

In Colorado, my family took us for a week to their cabin in the Rocky Mountains. It was heavenly. We could not get enough of the dry, crystal-clear air, the hot sun day after day, and the beautiful vistas from the crow's nest—a platform that Father had built high up in a tall pine tree, from which we could look out over the plains.

In California, Hugh's mother eagerly awaited our arrival. When news came that we had Nanny with us and several pieces of baggage, she secured a furnished bungalow next to hers, where we could set up housekeeping on our own.

As I had prophesied, Mrs. Butler could not withstand the appeal of a grandchild. She was wildly enthusiastic over Rosemary. She could not see enough of the baby. She hovered around her granddaughter all day long.

She went in every night to the nursery to talk with her before she went to sleep. She was almost too stimulating; we had to set up a rigid routine to protect Rosemary from too much attention. In this endeavor, Nanny was invaluable.

I was, naturally, eager to heal the rupture that our marriage had caused in Hugh's family. Rosemary helped both of us—mother-in-law and daughter-in-law—as only a grandchild can do.

During three busy months, Hugh spoke about English business methods to Chambers of Commerce all across the United States.

He paid a brief visit to Washington. Then we returned to England on the RMS Homeric.

We were overjoyed to be safely back in our own home, but it seemed almost impossible to adjust once more to the cool fall weather that greeted us.

Then in December, I dreamed that a beautiful baby boy was coming to us. I saw him in my dream as clearly as though he were there. Hugh was overjoyed. Like all men, he wanted a son in the family.

Nanny had by this time become a part of our family. She was an institution. Her routine, and that of Rosemary, never varied a hair's breadth from one day to another.

There were many things about Nanny that I found difficult, but my British friends assured me that I had a treasure in her. They said it was my duty to adjust myself to her, and this I proceeded to do. She was a slave to Rosemary, yet she did not seem to spoil her.

The only spoiling Rosemary got came from her parents, in spite of repeated warnings from Mrs. Gasquoine Hartley, a recurrent visitor to our home. I had kept in constant contact with Mrs. Hartley, who I came to know so well during long walks at the Fabian Summer School. I substituted her for a mother, I presume. Often she came to our home for tea when I would talk over the day-by-day family problems with her, or I would meet her in London at a vegetarian restaurant near the Strand for luncheon.

She was a strange woman, utterly uninterested in her personal appearance. She had thin, straggly, gray hair, which more often than not escaped the hat in the back and drooped about her face.

Like many British people, she had lost all her teeth. Her false teeth were badly fitted and loose, thus interfering with her speech. Life had been cruel to her, as her bent shoulders and drab appearance testified. Yet within that strange frame there was a soul of great wisdom and understanding. I could not understand her deep love for me. She would come at a moment's notice. So, one day I asked her why she was so interested in us and our family.

"I'm determined that you and Hugh shall make a success

of your marriage. And you, Jessie, have a gift seldom found in a woman. You are honest and truthful. How refreshing it is to find an honest woman! Your honesty was the gift you gave to Hugh, whose own home was enmeshed in a web of lies and falsification. No one there spoke the truth unless it came from Hugh's father."

Right or wrong, I sorely needed her confidence. I had many moments when I seemed to be walking in a dream so intangible that I scarcely knew where I was. Somehow or other I had built up what looked like a solid framework of home life, but I did not believe in it. Only I knew how frail it was and that the tiniest whiff could knock down my castle.

Always I felt apologetic to Hugh because of my lack of femininity. I dressed well. I looked like a woman. But I did not feel like one. And so Mrs. Hartley's words came like a balm to my troubled spirit. At least I had supplied something to Hugh that was needed—my honesty!

Our cook, Miss Jones, ran the household, as Eva Zorn's cook did. She bought the food and did all the housework, except for the help of a weekly scrubwoman.

She cared for three fires; cleaned our shoes, which we left outside our bedroom door every night; and brought hot, strong tea to our room before we got up. We had to have hot tea to get up the courage to face the icy, damp room. She turned on our gas fires and did everything else that had to be done.

But on the day that I asked her to set up Nanny's tea tray, because Nanny was so slow about it that Rosemary got hungry while waiting for her supper, Miss Jones resigned.

"I'm sorry, Mrs. Butler, but this is where I stand down," she announced. "The cook never sets up the nurse's tea tray."

"But, Miss Jones, you set up her breakfast tray in the morning," I replied, stunned and angry. Nanny and Rosemary ate their breakfast upstairs in the day nursery, to which Miss Jones carried the breakfast tray.

"The cook always sets up the breakfast tray, but never the tea tray," she replied with dignity.

So I dropped the matter until I could consult my friend, Lady Walker-Smith. That very afternoon I walked across the heath to her house in great trepidation. When once you have a complicated household, such as mine had now become, the resignation of the cook was a major disaster.

"She is quite right to resign," said Lady Walker-Smith. "The cook never sets up the nurse's tea tray."

"Why? She sets up the breakfast tray. Why not the tea tray?"

"Because that is the time in the afternoon when Cook must have her own tea in order to relax before preparation of the evening meal."

"But she serves tea in the drawing room when I have guests."

"That's different. She knows in advance, so she arranges her own time to fit in with yours. But she cannot also take on Nanny's tea tray. That is too much.

"You see, dear Mrs. Butler, all these household duties have been established through the years, and you cannot change them. You must never again ask the cook to set up Nanny's tea tray. She was quite right to resign."

Well, that was that. I had run counter to tradition. Then I realized that, within the confines of the traditional ways of doing things, we had a peaceful and harmonious household, where everything got done on time and as it should be done.

I returned home in a chastened state of mind, and naturally Miss Jones relinquished her resignation. I saw to that. I also developed a new respect for the so-called British "lower class."

The new baby was due in August. A letter arrived from Hugh's mother saying that she and his younger sister, Margaret, were coming to England on a cargo boat from San Francisco. They would be on the water by the time their letter reached us.

We had urged them to visit us, but that was before we knew Rosemary's brother was coming. Now the thought of this visit frightened me. But it was too late to stop them. Hugh's mother had seen to that! Immediately I was thrown into a spasm of fear. The black cloud in my frail little home would surely find the cracks! What was I to do?

I flew to Mrs. Hartley—clear on the other side of London— in a panic. It took two hours on the bus to get there. She agreed that their visit was most unfortunate from my point of view, with a new baby coming, so she suggested that we lodge them in rooms at Meadway Court, inviting them to join us for meals. This arrangement would be easy to excuse, as our one small guest room was rented.

I was still so scared that I invited Mrs. Hartley to dinner the first day of their arrival. Hugh's mother at once sensed that she was on exhibit for our guest. Always ready to rise to any occasion, she put on a show that first evening.

She danced Rosemary up and down on her foot, singing gaily as she did so, posing as the beautiful grandmother with her beautiful granddaughter. Rosemary had no hesitation in showing that she did not care for the experience. She was almost rude to "Nana," as we were made to call her.

Nana laughed and told gay stories, then sang for us, with Hugh playing an accompaniment on the organ.

All the while, Mrs. Hartley just sat there, stonily gazing into space. What a contrast they were! Mother Butler—glamorous, beautifully dressed, poised, and apparently sure of herself—and Mrs. Hartley—bent of back, shabbily dressed, with poorly fitting artificial teeth so conspicuous, and no glamor. She sat there honest, sincere, and wise in the ways of women.

Mrs. Hartley phoned early the next morning. "Come to town at once for lunch. I must see you."

There, with few preliminaries, she launched into the purpose of the meeting.

"Jessie, do you think I know women?"

"Yes, I would say you do. I would hate to try to fool you," I answered.

"Your mother-in-law is the most dangerous woman I have ever met. She is completely unscrupulous. She is determined to break up your marriage on this trip, and she can do it. Neither you nor Hugh are a match for her."

"What am I to do? After all she is Hugh's mother."

"You must never live on the same side of the United States with her. If she moves to your side, you must move to the other. She must never sleep one night in your house."

"Why, Mrs. Hartley, what could she do?"

"She would go to bed and never get up again."

"That would finish me! I can't take care of a sick person."

"Another thing, she must never be left alone with Rosemary for one second."

"Why?"

"She will poison Rosemary's mind against you and Hugh, and you will never be able to reach her again. She will cut the child off from her parents forever."

"But, Mrs. Hartley, she has already had a chance to do that. When we were in California, she used to go in and talk to Rosemary every evening as she was going to bed."

"Did you hear what she said to her?"

"No. I left her alone with Rosemary. I wanted her to love her granddaughter. I thought I should not be selfish but should share my baby with her grandmother. I hoped that it would reconcile her to me and to our marriage."

"I see. You thought you would use your baby to do a job you hadn't done yourself."

"If you want to put it that way, I guess I did."

By this time, a cold chill was creeping down my spine. "I guess I have been rather stupid, but you have awakened me now, Mrs. Hartley. If you will wait here, I will phone Hugh to join us. It's no use for you to tell me these things without having him know them too."

Soon Hugh was there, and I asked Mrs. Hartley to repeat to him what she had told me. He grew deathly pale. "I don't believe it. But I suppose you are right. What are we to do?" he said.

"You are to trust Jessie and her intuition implicitly. Whatever she wants to do, you must do. She will know because she is not so close to your mother as a son naturally is.

"Hugh, I am not so much interested in you and Jessie as I am anxious for Rosemary and her little brother, as yet unborn. You and Jessie are all they have to give them a chance at life. If you fail them, they haven't a chance.

"So, I am doing this for them, not for you. I want you to keep your home going for their sakes. Your mother has had her chance at life. Now it's their turn. Another thing, you must get your mother away from here at once, or she will kill that unborn baby of yours. She must return to America."

"How can we arrange for that?" Hugh said.

"I will come to dinner soon. I will manage it so that she will leave."

We took our guests sightseeing frequently after that, going out of our way to make their visit a happy one. During this time, we were again invited to a ball at Lady Astor's. Margaret, Hugh's sister, accompanied us. She was accustomed to being the belle of the ball in all her circles at home and looked forward to such an extravagant event. Generally gregarious and boisterous, she appeared lost and out of place in the giant ballroom full of hundreds of Londoners. Here, in the sophisticated atmosphere of the British, she seemed small and her charms found wanting. Lord Astor came to me after a short interlude with her and asked, "Are all young American women devoid of conversational skills and subject matter?"

Some days later, as we all sat closely around the fire in the living room after dinner, I opened a drawer full of baby things and began to show them to Mother Butler and Margaret.

"What does this mean?" she asked.

"It means that Rosemary's little brother is on the way."

She went white. "You fools!" she hissed, "bringing another baby into the world!"

She was evidently caught unprepared, and for the first and only time she showed her real self. She gathered up her possessions at once and left the house. Hugh was horrified. Her incredible reaction to the glorious news, coming as it did immediately after Mrs. Hartley's warnings, gave him a terrible shock.

We did not see Mrs. Butler again until late the following afternoon when she appeared, loaded down with many little presents for the new baby, all smiles and gaiety, as though the events of the previous night had never taken place.

Several days later we told her Mrs. Hartley was coming for dinner again.

"That awful woman! I had hoped I wouldn't have to see her again," she exclaimed.

This time there was no display of grandmotherly affection. Evidently it had become clear that such a display would be useless. As before, Mrs. Hartley said little, but sat looking off into space. The conversation dealt with conventional and objective topics, which are always useful in a tight situation.

The next morning at breakfast, Mrs. Butler announced, "We have decided to return to America. We found a boat leaving this afternoon, and we are already packed and nearly ready to go."

Hugh and I concealed our delight and surprise as well as possible, expressing sorrow at their sudden departure but helping them as much as possible to prepare for it. Late that afternoon they were off.

As soon as we were out of earshot, having said our goodbyes and presented and exchanged presents and all that, I pulled Hugh to one side quickly.

"Hugh, you must get me to the seashore at once. The baby has stopped all movement. At five months he should be moving more than ever! I must get out from under the black cloud I have been living in. The open country, the clean, fresh air, and the seashore will do it. Mrs. Hartley has an old inn at the seashore where we can go."

The next day, we all left for Bonchurch in the south of England. The blessed sun, the sound of the waves beating on the shore under our windows, and the release from tension did their work so that within a couple of days the baby was kicking away as usual, and we were all relaxed and happy once more.

We were mystified. What had Mrs. Hartley done to cause Mrs. Butler to depart so hurriedly and peacefully?

We soon found out. Upon our return to London we made a glowing report to her of our sudden recovery of health and happiness.

"What in the world did you do to cause Mrs. Butler to make such a sudden departure? She had indicated that she would stay here for several months."

"That was easy. I happen to know that people who have used hypnotism, as she has done for so long, are themselves extremely suggestible. They never suspect that anyone else is as clever as they are.

"At dinner that night, I just sat there and willed her to go home. 'You must go home. You must leave here at once. You must return to America at once,' et cetera. She did not know where she got the suggestion. Suddenly she knew she wanted to go home, and that was all there was to it."

"Well, I don't care how you did it. All I know is that you saved my baby, and me too. I'm sure of that. I'm so deeply grateful to you, dear Mrs. Hartley. You have given me a second chance. I'll never forget you as long as I live."

And I never have. Though she suffered a tragic death a year later, I have heard her speaking to me many times through the years, reminding me that she was counting on me to have the wisdom to make a success of my family life.

1928 was the last year that Court Presentations were held. This was the picture handed out to people who were presented at Court.

CHAPTER 30

Presentation at the Court of St James's: Queen Mary

"Why don't you see if you can be presented at court this season, Jessie?" my friend Eva Zorn suggested. "Your husband's diplomatic position should make it easy." Eva steeped herself in court tradition, as all British women did, even though going to court would never be possible for her.

"Why should I? We came here for serious purposes—to start our family and to make a study of England's social and economic problems. What has that to do with the royal court?"

"You'll not have a complete picture of England unless you see the part played by the royal family. All this is as much a part of English life as the subjects you have studied. Besides, if you remain here, as we hope you will, your children will be at a disadvantage when they go to school because they are Americans. Many of my American friends tell me that their children grow to hate America because of the teasing they receive from their schoolmates. They begin to think that America must not be a good country."

"What will presentation at court have to do with this? I asked.

"Everything. It is known within the school if a child's mother has been presented at court. And so the American stigma wouldn't stick for your children. These ideas must seem snobbish to you, but that's the way it is."

"But going to court costs too much. We're not rich people, Eva. We have to live on a government salary. And I have no jewels. Don't you have to have jewels to be properly dressed for court?"

"It needn't cost much, if you'll let me help you with your buying. People nowadays don't have money as they used to, so they resort to all kinds of expedients. For example, one of my friends lent her train last year to three other women because each of them went to a different court.

"And you can buy all the imitation jewels you need for one or two pounds. Most people today keep their real jewels locked up in the bank and wear copies anyway, so well-made that only an expert can tell the difference. It's much less trouble."

"I am interested in the young girls who go to court," I remarked. "How do they blossom so suddenly from the drab school uniforms and long black stockings, from the hair in pigtails and no makeup, into beautiful debutantes? I've often gone down to the Mall and peeked in at them as they sat in carriages, waiting to enter the palace grounds."

I was not alone in my peeking. Most of London did the same, from the cockney workman and his wife on up. It is part of the show which royalty puts on for the common people.

The palace gates opened at nine thirty. In order to get a preferred place in the throne room, the debutante and her mother sat in the carriage queues in front of the gates from six thirty on.

Some of the crowds came equipped with thermos bottles of hot drinks to keep them warm in the English evening chill.

"That's part of our system," Eva explained. "We try to keep girls young and natural until they are eighteen. Then they throw away school clothes and blaze forth looking like Cinderella."

"As a matter of fact," I said, "each year for the past six years, my name has been sent in automatically from our embassy to the Lord Chamberlain for presentation at court. But Hugh always sent back word that I didn't care to attend. Perhaps we should rethink our position."

At this Eva became excited. "Oh, dear friend, I do beg you to think it over again. I know you will never regret it. You have no idea what an experience it will be for you!"

One evening I asked Lady Astor whether she considered it important for an American woman to be presented at court.

"Everyone who can should go to court," came her prompt reply. "The British court is one of the few beautiful bits of Old-World pageantry that remains today. Do not miss it."

"After all, Hugh, we didn't have a very exciting wedding, did we?" I said one evening, while discussing the question of court.

"I never knew you wanted an exciting wedding," Hugh said.

"Every woman deep in her heart wants an exciting wedding. But it just wasn't possible for us, and I knew it. But I would like to go to court before we return to the United States."

I almost surprised myself at this unexpected sign of femininity.

Hugh consented, and my name was submitted again by the American Embassy. Soon the Lord Chamberlain sent the embassy the regulations governing the dress being worn by ladies presented at Court.

Eva kept her word as to expenses. The entire event cost $150 dollars, instead of the two or three thousand spent by many American women who were presented at the same time.

We began, as women always do, by going to the smartest and most expensive shops to see what was being worn. But we wound up on Shaftesbury Avenue, where actresses on small means found modish clothes. We settled on a copy of a French gown costing ten pounds, or around forty dollars. The dress became a great success, and the court photographer posed Hugh and me for a memorable shot that we kept throughout the following years. Soon after the Court, *The Times* singled me out and described my gown in the following words:

> *Black and white chiffon entirely covered with diamanté, pearls, and silver-lined bugles embroidered in an elaborate pattern. The train was made of silver lamé covered with ivory-white georgette and heavily embroidered to match the dress. It was lined with delicate pink georgette and fastened on the shoulder with a trailing motif in a lily design of white velvet and silver cloth. Mrs. Butler carried a sheaf of arum lilies.*

Court Photo of Jessie and Hugh

We found a sparkling necklace for a pound. The ornate tiara cost the same. Black satin shoes, long white gloves, the Prince of Wales feathers, and the veil, and I was ready. We bought the train at the shop where I bought the dress, and we ordered my bouquet on Bond Street.

Although I had never seen or heard of anyone carrying arum lilies (calla lilies), the clerk said they would make a statement.

I inquired about the curtsey from several American women who were also going to be presented. All were very casual about it. "Don't worry. Mrs. Houghton invites us to the embassy the day before and shows us how to do it."

There were 108 of us, all told.

We Americans were to enter the throne room at the Palace of St. James's tenth on the list of countries. We were preceded by the wife of the Spanish ambassador. She had the longest term of service in London. She was followed by women from Italy, Austria, Bulgaria, Japan, Romania, Egypt, Germany, France, then the United States, in order of the terms of service of their diplomatic ambassador husbands.

Eight of the American women had been presented the year before. For nine of us, it was our first presentation.

Just as we got into line to be checked off by Mrs. Houghton, there was a fanfare of trumpets and everyone stood at attention. The band played "God Save the King" as King George V and Queen Mary entered the throne room.

The next thing I knew, the line was moving forward. I saw Mrs. John D. MacArthur, who was directly in front of me, enter the throne room, letting down her train as she went in. Two gentlemen-in-waiting at once stooped to smooth it out.

Then we were moving slowly, as in a dream, into the great blaze of light. I could see the long line in front of me broken every few seconds when someone curtseyed and we inched forward.

The king and queen stood on a raised dais in front of high-backed thrones heavily encrusted in gold. They bowed slightly with expressionless faces as each woman made her curtsey.

I concentrated my attention on the spot in front of the king, making sure I did not tread on the train of the woman directly ahead of me.

The string band of the Irish Guards, seated at the other end of the throne room, played through the presentation. Although I could hardly see them through the haze, I dimly heard the lilting strains of "The Merry Widow Waltz."

Immediately upon turning into the throne room I heard my name called out in loud tones. As I proceeded, the sound of my name traveled along with me, passed from one courtier to another, until the words "Mrs. Hugh Butler" reached His Majesty at the same moment I did. The timing was perfect. This was very disconcerting, for it made the business of forgetting oneself almost impossible.

Then a strange thing happened. I kept myself completely cool and self-possessed until I bent low before the King George. All of a sudden, I went so limp that I rose from the curtsey with the greatest difficulty. But as I stepped to the side, as we had been taught, to Her Majesty Queen Mary, I felt wonderful again.

There she stood, regal in appearance, radiant with jewels and so evidently enjoying the spectacle and her part in it that I caught her mood and so gained confidence in myself.

His Majesty, on the other hand, seemed to wish he were elsewhere. For one brief second while curtseying, I had caught his mood.

Was it my imagination that, as the queen looked at my beautiful sheaf of lilies, she raised her eyebrows a tiny bit as she made her stiff bow? I had heard that her favorite flower was the arum lily and, after that, the carnation. So I was pleased to be the only woman who carried arum lilies that evening.

Immediately past the queen we came to the Lord Chamberlain, who with courtly grace picked up our trains and hung them over our left arms. Then we were ushered to raised seats, upholstered in scarlet, at the side of the throne room so we could see the other seven hundred presentations made that night. These seats were reserved especially for the ladies of the diplomatic corps.

After we were seated, our husbands were presented. They then took their positions in an open space in front of us, where they stood for the next two hours.

Hugh made a very dignified bow. He didn't seem a bit nervous.

An Englishwoman—thank goodness she was not an American—said just as she entered the throne room, "I'm going to be sick!"

Thereupon the gentleman-in-waiting produced his tall silk hat. She threw up into the hat, then proceeded as though nothing had happened! Sick or not, she had to get to the king as her name reached him or there would be confusion.

Three women from India, clad in colorful saris, were presented, looking demure and shy. I wondered what they thought about this great display of Western women, hidden as they were in their flowing robes. What a contrast between the East and the West.

After the presentation of the diplomats and their ladies, the king and queen sat down. But they continued to bow as the remaining guests passed by. Standing at the side of the thrones were Princess Mary, the Duchess of York, the Prince of Wales and his two brothers, and the ladies- and gentlemen-in-waiting. The king's Indian bodyguard wore a traditional, picturesque uniform from his own country.

Near the end of the procession, we saw Lady Astor and her debutante daughter, Phyllis. Lady Astor was glowing in a chiffon and velvet dress of love-in-the-mist blue. She wore her famous diamonds. Phyllis, gowned in pale yellow taffeta, walked with poise and sophistication.

Finally, the last lady curtseyed and passed on to the banquet hall. Another fanfare of trumpets sounded. The king and queen stood during the playing of the national anthem. Then pages came forward to take up Queen Mary's long train, and the King George gave her his hand.

In stately manner, they descended from the throne, stopping to bow to the cabinet officers opposite us, then to our husbands, and then to us. We returned the bow with a curtsey. They were followed by the Princess Mary, the Duchess of York, and the three princes, who each also bowed three times.

After "Mama," as the princes called the queen, turned her back to the throne and left the room, the three princes joined arms and swung off the dais with a gay and flippant manner, as if it were all a huge joke.

After that, the wives of the diplomats descended from their high seats to accompany their husbands into the nearby banquet room, where we were served a "stand-up-supper" on gold plates. The supper consisted of cold, sliced ham and fruit compote. I thought it pretty prosaic, but Hugh, normally a teetotaler, didn't complain because he so enjoyed the king's champagne.

CHAPTER 31

The Queen's Garden Party

The American Embassy sent us instructions to go to the left door of Buckingham Palace three days after the Court presentations to sign our names in the queen's guest book, which I did.

An invitation waited for us to attend the queen's party, held in the gardens on July 26. Every year, this garden party marked the high point in the social season. Afterward, the king, queen, and royal family left London for their summer residence, Balmoral Castle in Scotland.

The rest of the court and London society also scattered to country estates or castles in all parts of the British Isles to enjoy the month of August, which was a national holiday for royalty, government, and school children.

All those who had been presented at court earlier in the season were invited to the Queen's garden party. Government officials and many others, as well as visiting foreigners, were invited. Nine thousand in all attended, according to the estimates of the press.

It was a blistering hot day with bright sunlight. Lady Crawford, our neighbor, drove me and another Englishwoman down to the gate designated for the diplomatic corps.

There I met Hugh, attired in formal afternoon clothes that he rented—a fine heavy wool dress coat with tails, striped trousers, patent leather shoes, and tall silk hat. He looked very hot and uncomfortable, but handsome as usual.

I wore my street-length beige lace dress along with a beige hat with the tomato-colored feather. A fluffy georgette pom-pom of the same color as the feather and tipped with silver was fastened to the left shoulder of the dress.

The grounds at the rear of Buckingham Palace were surprisingly spacious and beautiful. They were located near Victoria Station and surrounded by heavy street traffic. All this spread out behind a high brick wall, which shut out the noise and isolated the palace grounds.

A good-sized lake, surrounded by an array of shrubs in full bloom, added natural elegance to a scene already gay with the colors in the gowns and hats worn by the women. Tall trees with tops like umbrellas afforded shade all around.

Several pavilions, covered with brilliantly striped awnings, were scattered about the grounds. Some of them housed bands, which played popular music whose strains wafted out over the lawns and the crowds strolling about in leisurely fashion. Other pavilions served refreshments while vibrant flags fluttered in the light breeze across their fronts and tops.

The back of Buckingham Palace is totally different from the front, which is cold and austere in appearance.

Soon the great door opened, and King George and Queen Mary appeared to the left, followed by their gentlemen- and ladies-in-waiting.

I tried to catch a good view of the queen, but the crowd was too dense, so I trailed along, keeping as close to the royal party as possible.

Hugh followed reluctantly. I had trouble convincing him that, according to the press, this garden party was one of the few occasions when Their Majesties mingled freely with their subjects, so we had every right to join the crowd trailing them.

I noticed many British people, both men and women, speaking to the king and queen as they proceeded over the lawns to their refreshment tents, pausing to chat pleasantly for a few moments with those they recognized.

Over to the side stood the Prince of Wales, holding a little court of his own. How shy and self-conscious he seemed, as though this were his first experience at a garden party instead of one of many!

He appeared awkward as he tried to shift his gloves and cane to his left hand so he could tip his tall hat with his right. It was difficult to picture him as the future king!

"Hugh, I want to speak to Her Majesty. Other people are speaking to her, why shouldn't I?"

"For heaven's sake, quiet down. You'll get us sent home yet if you're not careful."

"But Hugh, I may never get another chance to speak in person to Queen Mary. What a story that would be to tell the women back home! Please let me speak to her. You can go back to the rear, then no one will know that I am your wife and you needn't feel embarrassed."

So Hugh, who always hated to attract attention, vanished. I walked up to the elderly Lord Chamberlain.

I said, "Do you suppose I could speak to Her Majesty?"

"Yes, I think so. Have you been presented at court?" He smiled indulgently as he recognized my American accent.

"Yes, in May. You know American women are so interested in Her Majesty."

"What is your name?"

I told him.

"Just wait here until she comes by, and I will present you."

Down the walk, I could see Queen Mary, stopping first on one side, then the other, as she spoke to her guests, all of whom curtseyed when she offered her hand, which they touched lightly.

She was gowned in a tight-fitting Alice-blue dress—blue being her favorite color—buttoned to the throat. Her full bosom lent itself to the jewels and decorations, which she unfailingly wore. She also wore the famous Queen Mary turban.

I knew, by now, the reason for that style of hat. This style was her husband's favorite, and although she confided to someone that she would prefer a variation, she could not bring herself to change and risk disappointing him.

What wifely devotion to wear the same style hat for years to please a husband!

She certainly had a peaches-and-cream complexion, but as she was not smiling, I could not be sure if she were wearing enamel.[34] It could be that she had some on.

Out of the corner of my eye, I could see Hugh at the rear of the crowd, mopping his brow, wet with perspiration from the heat, and from anxiety too, I feared.

Soon the queen came near.

"Your Majesty, this is Mrs. Hugh Butler from the American Embassy," said the Lord Chamberlain, the perfect model of a courtly gentleman.

"Oh, so you are from America?" she said as I curtseyed properly. She lifted her eyebrows. No enamel on the forehead, else it would have cracked.

"Yes, Your Majesty. And do you know that the American women are very much interested in Your Majesty?" I added.

"Oh, indeed! And why are they interested in us?"

"I think, Your Majesty, they would like to know just how good a housekeeper you are."

At this, she threw her head back and laughed heartily, a deep, throaty "Ha! Ha!" which finished the gossip about the enamel completely. All down the line, heads pushed forward to try to see or hear what had been said to cause such frank and open merriment.

"Well, you know, one must care for one's house, mustn't one?" she said, and with that she started to pass on as I made another curtsey.

Soon Hugh joined me. "What in the world did you say to her?"

When I told him, he said, "At what moment did you decide to say that?"

"As I walked forward to meet her. I've been reading lately about the many details the queen personally sees to when the time comes to close Buckingham Palace before going to Scotland at the end of the season.

---

34   Face enameling (applying actual paint to the face) became popular among the rich at this time in an attempt to look paler. This practice was dangerous due to the main ingredient often being arsenic.

"Remember, she is German. She is very proud of her housekeeping abilities, as the stories the newspapers print about her constantly show. So, I knew I would strike the right note by mentioning housekeeping."

Then Hugh and I went to the refreshment tent to eat the largest strawberries I ever saw, in the thickest Devonshire cream I ever tasted. After that, we visited the adjoining pavilion for tea and cakes.

Too soon the afternoon came to an end, and I met Lady Crawford and her friends to drive back to Golders Green, while Hugh left to return his rented clothes.

On the way back, the ladies were exchanging experiences and comparing notes as to how close they had been to the queen. One had been able to get within ten feet of her.

I recognized this as an opportune time for an American to keep quiet. If I told them that I asked to meet her personally, they would have said, "How like an American!" or "Wouldn't you know that an American woman would do such a dreadful thing as to ask to meet the queen!" I couldn't bear to give them that much satisfaction, so I did not report on the lack of enamel.

Queen Mary

CHAPTER 32

The Queen Takes a Hint

Within a day or two after the garden party, there appeared a long column in The Times, titled "THE QUEEN AS HOUSEKEEPER," with the subtitle "Queen Mary Supervises the Details of Her Many Households in Person."

The lengthy story told of how she knew where every chair or picture in Buckingham Palace belonged and how she made regular visits to the vast kitchens to inspect cupboards, pantries, and pots and pans. I decided that my question must have touched a warm spot in Queen Mary's heart. After all, she was a woman before she was a queen!

For days after, I could not get back to earth. I knew that I had participated in an event of deep historical portent, a sort of cosmic event, which tied up the past, the present, and the future.

All that the British Empire stood for was symbolized and expressed in the pageantry of the royal court. A mixture of fantasy, fairy tale, and deep realism permeated the event. Men and women became participants, lifted out of the daily run of living into a sort of heaven of majesty and nobility.

Eva Zorn was right. I had shared in an experience, which I would never forget as long as I lived.

May 8, 1928, held a double significance for me. Thirty-two years prior, on May 8, 1896, my mother died a tragic death in her pioneer home in Pueblo, Colorado, when I was ten years old.

Think of the contrast: the grandeur and elegance of the British court, patterned on generations of history, compared to Colorado in the United States, a new experiment in living and government.

Destiny placed me to experience a great national difference of living between our two countries. Little did my mother dream that her first child would witness such a miracle of growth!

Our final year in London coincided with the end of an era in world affairs. The old way of life was dying. It was not clear what the new way would be. Every week or so Winston Churchill, in impassioned speeches, warned the House of Commons that another World War was in the making. But no one listened. The British people wanted to be left alone to pursue life as usual, enjoying their gardens, their sports, and their family life, undisturbed by rumblings from the rest of the world.

At tea parties in those days someone would ask, "What happened in the House today?" What occurred in the House of Commons usually came first on the list of topics for conversation.

"Oh, that old warmonger, Winston Churchill, was at it again! I wish he would let up!"

Then the teacups would rattle with annoyance until the conversation changed to a more pleasing subject.

But that "old warmonger" never let up. In booming tones he continued to ring out, though few paid any attention to what he had to say. He kept right on trying to find words to awaken the British people to their danger.

The American newspapers predicted the highest tariffs in history. It was obvious that England could not continue to pay the war debts she owed the United States if she no longer received the payments from Germany, and was no longer able to sell her goods in the American market.

At last Winston Churchill's warnings began to be taken seriously. The British Government, in self-defense, prepared to set up tariff walls of its own, for the first time since the days of Cobden and free trade. They hoped through this artificial means to safeguard the Empire markets, without which England could not maintain her positions as one of the leading industrial nations of the world. Many men in Government positions and in business in the city openly prophesied that what was happening would inevitably lead to another World War.

CHAPTER 33

Three Funerals and A Ball

Soon after my presentation at court, in early June, the London papers carried news of the death of Mrs. Emeline Pankhurst. Two months before her death, she sat in the gallery of the House of Commons to listen to the second reading of the act of 1928, which gave women in England the vote on the same basis as men.

The press recalled the days, fourteen years earlier, when this frail little woman with the sensitive face and the deep, soft eyes demanded that her government give women equal political status with men and embarrassed those in power with her hunger strikes and her militant methods.

I decided to attend Mrs. Pankhurst's funeral to pay her memory my deep respect and to express my personal gratitude for what she had done for women.

Although June, the day grew damp and cold. A slow drizzle dusted my hat as I hunted up the smoke-stained, dreary little church where the funeral took place. I saw among the mourners many men and women of importance in English political and social life. The atmosphere felt especially mournful.

The setting of this funeral seemed quite different from that of another I had attended the previous October. When I learned from *The Times* that Mrs. H. G. Wells had died and that her funeral service was to take place at the crematorium near Golders Green, I could not resist going.

On that bright and sunny day, the cheerful chapel was filled with bouquets. Opposite the entrance and back of the pulpit, wide doors opened on a vista of beautiful flowers bordering a long walk. Soft music filled the air. A gentle breeze blew through the chapel, bringing us the fragrance of the hothouse blossoms heaped upon the casket.

The room filled with well-known writers and artists, with society leaders and people of importance in political circles. On the front seat, apart from the other mourners, sat H. G. Wells, with Bernard Shaw by his side.

London had been shaken for years by the controversy between these two men. They were utterly different in character. One of them was known to have had many extramarital love affairs, and the other had been an ascetic in his personal life.

"There they sit, side by side," I said to myself, "two men, who through the power of the written word, have certainly changed the thinking of a generation."

A popular hostess, Mrs. Wells had been greatly loved by all who knew her. She had edited and proofread many of her husband's books.

***Cliveden – Lady Astor's country home
where many formal Balls were held***

Many stories were told about Mr. Wells's extramarital adventures. His wife, from all accounts, had shown herself capable of forgiveness to a most unusual degree.

The gentle, old clergyman announced that he would read a tribute to the dead woman, written by her husband. As he read in rich, mellow tones, Wells began to cry. When he buried his face in his handkerchief and wept without restraint, so did I. So did many others.

Through it all, Bernard Shaw sat erect and motionless without a tear. Somehow I knew why he was there. There seemed to be a kind of spiritual power about him, which few possess. He used this power to help H. G. Wells, and perhaps Mrs. Wells too.

Around the same time, Lady Astor gave a ball in honor of the ninety Rhodes Scholars[35] at Oxford. I wore my court dress to this ball. There were some three hundred guests in all.

What unpredictable people the British are! On most occasions, they are shy and modest and badly dressed, both men and women, but at parties, they reveled in wearing the most beautiful costumes they could assemble. The effect proved both gay and picturesque.

We saw Winston Churchill sitting in a corner talking to Wickham Stead, the editor who had just come back from a visit to America. Over in another corner, I observed a strange-looking man with a great chain of decorations hung around his neck. He stood alone, looking shy and unhappy.

"Who is that little man?" I asked someone.

---

35   The Rhodes Scholarship is an international postgraduate award for students to study at the University of Oxford. It was established in 1902, making it the first large-scale program of international scholarship. The Rhodes Scholarship was founded by English businessman and politician Cecil John Rhodes to promote unity between English-speaking nations and instill a sense of civic-minded leadership and moral fortitude in future leaders irrespective of their chosen career paths.

"Why, don't you know? That's Sir James Barrie."[36] Imagine!
(Peter Pan)

And so I went to speak to him. His shrewd Scottish eyes peeked
out at me from under his overhanging brows. I found it almost
impossible to know what to say to him.

I'd heard of the four boys he had adopted after their parents
died, and I knew that all four had been killed in World War I. Now
he remained quite alone, except for a faithful servant and a dog.
Such a tragic-looking man! Recently he generously endowed a rest
home in honor of his mother, where poor women could go for care
after childbirth.

Ellen Terry,[37] the English Shakespearean actress died. Again I
attended a funeral at Golders Green Crematorium.[38] By this time I'd
become quite an authority on funerals!

Mrs. Pankhurst's funeral had been filled with sorrow; Mrs. H.
G. Wells's funeral had been radiant with victory; Ellen Terry's
marked the end of an era in British life. She always seemed
unreal to me—a tradition rather than a living woman. But when
the clergyman said, "Ellen Terry, I commit thee to the flames," I
shuddered. How absurd to think anyone could ever commit that
gay spirit to the flames!

Among the mourners sat Gordon Craig, Ellen Terry's son who
had been one of the many men in the life of Isadora Duncan and
the father of her first child. He looked rather seedy, I thought, with
his very high, stiff collar and thin hair. It's a good thing that tastes in
men differ, for he was surely not one to set me afire as he had done
Isadora Duncan!

---

36 Sir J. M. Barrie, the Scottish playwright and novelist, wrote Peter
Pan in 1904.

37 Dame Alice Ellen Terry (1847 –1928) was an English actress who
became the leading Shakespearean actress in Britain.

38 Golders Green Crematorium and Mausoleum was the first
crematorium to be opened in London and one of the oldest crematoria in
Britain, with a list of notables whose ashes are interred there including
Sigmund and Martha Freud, Bram Stoker, and Peter Sellers.

Isadora Duncan, Maria Montessori, and I Get Homesick

About this time, Isadora Duncan's autobiography fell into my hands. I admired the woman, who was primarily an artist and yet met tragedy when she tried to be a woman. She depicted the conflict between creative genius and the demands of womanhood.

To use the words of a reviewer, "She had a rapid transit across the civilizations of two continents, from her cradle by the Pacific in California to the horror of her death in France a few months ago."

The following quotation from Isadora might easily apply, though to a lesser degree, to some of us today:

> *Just as there are days when my life seems to have been a golden legend studded with precious jewels, a flowery field with multitudes of blossoms, a radiant morn with love and happiness crowning every hour . . . when I have found no words to express my ecstasy and joy of life . . . when the idea of my school is a great success . . . when my art is a resurrection . . . so there are other days when, trying to recollect my life, I was filled only with a great disgust and a feeling of utter emptiness.*
>
> *The past seems but a series of catastrophes and the future a certain calamity, and my school the hallucination emanating from the brain of a lunatic.*

As I read Isadora Duncan's autobiography, I could not help thinking of Lady Astor, also a genius in her own way. She had produced six children while being the first woman member of the British House of Commons. Loved by men and women alike, Lady Astor used her political influence to help humankind. Regardless of her tangible accomplishments, her greatest contribution, in my opinion, was her skill at harmonizing her talents as a person with the demands upon her as a wife and a mother. Lady Astor showed, by her life, that the conflict between genius and wifehood could be resolved.

Lord and Lady Astor, who were both Americans

One day in the fall of 1928, as I walked across Hampstead Heath, I suddenly felt a great longing to return to the United States for good. Now over eight years since Hugh and I had come to England, I was becoming weary of the old men and women who dominated the country. I wanted a house in the suburbs, or a cottage by the sea, or a cabin in the mountains, and a car, and all the comforts of American suburban life. I wanted our children to grow up in youthful America, where anything can happen, because we belonged there.

Hugh told me that he expected soon to receive an offer to take charge of the New England office of the United States Department of Commerce, located in Boston. The time to move seemed propitious.

"If I were you, Mr. Butler," Ambassador Houghton told Hugh, "I would take my children home to be educated. America is the country of the future—it is based on real democracy. Over here, our American children feel that they don't belong—they are thought queer by their classmates. If they have no chance to become acquainted with their own country, they may grow up feeling that they don't belong anywhere."

That day at luncheon, Mrs. Curtis-Brown seconded what the ambassador had said. "Our own children have grown up without a country, Mrs. Butler. They have come to feel just a little ashamed of the United States, yet they have never felt that they belonged here either."

Never did our garden look so lovely as it did during that last spring, as though trying to persuade us to stay on and care for it. Hugh's mother had sent us prize dahlia bulbs from California, which were the pride of our English gardener.

The delicate blue lupines, standing in stately rows against the fence, the tall snapdragons in many pastel colors, and the rhododendrons in the front garden were all heavy with bloom. We enjoyed a solid bed of forget-me-nots, backed by the pear tree hedge that lighted up the far end of the garden. Rambler roses of many different colors covered the fences on both sides of the yard.

Hugh usually invited me to walk with him down the winding garden path to the shimmering birch trees in the evening before retiring. There is a silence and peace about flowers at night that is calming to the soul. A garden at night is even more beautiful than in the daytime.

In the dead silence we seemed to hear the vibration of the earth. At other times, he insisted that I accompany him to Hampstead Heath early in the morning to listen to the songs of the skylarks as they hovered high in the sky, sending out burst after burst of exultant music.

Dr. and Mrs. James J. Hadfield were our last dinner guests in London. Miss Jones, our cook, outdid herself on this occasion, serving a wonderful meal. I remember how astonished the Hadfields were to see the house in perfect order, with only an occasional trunk about, when we were scheduled to sail for the United States in three days, taking all our antique furniture with us. As usual, the British method of packing and moving was done in an orderly and efficient manner.

The week before this dinner party, I'd heard a lecture by Madame Montessori, whose words rang in my ears that final evening:

> *We have witnessed the emancipation of women in this generation. In the next we shall witness the emancipation of the child who is still in slavery in the adult world.*

Hugh and I had enjoyed eight years comparatively free from family ties and obligations, in which to establish our marriage and the birth of two children. We had been blessed in this respect.

We took with us Miss Jones and a governess named Emmy Turnbeer, whom we had brought to England from Switzerland.

At seven o'clock on a brilliant May morning in 1929, the four Butlers, with Emmy and Miss Jones, walked out of our beloved home in London, which had been sold. Our furniture and other belongings were to be packed and shipped after us.

On the last morning, Hugh and I took our children, Rosemary and Richard, down through the garden, all wet with dew, to give them a final swing. Never had the place looked lovelier. The apple tree in the grove of birches in the rear was covered with pink and white blossoms. The blue forget-me-nots danced in the bright light of the morning sun. Every tiny leaf shimmered with color, for when the sun does shine in England, it makes up in radiance for lost time.

In a few hours, we were on the SS America, en route to our homeland. We had left the United States with one large wardrobe trunk and several small suitcases. We were returning with two children, a governess, a cook, and enough furniture for an eleven-room house. We brought twenty-six pieces of extra baggage!

In addition, Hugh had become an author. During his last year and a half in the London office of the United States Department of Commerce, he had planned and produced two books, which were destined to become best sellers in their own field. He became an authority on Anglo-American relations to England. The first was a thousand pages, *The United Kingdom: An Industrial, Commercial, and Financial Handbook*. The second was a short book, titled *The Irish Free State*.

We learned many useful things from the British people. "The gracious art of living" left its mark upon us. We were determined, wherever possible, to keep the best of both civilizations. We became convinced that the destiny of the world lay in the hands of the British and American people working together.

At breakfast, on the day after the SS America left the shores of England, our daughter suddenly remarked, "Oh, Daddy, I like America so much better than England."

"Why, Rosemary?" he asked.

"Because the skies are higher."

Sure enough, we looked up and the low-hanging ceiling of London skies had disappeared. The spaciousness of the heavens over the open ocean appeared so striking that even a five-year-old child notice the difference.

Hugh with Rosemary and Richard

Miss Jones, of course, was in third class, while we were in first class on government passage. As soon as I had my sea legs, I went down to see how she was faring.

Hugh had written to the third-class purser to look out for her especially, so she had a room to herself. It was clean and comfortable and quite good enough for anyone, but Miss Jones was furious. She did not understand why she could not be with us in first class.

"For the simple reason that you could not afford first class. It would have been foolish for you to pay out so much of your savings for a first-class passage. You will need all the money you have to help you get started in the United States—it's costly there. Believe me, I know what I'm talking about."

Of course Emmy, the Swiss governess, stayed with us in our quarters to help with the children, and that was a bitter pill for Miss Jones. She quoted remarks her fellow passengers had made about America, to the effect that there was no class system in the United States and she should have insisted on being in first class.

I saw that she did not intend to listen to my words of caution, so I consoled myself by thinking, "Well, in three months she can go off on her own—then she'll learn!"

It was a heavenly passage, smooth and sunny all the way, and soon we were within a day of landing. What a thrill that was, after eight years of life away from the United States! We would now rediscover our own country!

As we sat out on deck in the warm sun, I brought up the question of Hugh's mother once more. She had come to New York City from California especially to greet us on our return. She was staying with Hugh's sister, Margaret, now married and living on Long Island.

Before sailing, we engaged a summer cottage just out of New Bedford on the sound for the summer. Hugh had three month's holiday before due to take up his new duties in Boston as manager of the United States Bureau of Foreign and Domestic Commerce for New England. He looked weary and suffered from a painful infection on his hand, which had to be lanced by the ship's doctor. We were both exhausted from the strain of moving and from the trying British winter we had just experienced.

"You won't forget, will you, Hugh, that we agreed not to have visitors until we are settled? We need to become accustomed to America after eight years away. We must get into our new home and be rested before we can take on any family problems. Isn't that so?" My pleading tone indicated how scared I still was.

"Having Mother needn't interfere with our resting. I don't see why we need so much time to get ready for her visit," Hugh protested.

My heart sank. "Oh, dear Lord," I thought, "the conflict is still with us. Help me to have courage to work out a plan that is right for our family . . . for all of us."

"I'm sorry, I don't want to be difficult, but I need time to get ready for any visitors. Rosemary is still not out of the woods. We must keep our home peaceful and serene for her sake, so please cooperate with me on this! As soon as we land, let's take a train for New Bedford and get settled in our own little place. Please stand by me on this matter, even though it may seem foolish now. I'm sure you will see later how much we need time to get adjusted."

"Oh, all right," said Hugh, still unconvinced and slightly annoyed.

One night at dinner, Rosemary said, "There's another reason why I like America more. The spinach tastes better."

From that moment on, Rosemary seemed to want to forget that she'd ever lived in England. In no time at all, even her correct English accent began to disappear. She became quite obviously already an American child.

We all rose early on the day of the landing, eager to see the sunrise on our new life. Oh, the blessed sun! So bright and so warm to the very bones! How good it felt! It seemed like years since we'd been warm.

"Americans should never forget what the British endure with their climate and what their climate does to give them hardihood," I commented.

"Yes," Hugh replied, "in some ways, I like their mild climate, never too cold or too hot. That also must affect their temperaments, which blow neither hot or cold."

Now our eyes turned away from England, toward our own country. Yet we no longer possessed the same point of view as when we left the United States. Almost at once, we began to see and hear things differently. For one thing, the noise! And the confusion. The sound of cars honking, people rushing to and fro, yelling and waving and jumping up and down like jumping jacks. Such restlessness!

We found Hugh's mother and sister waiting at the pier, looking very surprised when they saw what we brought with us: two children, a governess, a cook, and twenty-six pieces of baggage!

They came prepared to invite us to their small seaside cottage on

Long Island. It was impossible for us to accept the offer, so after we finished the greeting, we found ourselves on the train for New Bedford.

Miss Jones, all smiles again as she shared a seat with Emmy, felt included once more as part of the family. She reluctantly admitted that the ocean passage had not been too bad!

On the train, Hugh turned to me casually and said, "Oh, by the way, Mother is coming up to visit us next week. I felt sure you would be ready for her by that time. She is so anxious to see the children. She can't wait any longer."

"When was this decision made?" I asked, stunned. "Hugh, can't you see I'm tired? And you're tired. We need time to get adjusted to American life once more. You have three whole months' vacation. What is the hurry?"

"It sounded so silly to ask my mother to wait indefinitely. I simply couldn't do it. What reason could I give?"

"Listen, Hugh dear, it's natural after all these years that your mother should be eager to visit us, but we have to think of our family first now. And after all, your mother is not the head of our home. You and I are the heads. And I have the right to decide who is to visit us and when, because it is my responsibility as a hostess to see that my guests are comfortable. We agreed on this in London and again yesterday on the boat."

"But what could I say when she said that she wanted to come now?"

"You could have said that you would have to talk it over with me first. You could have explained that we were both tired and needed time to get settled, and that we would let her know when we were ready for her visit.

"Now we have a crisis developing. You have forced me to be rude to her. Think what trouble that will make with your sisters! I'm not ready for any guest, and you will just have to write and tell her so. You will have to fix it up somehow."

"What am I to tell her? It's all settled. She will be very much upset if we change her plans. I can't keep her waiting for such foolish reasons as these."

"All right then, you go to New York and stay with her until I'm ready."

Our seaside house became ideal—just big enough for the family and our "ménage," as our friends called it.

We went swimming twice a day. We reveled in the lovely fresh vegetables and fresh fruit. We ate simply and lived simply, so as to have as much time possible on the beach in front of the house, sunbathing.

Hugh and Jessie return to America

Old Boston friends began to drive down to visit. They all emanated a glow of excitement. The stock market was booming. Everyone made money overnight. They all drove shiny, new modern cars.

The conversation consisted chiefly of stock market reports, and when it didn't, our guests exchanged information about private sources of liquor, for Prohibition still ruled the land and bootleggers were thriving.

Hugh and I felt out of everything. Our financial reserves were small; we had no car, almost unheard of with that bunch! How in the world were we to fit into this new progressive setting?

Some old friends came down for the day and proceeded to give us some sound advice. "If you have any cash laid away, Hugh," they said, "we would advise you to buy some good stocks at once. Just tell your broker that if the market goes down to the point at which you bought, he is to sell. You can't lose!"

"We bought a new house last year, but we have made so much money on the market that we are selling that house and buying another, much larger and more modern. Investing in the stock market is the only thing to do if you have any cash lying about."

"But we wouldn't want to get money that easily," I protested. "We have always worked for our money. It would ruin our integrity to get money as easily as you say you do, without any effort on our part."

They threw back their heads and roared with laughter. I heard later that my fear for our integrity became table talk at dinner parties. All our acquaintances were playing the market. Nice, professional, cultured people they had been when we went to England, but now the stock market monopolized their thinking, time, and conversation. Literature, culture, everything else—thrown out the window. We felt like crawling into a hole and pulling in the hole after us. It seemed that we no longer shared anything in common with our own people.

Miss Jones took a great interest in swimming, so I began to teach her the mechanics of it in the ocean outside our cottage. She seemed to be improving everyday and loving every minute of it.

About a week later, Hugh, looking very glum and thoroughly critical of me and my queer ways, departed for Long Island to stay with his mother. I felt guilty and selfish and unreasonable, yet I knew that I was not ready for Mrs. Butler's visit and whatever might develop from it.

Finally, after two weeks of rest, sunbathing, and meditation, I wrote Hugh that I was ready for his mother's visit. I found a room in a small hotel on a hilltop behind the cottage, where she could stay and come to us for meals. I explained that all the space in our house was taken. They arrived within a few days.

Hugh looked terrible, ashen-white and exhausted. "I have been in hell," he said when we were alone.

Mrs. Butler stayed for two weeks. She seemed happy to have a place to herself for quiet thinking, which had been a lifelong habit for her. I can see her now as she walked daintily down the hill for lunch, carrying a colorful umbrella. Her greetings were always full of enthusiasm and gaiety. What a great stage diva she would have made! I could picture her bowing before large audiences, which she would charm with her voice and personality.

It was difficult not to fall under the hypnotic spell of her charm. It would have been easier to excuse her, to make allowances for her, and to let down the bars. I had to keep reminding myself that her difficulties were not my problem. I could not make right the mistakes of another.

Right now my problem I need to care for my family, my children. I often thought of the popular play The Silver Chord, which we had seen in London during our last year there. Some day, I decided, I would try to write about this experience, to help other women who lacked a Mrs. Hartley to help them.

One evening I retired early, exhausted from the strain that existed in our family. Hugh and his mother were alone in the living room below the bedroom, but I could hear every word she said. She protested to Hugh because he had ceased studying Christian Science as he once did.

"Well, to tell the truth, I got my bellyful of Christian Science, and I don't want any more of it," I heard him say.

I never before heard my polite husband use such strange words, so I began to have some hope for the future. But the chasm ahead of us still loomed.

Mrs. Butler was never left alone with the children. To all outside appearances, all was harmonious in our home, when out of the blue, Rosemary caught a dreadful chest cold. Emmy and I put her to bed, where she had to stay for days, missing the beautiful warm sun and the swimming.

Mrs. Butler became very critical of our nursing methods. She begged us to let her try mental treatments with the child, but we held firm and kept her away. Finally she decided to return to New York for another visit before going back to California.

Hugh and I drove her to the boat in New Bedford. On deck, I sensed that she wanted a last word with Hugh alone, so I stepped around the corner for a few moments, hoping it might be a long time before we saw her again.

On the way home, Hugh suddenly said, "Oh, by the way, Mother wants to come to New England to visit us before she starts back. She is eager to see our new home before we get settled. I thought you wouldn't mind, just for a few days."

I was so astonished that I nearly fell out of the car, to put it literally. The naiveté of the man seemed almost unbearable at this point!

"Oh, Hugh! Now you have really done it! We had her stay at a hotel at the seashore because there was no room in the cottage. But in New England, where we hope to get a bigger house, how will it look to have your mother living outside our home?

"I thought we had agreed once and for all that she was not to visit us without advance planning by both of us. She's had her visit. Why must she come to New England?"

"She doesn't want to stay. She just wants to see our new home, and then she will leave."

It all seemed utterly natural and harmless to him. How right Mrs. Hartley had been! We were no match for Hugh's mother. Once she got into our home, what next would she concoct? What in the world was to be done? If she got into our house and took to her bed, as Mrs. Hartley had prophesied she might do, that would surely ruin us.

Finally, in the deepest dejection of my life, I told Hugh that I could not go to New England with him. He seemed to want to have his mother around, so he had better take her along to the house, and the children and I would go off on our own. I could no longer live with a man whose mother could dominate our home every time she felt in the mood or had some ideas she wanted carried out for her own purposes.

But since Hugh evidently wanted it that way, that was the way it had to be. I just had to make the best of the situation. After all, he had eight years of life with me. If he wanted to go back to his mother, now was the time to go.

Hugh looked stunned at this "silly, foolish crisis," which he said I was creating over "nothing." We had three terrible days when life seemed to come to a standstill. Finally Hugh promised that his mother would not sleep in our house, if she came to New England.

The day after Hugh's decision was made, we bought a secondhand car and camping outfit and left on a trip to New England without the children. We hoped to regain our equilibrium in the deep woods of New Hampshire.

Emmy and Miss Jones urged us to go, assuring us that everything would go along on schedule during our absence. It had been a joy to see the way Miss Jones had blossomed out in the warm sun and the free and easy atmosphere of America. Apparently she was the type of newcomer who would take our country in her stride from the very first step stateside.

Emmy, the nanny from Switzerland, who came to America with the family when they returned from England

Just north of the Massachusetts line, in the New Hampshire woods, an old log cabin was lent to us by the director of a summer camp for girls. We could eat our meals with the girls whenever we liked.

So we dropped a card to Emmy and Miss Jones, telling them where we were, and proceeded to revel in the stately pinewoods, swim in the cold, fresh lake water, and relax. Our joint love for the out-of-doors, as always, healed our spirits.

Late one evening, as we came in to dinner, the camp watchman stopped us.

"New Bedford is trying to get you on the long-distance phone," he said. "They have left a number for you to call. They said it was very urgent."

My first thought was, of course, that something had happened to the children! The operator was called immediately, and a voice was heard saying, "This is New Bedford. The undertaker of New Bedford wants to speak with you." It was all I could do to hold onto the phone without fainting.

"This is the undertaker in New Bedford," said the next voice I heard. "Your cook, Miss Mary Jones, went out swimming today and was drowned. What am I to do with the body?"

We promised to return to New Bedford at once and give him instructions. We started back on the return journey with heavy hearts. Soon we were in New Bedford, and there was Mary Jones, dressed in her prettiest American dress, which Emmy had sent over, looking so peaceful and natural.

After lunch the day before, she went out gaily for her afternoon swim. I had been teaching her to swim, though she had been very nervous about going in too deep because of a "bad heart."

"Emmy, I'm really going to swim a long way this time," she said. "I'm so excited over our party tonight. What fun we shall have!"

The guests for the party, it turned out, were two men who they had picked up one evening on the highway at the top of the hill and invited to the cottage during our absence. The men were to bring along bootleg drinks to add to the festivities of the occasion!

Jessie's sister, Emily, in New York

I found it hard to believe that sedate Miss Jones and proper Emmy were planning to use their employers' living room to entertain strange men—an unthinkable proceeding in the Old World—and with children in the house. Emmy had been filled with misgivings over the whole procedure, she said, but trusted Miss Jones because of her mature years.

Out she went, they said, swimming with strong, sure strokes, until suddenly she realized that she had gone rather far. To reassure herself, she put her feet down only to find that she could not touch the bottom. She started to scream and thrash about, but when the men onshore got to her, she had gone under.

They applied artificial respiration at once, but she never breathed again. What she needed was adrenalin, but of course no one then knew that she had a bad heart. They said she had swallowed no water—it was her heart that failed, not her breathing.

Fortunately she had enough money in the bank to pay for the funeral. We buried her in a beautiful spot in the New Bedford graveyard and found quite a sum left to send back to her mother. The children never knew what happened to Miss Jones.

Within five months after our return, the Depression descended upon us.

CHAPTER 35

A New Home Near Boston
and Two Mrs. Butlers

S oon Hugh and I found a new home for ourselves in a typical New England town called Needham, Massachusetts, outside of Boston. A large, old-fashioned, white clapboard house, with a wide porch across the front and tall oak trees in the yard, gave us plenty of space for the children to play.

Home in Needham Massachusetts

It included a two-room apartment with bath on the top floor to rent to schoolteachers to help cover the monthly mortgage payments. It also featured a large front room for the children's day nursery. On the second floor were two sizeable bedrooms for the children and the governess, a master bedroom, and a study for Hugh.

In the fall of 1929, just three weeks before the Great Depression hit the country on October 29, we safely settled into our new home. Our lovely antique furniture, which had arrived with scarcely a scratch, was even more beautiful in our new spacious rooms than it had been in England.

The big entrance hall held Hugh's organ, which showed none the worse for its many travels. It fit nicely into the vast stairwell— ideal acoustics for organ music. The grandfather clock and the little oak table with clubfeet kept it company. Our Oriental rugs glowed in the soft light from the huge windows. Off the dining room, heavily paneled in fine-grained oak, we enjoyed a glassed-in conservatory filled with coleus, a tall rubber plant, and baskets of wandering Jew.

Since there were no storm windows on the house, we tried not to think of the future cost of fuel in this cold New England climate. We knew we would have a car to keep up; the fuel bill would be heavy— two or three hundred at least—and household help would cost four times what it did in London.

Shortly after we moved, Hugh's mother wrote that she was ready to visit us, en route to California.

"What are we to do? Where shall we have her stay?"

"I'll find a room near here," Hugh replied.

Mrs. Butler arrived just before dinner. She went right up to the day nursery to see the children. The apartment next to the nursery was in order, though not yet rented.

"Are you going to stay next door, Nana?" asked Rosemary in her childlike innocence.

I had to take the bull by the horns, then and there.

"No, Daddy has found a nice room near here, where Nana can stay and be more peaceful and quiet. But she is having her meals with us and will be here all of the time, except at night." And with that, we went on as if nothing had happened.

The next night we gave a dinner party in her honor with several neighbors and friends as guests. The dinner party was to precede her departure early the next morning. Hugh had been summoned to Washington by President Hoover for a special conference of all local Department of Commerce officials and would leave on a later train.

In the middle of the dinner, Mrs. Butler suddenly excused herself from the table and went upstairs. After dessert I hurried up to see what was the trouble. Imagine my shock to find her curled up between the blankets in our bed. Was I imagining things, or did I see a look of triumph on her face?

Hurriedly, I summoned Hugh and told him where she was.

"My heavens!" he said. "Just what Mrs. Hartley said would happen! Leave it to me. I'll take care of the situation."

Before long, he went up to her, and soon they came downstairs together, bade the guests goodnight, and departed. Afterward Hugh reported what had happened.

Without a word of sympathy, he said to her, "Come on, Mother, get up now and come along to your own place. You have an early train to catch, and soon afterwards I must leave for Washington."

Whereupon, to his utter amazement, she scrambled briskly out of bed, fixed her hair, got her coat, and went along with him. When they got there, she hurried quickly to her closet, where she undressed. Soon she got into her bed, bringing out the Christian Science lesson to read out loud to Hugh, as in the old days.

Hugh said, "I have to get to bed, Mother. I have a long and important day ahead of me tomorrow, and I must get some rest. You go ahead and read to yourself, and I will ask the landlady downstairs to bring you a hot-water bottle. You'll soon be all right." And with that, he kissed her goodnight and came home.

The next morning Hugh said, "You'd better go with us to the station, just in case I need your help."

So we got out the car and drove around for Mrs. Butler. She sat in the rear. She said nothing about her health, but I noticed that whenever she thought I was looking at her in the mirror with concern, she would slump into the seat and groan. Then as I looked away, she would straighten up as bright and pert as you please.

"What a consummate actress she would have made," I thought, "as well as an opera singer. She is putting on an act, which would surely have fooled me had I not been prepared for it."

When we got to South Station, Hugh went for his mother's bags. Turning to me, Mrs. Butler said, "I'm going to faint right here on the floor of the station."

"Oh no, you're not," I answered. "If you faint, I shall call the station master to come with a stretcher to carry you onto the train."

I looked at her without fear for the first time since my marriage because I knew Hugh had my back! And so did she. What a wonderful moment that was for me!

Soon Hugh returned with the bags and escorted his mother to her berth. After handing the porter a handsome tip to assure her plenty of personal attention, the train took off.

"Whew! What a close call! Who would ever believe such things could happen? Thank God she is on her way at last! And now we can get on with our new life here in New England." Hugh sighed with relief.

Just to complete this side of the story, I will relate what finally happened to Mrs. Butler. For a long time she lived in a modern hotel in California, quite the grand lady, but with increasing health difficulties.

Eventually her trouble was pinpointed as stomach ulcers and cancer of the lower intestines. She knew many well-known Christian Science practitioners who treated her illness, diagnosed by some to be connected to her inability to reconcile herself to the marriage of her son.

Though nearly seventy-five years of age, she had never before spent a day of her life in a sick bed. She had never even had a tooth filled. Her physique was most unusual to the very end.

When told how ill his mother was, Hugh went out to California to see her. She made every effort to make Hugh's last visit with her harmonious. Gaily, without a tear, she bade him goodbye, apparently still in fair health. He never saw her again.

Emmy still worked for English wages, but when her temporary visa expired after six months, she would have to return home, and I needed to find an American governess. I would either have to do the housework myself, as well as care for the children, or earn enough money to replace myself at home.

I knew I wasn't cut out to do the former. So, taking my courage in my hands, and against the advice of family and friends, I proceeded to get our household in order, on the theory that I would soon be making enough money to pay the necessary help.

I kept in contact, through letters, with Lady Astor, who had become a good confidant from across "the pond" and was to play a large part in the future of my career.

One day, after our arrival in town, the program chairman of the Woman's Club called. Club members heard that I had lived in England for a long time. They wondered if I would be the speaker at their anniversary program in November, depicting some aspect of life in England as my subject.

"Would you like a talk on the presentation at the Court of St. James's?"

"That would be a wonderful subject!" came the enthusiastic reply. "Could you bring your court dress, and after the lecture put it on with the train and feathers to show us how you did the curtsey?"

"I think I could manage it, if I've not added too many pounds since returning to America. Would you invite the program chairmen of surrounding clubs as guests so that they might hear the speech, and then perhaps I could repeat this lecture for a fee? I would like to do some lecturing professionally," I stated.

I delivered my first lecture in the United States before our local women's club, where several hundred attended. The talk included an excellent musical program, and the stage was decorated with beautifully arranged garden flowers. Someone even softly played the same music from court, "The Merry Widow Waltz," as I slowly entered from the wings in my court dress, wearing all the trimmings, to make curtseys to the audience after the lecture.

The presentation covered the details of going to court, with additional remarks on other British customs on childcare and household management, which I thought an American audience might like to hear. It was not all frills—I saw to that!

Jessie dressed in beaded court dress with Calla lilies

This began my series of lectures before small and large women's clubs over the next four years in New England. I delivered an average of ten lectures a winter, from fifty dollars to 150 dollars each.

The lecture was titled "Pomp and Pageantry at the Court of St James's." I always displayed the court finery, for the curtsey was considered an important part of the presentation. I found a spray of artificial Calla lilies to go with the costume to replicate the fresh bouquet I actually carried at court.

During our second year back in America, they asked me to discuss family life in England at the annual youth conference of the Massachusetts Federation of Women's Clubs, held at the Statler Hotel in Boston. Six hundred young mothers attended. The title of this talk was "English Family Life: Can America Learn Anything from England's Home Customs?"

During the winter of 1930, a sympathetic president of the Women's City Club of Boston, held in a beautiful clubhouse on Beacon Hill, asked me to organize some classes in public speaking there. The classes were small and the fees modest, but now as I look back on them, I am proud of the fine women who attended these courses.

I taught Mrs. Leslie Cutler,[39] who lived near us and who had, for years, been the public health officer of the town. Mother of four beautiful children of her own and an adopted son, she had the financial security that allowed her to devote time to public work. She wanted to become a member of the Massachusetts Senate for my district. She knew that public speaking was vital to her election.

I remember the first time I heard her speak at the women's club in our town on public health. Evidently a hard worker, she had laboriously written out and memorized the speech, which she recited in a strained voice, with a fixed stare, first into one high corner of the room and then into another.

---

39   Leslie Bradley Cutler was an American politician who served in the Massachusetts Senate.

A tall, stately woman, elegantly dressed with beautiful, sad eyes, Mrs. Cutler exhibited a brilliant mind. She only needed a little help in the public speaking department.

Later I invited her to attend my first class in Boston. She came reluctantly. Afterward she confessed that she feared I taught some old-fashioned form of elocution, which would not fit her needs. But when she learned that I was more interested in the content of the speech than the delivery, and found my teaching practical and

Jessie enjoyed national success as a lecturer and teacher

suited to everyday demands, she became enthusiastic. A woman who knew how to think logically, she was soon preparing speeches from outlines and delivering them as though extemporaneous.

Defeated for the House four times, Mrs. Cutler never gave up. Finally elected, she served for ten years until elected to the Massachusetts Senate, as one of the first women in the United States to serve in a state senate.

Mrs. Cutler told me that during an election campaign she could now deliver as many as seven speeches a day, all different.

Among many others, Mrs. John Winant, wife of the governor of New Hampshire; Mrs. Leverett Saltonstall, whose husband became the governor of Massachusetts; Mrs. Richard Russell, whose husband was mayor of Cambridge and later served in Congress, joined the classes and many more.

I found it gratifying to see the way all these students improved as they studied techniques and practiced their speeches in class. I found that in eight lessons, students who did their homework were often speaking as well as or better than anyone who had been on the platform for years without formal training.

Some of the most unpromising pupils in the opening classes turned into the best speakers.

As time went on, I became convinced that, deep down, every human being longs for the opportunity of full expression. Words, not swords, have always been a woman's weapon, but often she did not learn to use these powerful weapons outside the home. I believed women needed to know how to use the power of the spoken word in public affairs, as well as in the home.

Students began saying to me, "Do you know, I feel as though I have been made over. With your guidance, my study of public speaking has done something to me. I feel so different, so much freer. I have less fear and more self-confidence than I have ever known before."

I told Hugh, "You have found a wonderful hobby for me, but whether it will ever develop into a profession that pays remains to be seen."

"What do you care how long it takes? If you can earn enough to finance necessary household help—and some expensive clothes, I might add—you can carry on and have the satisfaction of knowing that you were doing something for American women, and men indirectly, along the way.

"Frankly, I'm jealous of you. I wish I had a career as fascinating as yours. You are a free agent. You can run your own show as you please." Hugh felt conflicted about his own situation with United States government, and all its internal politics, rules, and regulations. For like me, Hugh also remained an individualist at heart.

"Stop being jealous! What wouldn't I give for a real office once more, with the secretary to answer the phone and regular hours of work! How would you like to do your work in the bedroom amidst the distractions of a household and small children, with the phone ringing at all hours of the day and night?" As usual, the other fellow's grass looked greener.

The Depression of the 1930s rapidly came to a climax. Foreign trade, like domestic trade, remained in a bad way. In 1933, Franklin D. Roosevelt became president. All of a sudden, on July 20, 1933, Hugh was appointed to organize the National Recovery Administration (NRA) in the six New England states. The country that summer stared into an awful abyss. The NRA centered the nation's hope on economic salvation, and Hugh became the key to that crisis in New England.

He worked nights and days, seven days a week. Because conservative New England endorsed the NRA, it became easier to win it over in the rest of the country. The Boston office received Washington's award for the most efficient NRA in the nation.

The job ended abruptly, so we rented out our house and headed back to Washington, D.C., almost bankrupt. I approached my dear friend, Lady Astor, to ask her to use her influence to persuade Eleanor Roosevelt to recommend Hugh for a position in the administration.

Mrs. Hugh Butler
1922 Sunderland Place, N.W.
Washington, D.C. U.S.A.
4 ST JAMES SQUARE
LONDON, S.W.1
December 2nd, 1935

Dear Mrs. Butler,

 Very many thanks for your letter. I only hope
that what I have done for you may be of some help.
Do let me know as soon as you hear the result.
 Thank you, too, for your kind congratulations.
 We women have a very hard fight trying to get
into Parliament, but we have not done so badly
this time. Most of the women candidates are given
really bad Constituencies, and it is a wonder that
so many get in. On the whole, the Conservatives
have done very well.

 Nancy Astor

The image of the letter above, is below

4,ST JAMES' SQUARE,
LONDON, S.W.1.

December 2nd, 1935

Dear *Mr Butler*

 Very many thanks for your letter.
I only hope that what I have done for you
may be of some help. Do let me know as
soon as you hear the result.

 Thank you, too, for your kind
congratulations.

 We women have a very hard fight
trying to get into Parliament, but we have
not done so badly this time. Most of the
women candidates are given really bad
Constituencies, and it is a wonder that so
many get in. On the whole, the Conservatives
have done very well. - *Bud Us* -

TAPLOW,
BUCKS.

CLIVEDEN.

December 27th 1935.

Dear Mrs Butler,

    I enclose a copy of a letter I have

received from Mrs Roosevelt. I am afraid it does not

sound very promising, but I wanted you to know that I

I have really done my best.

    Do forgive this, I am just off to Switzerland

for the first real rest I have had since the Election

campaign, and I must say I am very glad to be going.

Mrs Hugh Butler,
~~The White House~~,
Washington, D.C.
~~U.S.A.~~

```
Mrs. Hugh Butler
1922 Sunderland Place, N.W.
Washington, D.C.
U.S.A.


CLIVEDEN


December 27, 1935


Dear Mrs. Butler,


        I enclose a copy of a letter I have
received from Mrs. Roosevelt. I am afraid it does
not sound very promising, but I wanted you to know
that I have really done my best.


        Do forgive this, I am just off to
Switzerland for the first real rest I have had since
the Election campaign, and I must say I am very
glad to be going.


Nancy Astor
```

The image of the letter above is on the previous page.

Dear Friends in England,

Hugh, now Research Director of the United States
Maritime Commission, is coming to England for a short
trip of about six weeks and I have persuaded him that it
is his duty to bring me along and this is the reason.
In March I had a ten day speaking tour in and near
Chicago. Most of the time I talked on the Reciprocal
Trade Agreements. My talks were well received because
I concentrated on the British goods which our women
would like to buy and similarly what we make that you
would like to buy. At the same time we would build sound
foundations for peace. So the excuse I have to come will
be in order to secure additional speech material.

Also because of your terrible difficulties with food,
I shall have a package of food shipped to us each week.
I am told you all carry your food about in suitcases
while visiting; so we will follow your example.

I shall sail on the U.S. Cargo Ship, Marine Flasher,
leaving New York City April 18th and arriving in
Southampton on the 26th. Hugh will come on a later ship
arriving about May 8th.

Why am I writing all this to you? I do not want
to cause any trouble or inconvenience but I would be
deeply grateful if you could send me suggestions for
my short study of English life whereby I may secure
some interesting speech material to continue to further
Hugh's and my hobby, which is the basic need of Anglo-
American world wide cooperation.

I am leaving a week ahead of Hugh because I must be
back in America to conduct a public speaking seminar for
75 leaders in Cleveland, Ohio, June 16 - 20th and four
public speaking classes for the General Federation of
Women's Clubs Annual Convention (3,000 attending) in New
York City, June 23 - 29th, in both of which places I will
be able to make immediate use of the material secured.

Looking forward to seeing as many of you as possible.

Cordially and Sincerely yours,
Jessie Butler

Chapter 36

Getting Back on Our Feet
in Washington, D.C.

Hugh preceded me to Washington, where he obtained a further position in the Resettlement Administration. He received practically the same salary he had when we were married, but we were grateful for any salary at all. Many of our friends were left without jobs for a long time, with no money coming in.

Some of Hugh's former associates began suffering nervous breakdowns and health problems of all sorts as a result. We at least kept afloat. We retained sufficient reserves to take care of ourselves and our children and found a temporary a place near Dupont Circle.

The loss of prestige, due to financial failure, caused almost as much suffering as the actual hardship. Hugh had worked in his own office for four years, with thirteen assistants and the excitement and notoriety of launching the NRA. Then suddenly, prestige and position disappeared.

I felt free and full of courage. At last I returned back to the world where I felt at home. I found it easy to laugh at Hugh and his fancy troubles. It turned out to be a good thing we could laugh, for we both needed plenty of humor at this time.

Hugh "sweat it out" in one new agency after another. One of his friends, a man long in the diplomatic service, used to entertain us with humorous descriptions of his experiences job hunting, telling us about the shoe leather he had worn out pacing the streets and the marble corridors of government offices. He helped us to see the funny side of what we were going through.

"I'll tell you, Hugh," he said, as parting words of advice after landing a job in Thailand, "in this world of today you have to be like a man jumping rapidly from one floating cake of ice to another in a swiftly moving stream. The trick is to avoid falling between the blocks of ice. When you come to think of it, it all adds up to additional experience.

"Any man is a fool who allows himself to become too much of a specialist in one department of the government. But you and I are specialists in public service. This is a broad enough field for anyone. The United States is getting ready to go into world affairs in a big way, so there is a future ahead for men trained as we are. Stay with it, Hugh, that's my advice.

"The pay will never be large, but the satisfaction that goes along with public service well done more than makes up for the low pay. After all, money isn't everything."

And Hugh did stay with it through thirty-two years of government service—some tough, some fine, but on the whole satisfying.

We enjoyed many outdoor picnics in Rock Creek Park, grateful to the men whose vision had supplied the very spot for picnic suppers by the cool Broad Branch stream.

This park extends through the middle of Washington for nearly ten miles. It offers an oasis both summer and winter, which to this harried couple proved to be a lifesaver. In the fall, the vivid colors taken on by the trees splashed up and down the hills were always a joy.

One day I called on a former friend, Florence McGill Kiefer, a well-known singer and student of Christian Science. She often sang in the All Souls Unitarian Church on 16th Street. She showed enthusiasm for any new artistic idea that came along, always eager to lend a helping hand to an artist whenever she could.

When she heard about my public speaking classes in New England, she promptly invited me to teach a class in her studio on G Street. So, on October 30, 1935, I opened the first class in public speaking in Washington, D.C., and began my new career in our nation's capital. That first class included many women who were then, or later became, prominent in public affairs.

I soon received invitations to teach at both the Republican Party Club and the Democratic Club. Women from both parties recognized the value of learning to make effective speeches. Without trying, I became a bipartisan teacher.

During the summer of 1937, Hugh held onto a fairly secure position with the Social Security Board, first in the training division, and later in the actuarial section.

"I'm glad I got caught in the Depression," Hugh said one evening. "It's good for any man to be without a job, to get down to rock bottom at least once in his life. I've learned a lot.

"And I've become familiar with more departments of the government. That's necessary too if a man is to spend his life in government service. I have a more rounded-out picture of the whole than if I'd stayed in the Department of Commerce all my life."

"Well, I'm glad we got out of New England, though I still love it," I replied. "We didn't belong there anyway. You would never have gone far in business because of the tradition favoring the sons of old New England families, the Harvard graduates who belong to the right clubs, and the likes.

"It's a sweet place to live all right, if you have your roots there. Otherwise it's a good place to leave. I'm beginning to like it here in Washington. It's a wonderful time to live here."

Finally, we found a home at 1559 44th Street, in Foxhall Village, built on the edge of Foundry Park, just west of Georgetown and not far from the banks of the Potomac River. The village, copied after the Hampstead Garden Suburb in London, was built in the same Georgian style of architecture, so we felt at home there at once. The furniture arrived by fall, and once again, the dear old organ found its place.

An intelligent and faithful black housekeeper, Dora Bailey, took over the mechanical details of running the household.

By the middle of September 1937, Hugh had retained a position that he liked. I made a good beginning in a promising new career conducting speech classes for both the League of Republican Women and the Democratic Club on New Hampshire Avenue. Rosemary received a scholarship in one of Washington's outstanding preparatory schools, the Holton-Arms School. Richard attended the Rose Lee Hardy School up the hill in Foxhall Village until he entered Western High School.

President Roosevelt appointed Hugh to put together and head up a department in the new Social Security Administration.

CHAPTER 37

A President's Wife Lends a Helping Hand

By 1938, activities of the Congressional Club, where we held our public speaking classes, grew so diverse with both political parties that it became necessary to move the public speaking classes to a different location. A faithful and enthusiastic student, Mrs. Harry Englebright, whose husband represented California, asked one day how we could get busy women to attend classes at some distance from their local club.

Mrs. Englebright eventually made an original suggestion. "Let's ask Mrs. Roosevelt to be the guest speaker at our next meeting."

"Will you write the letter?" I asked. "If you will write to her, I feel sure she will come and help us get a start."

"I'll be glad to," Mrs. Englebright promised.

To our astonishment, Mrs. Roosevelt accepted the invitation. On January 12, 1939, the opening meeting of the public speaking classes took place in Pierce Hall of the All Souls Unitarian Church, at 16th and Harvard, with Mrs. Franklin D. Roosevelt as the guest speaker.

Mrs. Jed Johnson, wife of Congressman Johnson from Oklahoma, another enthusiastic student, was selected to introduce the distinguished speaker to the audience.

Mrs. Englebright, our chairman, was very excited that day. Seldom does a congressional wife have the opportunity of presenting the wife of the president of the United States at a public meeting. All the Washington newspapers had been alerted.

> **Mrs. Franklin D. Roosevelt will be the guest speaker**
>
> at the opening meeting of
>
> **Mrs. Hugh Butler's Winter Course in Practical Platform Speaking**
>
> The Chairman will be Mrs. Clarence Cannon, wife of Congressman Cannon of Missouri; Mrs. Karl LeCompte wife of Congressman LeCompte of Iowa will introduce Mrs. Roosevelt.
>
> Congressional wives active in the recent campaign The Junior League, The P.T.A.; Army wives, Columnists and Club Women will be represented by able speakers.
>
> You are cordially invited to attend the meeting at
>
> Pierce Hall, All Souls' Church, 16th and Harvard Streets
> Entrance on Harvard Street
>
> Thursday Morning, January 9, 1941, at 10.30 o'clock

First Lady Eleanor Roosevelt was a guest speaker at many of Jessie's public speaking courses

Mrs. Englebright, a very short woman, looked out of place next to Mrs. Roosevelt, who stood at almost six feet. A large, avid audience waited as the chairman pinned a camellia on her distinguished guest.

Finally, Mrs. Roosevelt said, "Are you ready? Let's go." I stood back of them, but soon I saw Mrs. Roosevelt leading the way. In those days, Mrs. Roosevelt did not walk, she loped, and Mrs. Englebright had to run to keep up with her.

By this time, Mrs. Englebright became so excited that she forgot to sit down to catch her breath. She dashed up to the speaker's table and, without a pause, began her welcome speech. But no sound came because she had no breath to push the sound out.

Her mind went blank, and she forgot what she meant to say. With a stricken look, she realized that her notes and her glasses were still in her purse. She opened her purse, packed full as most purses are, whereupon everything fell to the floor. Both the chairman and the guest of honor, the First Lady, bent down on their knees to pick everything up off the floor!

As for myself, I blacked out, figuratively speaking of course. The entire incident was my fault, for I realized that I hadn't forewarned my students: when conducting a meeting, sit down first; breathe deeply from the diagram to fill the bloodstream with oxygen; give the speaker a chance to size up her audience, to collect notes and ready glasses, if needed. When I finally came to, so to speak, the meeting was proceeding as scheduled, everything in order. Mrs. Englebright proved to be a most gracious chairman.

Mrs. Jed Johnson gave an original, yet suitable, introduction. She carefully avoided the personal remarks that do nothing for the introduction, but stressed the contribution that Mrs. Roosevelt offered to the women of America. The meeting turned out to be most inspiring and satisfactory. A large class formed the next week.

After Mrs. Roosevelt's speech, Mrs. Englebright conducted a question-and-answer period. One question asked and answered by the guest speaker provided a guide for women in general:

> *Question:* How do you learn not to mind when there is an unfavorable criticism?
> *Answer:* You have to remember that history shows that whenever there has been progress, there was also unfavorable criticism. You have to be sure that you are doing what you think is right . . . that you know all of the facts . . . and that you have integrity of purpose. Then go ahead and don't let the criticism bother you.

Mrs. Roosevelt knew that women, more than men, find political brickbats *[insulting remarks]* especially vexing. I suppose this is because women want to be liked. It is their nature to court and receive words of praise. But if they are to enter the political arena, they have to learn to take personal attacks on the chin. Our speaker knew from experience of what she spoke, or she would not have been able to give such wise advice.

In 1943, my dear friend, Mrs. John L. Whitehurst, president of the General Federation of Women's Clubs (GFWC), visited England and learned that many young women were anxious to marry in the traditional white dress, but resources made it impossible. She decided to enlist American women to help and asked members of the GFWC to donate their own wedding dresses. Fifty gowns were donated by American women for British servicewomen to wear. Each dress was loaned and passed to the next woman to ensure that it was worn by as many brides as possible until it was worn out.

Famous donors included Mary Pickford and Eleanor Roosevelt.

Each gown had a little gold label providing the name and address of the dress donor. British women confirmed that this scheme allowed many young brides the opportunity to wear a white wedding dress.

Excerpts from letters to family about some of the times with Eleanor Roosevelt

[More letters to family about Mrs. Roosevelt in Appendix, page 282]

Dec. 22, 1938

Dear Folks at Home,

On Christmas Eve, the President goes from the White House to the Park in front to light the big Christmas tree and we are going to take Richard, so if it comes in over the radio you can all picture us there looking at the President and listening to the big band. The next day, we are going to the church where he goes to see him and his family at church. We saw him last Christmas Day — and we shall never forget it. You forget what a cripple he is when you see him in the movies so you would get a shock if you could see him stumble in on his canes with his face and neck red with the effort and downright pain which walking causes him. What a wonderful man to carry his great burden and yet to be a cripple!

April 15, 1939

Dear Folks at Home,

As you know Mrs. Roosevelt came to open my first meeting of wives of members Congress and was our first speaker. As a result I had 25 in the winter course and have had 12 since in other classes besides some private pupils.

Last month the Democratic women from all over the country were in Washington and had me give them a short lecture on Speech Preparation and Delivery. As a result of that talk, I am to go to Harrisburg, Penn. in May to the State meeting of the Democratic women to give the same speech for $25 and expenses; also to Norfolk, Va. and to Springfield, Mass. and Holyoke, Mass. Don't think I am turning Democratic; I would do the same for the Republicans if they asked me to. (After working with Eleanor Roosevelt, Jessie did become a Democrat for the rest of her life.) My desire is to help them all become good speakers. Also the Democratic National Committee here is now assigning some of my speakers to their state meetings; then the speakers come to me for private lessons and so it works all ways around. Hugh says "I have arrived" and it looks as though I have. In a couple of more years by the time Rosemary gets into college, I should be making enough to help out the family budget.

[Author's note: After that first speech, Mrs. Roosevelt invited Jessie to hold speech classes in the East Room of the White House. Later, Mrs. Harry S. Truman sponsored Jessie's classes in the same room.]

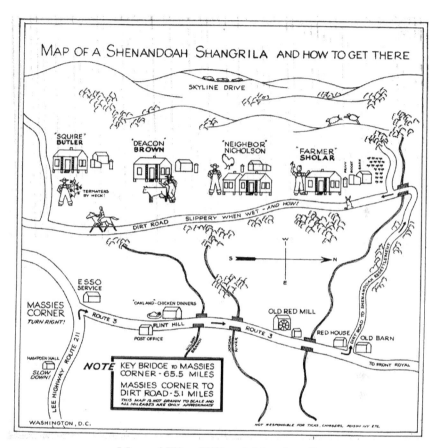

Map of Flint Hill neighborhood

***Jessie and Hugh with Richard and Rosemary
at their Shenandoah hideout***

CHAPTER 38

A Deadline to Write a Book:
Time to Speak Up

Just one obstacle stood in the way of my amazingly successful public speaking classes for congressmen's and diplomats' wives. (Even more important were the speech workshops at the annual meetings of the General Federation of Woman's Clubs held in Chicago.)

No speech textbook existed for women's classes, and the speech textbooks for men were inadequate. They were stuffy, artificial, and dry, which would not do for women students.

Jessie speaking at a National Convention — one of many

So I attended the annual meeting of the Speech Association of America in 1944, held that year in the Mayflower Hotel in Washington, D.C. The founder of this association, Norwood Brigance,[40] a famous professor of public speaking at Wabash College, was the highest paid speech teacher in the United States.

"He ought to have the answer to that one," I hoped. "If he is so famous, surely he will have a speech textbook for women on his to-do list."

I told him briefly what I had been doing in Washington to further the training of women and that I even taught a men's class for diplomats. The answer from this great authority shocked me: "No such book has ever been written. It's badly needed for this country. I know the need from my own experience as a lecturer. Why don't you write the book? You will perform a service for public speaking by writing a textbook for women."

"I don't know how to write," I replied.

I felt more shy about such a task than I did about speaking in public. It seemed to take exceptional nerve to even think about writing a book—almost as much to undress in public! The very idea gave me a cold chill.

"Can you compose on a typewriter?" he asked.

"Oh, yes," I said. "I've typed my own letters for years. I don't know what I would have done without a typewriter."

"All right then, all you have to do is to get out your typewriter, put in some fresh paper, and start to write. Write a chapter as soon as possible and send it to me," he insisted. "I'll edit it and tell you if it's any good. Now, when do I get that first chapter?"

Evidently Professor Brigance knew the value of a deadline. I opted for the middle of June, which coincided with the coming of summer. I knew I would be in our retreat in the mountains then, and I could work uninterrupted. I would be free to write.

---

40   William Norwood Brigance (1896–1960) was an educator at Wabash College, as well as an author and lecturer.

Way back in 1939, we scoured the countryside around Washington in search of a summer escape. We wanted a hideout, however simple, where we could go for weekends and holidays and yet be within easy driving distance of Washington.

Shenandoah hideaway at Flint Hill, Virginia

We decided to locate in Flint Hill, Virginia, near the foot of the Blue Ridge Mountains. The country around this area was lovely, combining the wild, untamed beauty of the mountains with the "hillbillies" found living up in the "hollers."

We were able to purchase a small white house, built by the Resettlement Administration, seventy-two miles from Washington. Located on a hilltop, it revealed a wide view of the mountains and the Shenandoah Valley. Farm neighbors lived on all sides, from whom we purchased milk, eggs, and fresh vegetables. Our nearest neighbor, Luther Adkins, had six little girls. The older ones came up the hill during the canning season to help put some of their surplus fruit and vegetables abounding in that region into our jars for the winter.

Here on the hilltop, our family let go of all our tension and strain to live informally. We slept, read, and swam together as a family. Rosemary rode horses that belonged to our neighbor, Scoot Welch, in exchange for helping Mrs. Welch peel peaches or tomatoes for canning. She enjoyed learning about farm life. Richard worked as a farmhand for Fred Dotson down the road, helping with the milking, feeding hogs, and haying.

Martha Ellyn's Platter Chatter

Home Canning Is Delightful Experience Rather Than Chore for Mrs. Hugh Butler

Shoulders have been put to the wheel in many ways since our lives have been changed by the war. Many women who had never turned a hand or furrowed a brow about laundry, houseclean-ing and other household respon-sibilities have taken to these ac-tivities, not in a resentful way, but with an I-can-do-it attitude.

Mrs. Hugh Butler, who is known in Washington as one who is always out to improve even the shiny hour, took on a new inter-est this summer. Learning to can products grown on the Butler country place and from the sur-rounding country, is according to Mrs. Butler, one of the most en-gaging things into which she has ever entered. If you take a re-sume of the life of this energetic woman who has fingers in various pies, you would realize that the comparison is a notable one.

Educated at a school where lib-eral arts made up the studies, Mrs. Butler wasn't subjected to the learning of those things which would especially fit her for homemaking. This in the opinion of Mrs. Butler, is a minor tragedy in a girl's life—not to be fitted for homemaking. She has learned from experience, and not from training in home economics, that it is just as important to know the A, B, C's of running an effi-cient household as it is to play Beethoven's "Seventh Sym-phony," know how to copy a Corot, or speak as an expert lin-guist.

Mrs. Butler has done much to bring about a common interest between the British and Ameri-can women in Washington. A series of teas was one medium by which she brought them to-gether. As a teacher of effective speaking she has helped many women to reach out to newer and wider horizons.

A New Thrill

In a recent interview, Mrs. Butler said that she has had no greater thrill than when she first viewed the products she canned throughout the summer at their Virginia home which is situated near the Flint Hill project of the Farm Security Administration program.

It was through the help of the women of the families who live on the farms of the Flint Hill project, that Mrs. Butler learned about canning. Without benefit of pressure cooker she canned several hundred cans of food. Chickens were canned in several ways. The choice pieces were fried and canned. The bony pieces and feet were cooked and processed for soup. The older chicken were canned for making stew. Green beans, sauerkraut, raspberries, pickles, tomatoes, corn, applesauce, and many other foods were canned by Mrs. But-ler.

I ate a dinner from products she canned. If everyone who canned home products this year is as successful as this energetic woman, they can assure them-selves that meals will not be skimpy or lack good nutrition this winter. The following is the

Jessie took up gardening and canning for the war effort and inspired other women by participating in newspaper and magazine interviews.

1559 — 44th Street, N. W.
Washington, D.C.
November 17, 1943

THE BUTLERS' LOG — 1943

Dear Friends (American and British),

June and July I spent on our mountaintop in Virginia. Then I returned to Washington with over 200 jars of food, including 55 chickens. The country girls all asked to help--the food was there in lavish quantities and so I couldn't resist the temptation to preserve it. I lost some 15 pounds in the process and returned to Washington greatly rested. Life on a hill top with no phone, no radio, and little diversion except the 8 new puppies presented to me by Richard's dog, Amiga, is a cure for the dark moods which assail one in a world such as this.

There was an interesting aftermath to my experience. Martha Ellen, who writes Platter Chatter in the Washington Post, asked to come out and take a picture of my shelves. This she did. I sent the picture and article to Mrs. Roosevelt and offered to come and tell her about our experiences in the country with the Farm Security folks who had been helped during the past years by the President's program for farmers. In a few days a letter arrived inviting me to the White House to tea, and last week I found myself in the sitting room on the second floor of the White house talking to a very wonderful person. We talked some of the farmers, but Mrs. Roosevelt's burning interest at the moment is concerned with our boys coming back from the war badly crippled and needing adjustment to civilian life. She talked of her trip to the South Pacific, and as I left, I found myself agreeing with Ernie Pyle, the newspaper correspondent, who had had tea there and who wrote about her: "I had been talking to a woman who is unique; who is remarkable, and who is all good." So you see what a fascinating experience my little jars led me into.

Jessie

***Mrs. Hugh Butler** proudly surveys the array of foods she canned during the summer. Although this is the first time that she has done home canning, yet she processed fruits and vegetables and poultry. Apples and potatoes too were brought from the Butler country place so they will be assured of adequate nutrition when winter comes.*

When I told Hugh how scared I felt at the very thought of starting the book, he said, "I don't see what you're waiting for. You have three months with nothing else to do and a place where you will have no interruptions. You said it all hundreds of times in your classes. All you have to do is make an outline of the chapters exactly the way you teach. Just record what you've been saying now for over fifteen years."

I found nothing left to do but start. And that proved the most difficult of all. I put off starting as long as I could, finding all sorts of little jobs, which I told myself needed doing first—anything but to sit and start. Earlier in the year, when I first decided to write the book, I wrote to my dear friend, Lady Astor, to ask her to write the foreword. She consented.

```
9 Babmaes Street
Jermyn Street
4 St. James Square
SW1, London

11 October 1944

Dear Mrs. Butler,
    I was so glad to have your letter of last week. Thank you
so much.
    What you tell me about your book interests me very much
indeed. I can't think of anyone better fitted to write it.
    It is really kind of you to invite me to write the
Preface, and I do appreciate it. I will with pleasure, do
this for you. I have read the draft you enclosed, but I
think it is much too long. If you can wait a little until I
am less rushed with work, I will write one and send it on. I
feel that a Preface is much more effective if it is short. Do
you agree? Anyway, when you read mine, please tell me quite
frankly what you think.
    These last few weeks have been hectic with the Town &
Country Planning Bill in Parliament. As you can realise, it
is vitally important for Plymouth and other blitzed cities
throughout the country, and we are anxious that it should be
the best possible. In spite of a rather stormy passage, I
think we will win, but it has not been easy.
    How I envy your little corner in Virginia!
    We managed to get a few weeks in Cornwall in August; We
needed it badly, and we got it.

        Nancy Astor
```

One Monday, early in June, I rose at the crack of dawn. And what a display of color spread across the horizon! The whole eastern sky appeared before me bathed in rosy hues. The air filled up with the twittering of all kinds of birds preparing to take off for breakfast. The cows down in the Welch pasture moved in unison toward the barn for our neighbor, Lulu, to milk. Sweet scents of honeysuckle and wildflowers saturated the air and dotted the rolling green pastures with bright, gay colors. Over in the west, the Blue Ridge Mountains stood immobile, shrouded in dark shades of blue, which were almost black in spots. From my hilltop, I could look up and down the valley and watch the first rays of the rising sun as it penetrated the fields and hills, lighting up the small white farmhouses scattered over the landscape.

I once heard Bernard Shaw say, "If you sit down and quiet your mind, inspiration will pour through."

"All right, Mr. Shaw," I said to myself, "let's see if you know whereof you speak!"

Professor Brigance enthusiastically endorsed chapter one. "This is the first time I have ever seen 'conquest of fear' put into a speech textbook!"

I took the title *Time to Speak Up* from an editorial written by Malvina Lindsay, editorial writer for *The Washington Post*, which appeared in that paper on February 18, 1944. Her editorial was printed in the original edition of the book, as well as a foreword, written by Lady Astor, and an endorsement from First Lady Eleanor Roosevelt.

There are fourteen chapters. The appendix included sample speeches delivered by well-known women.

By that fall, the book was accepted by Ordway Tead, editor of social and economic books for Harper & Brothers, and the manuscript went on its way to the publisher.

Ordway Tead had been a member of the Little Fabian Society in Boston many years before when we were both much younger. He remembered my name, which evidently helped get my book published.

The regular hours of writing, five days a week, brought a sense of accomplishment and satisfaction such as I have never known before.

By the end of that same summer, I was glad to have Rosemary join me on the hilltop. She came after six weeks' attendance at the School of Citizenship in New York City.

One warm summer evening we decided to attend the tent meeting of the Pentecostals near "Little Washington." There loomed something elemental and primitive about these tent meetings, crowded with farm families and their children. Such assemblies fascinated us both.

The rhythmic singing of Pentecostal hymns rocked in a rapid tempo during an emotional summons from Preacher Scroggins. With hands upraised, in a singsong voice, he called his congregation to come to the altar and give themselves to Jesus. He created a dynamic and moving environment. Several of the worshipers fell to the ground unconscious in convulsions, hands and feet jerking.

On this particular night, the tent audience remained singing, praying, and preaching until the unconscious ones rose and returned to their seats, looking natural once more.

By 11:30 that night, Rosemary and I returned home still singing, refreshed as though we too had experienced an emotional cathartic. We came into our little sitting room on the hilltop, all dark outside and cozy and bright inside, lit by the glow of a red-base lamp.

```
3 Elliot Terrace
The Hoe, Plymouth
9 April 1945

Dear Mrs. Butler,

     Here is the introduction. You can change it if you
like and I've no doubt you can improve on it, but that
is the sense of it. It comes with my love.
     I have had a very difficult time lately, but I am
not alone in that.
     I do hope and pray that this is good enough, but
as I say, you've got the sense of what I've tried to
say and you can make it much better.

                    Nancy Astor
```

FOREWORD[41] to *Time to Speak Up*

Bernard Shaw wrote a long book on *An Intelligent Woman's Guide to Socialism.* I tried to make him see that Intelligent Women could not be Socialist—that is if they were Mothers of many children. This is what I meant. At a political meeting some years ago an irate woman yelled out that her children were as good as mine. I replied, No doubt, madam, but which of my children are you referring to? There are so many and they are so very different. She replied, What do you mean? I explained that I had one son who had certain qualities: that if he were put into a dark forest I could rely on him to get out, and he would very likely come out leading the natives. They would be right to follow him as he would know where he was going and not let them down. Whereas I had another who was equally nice but hadn't got those qualities and if he was down a mile from home he would probably lose his way.

Women who are wise are not theorists. They face facts and use their common sense combined with humanity. Mrs. Butler has both and I believe her book will be a Woman's Guide to Useful Citizenship. We women who care passionately about a safer, saner world must be awake and on our toes. Else this freedom which so many young lives have been given to save—will be lost. We who belong to the English-thinking Democracies must be quite certain that nothing separates us. Together we can <u>almost</u> guarantee a better world—for all mankind.

Six years of war have shown us what makes strong nations, and what makes weak ones. Let's thank God for the vision and courage of our Freedom loving Ancestors. Never forget that the Bible in the common tongue was first read by the English-speaking people and it certainly seems to have made them a very uncommon people. Our foundations guarantee freedom to all people of goodwill and I refuse to carry on inherited hatreds. The world was never more in need of our goodwill and our good citizenship, and I myself am grateful to Jessie Butler for having written this book.

---

41   This is the Foreword of *Time to Speak Up* by Lady Astor (with slight changes to punctuation).

CLIVEDEN
31 May 1945
Dear Mrs. Butler,

Thank you so much for your interesting letter and enclosures.

On reading my Foreword again, I agree with you that it's extremely good! I feel like Baalam when the ass spoke!!

I am deeply interested in all you say and feel like coming over to America and attaching myself to Colonel Himmatsinhji[42] and touring the country. I would do anything in the world to keep our two countries together and save what little civilisation we have got. You think about it!

What a pity Olive Butler can't see things our way! I am amused at Drew Pearson's[43] articles. Winston Churchill would have a fit if he heard himself described as a member of the Cliveden Set.[44] Do tell Mr. Pearson the Cliveden Set was composed of Lord Halifax, Lord Lothian, Dr. Tom Jones, Lionel Curtis and such like. Winston wouldn't have touched them with a barge pole. He never forgave Philip Lothian and the others for trying to stop his intervention in the Russian war. However, Mr. Drew Pearson couldn't think less of me than I do of him in his writings.

I still feel sad at leaving Parliament and think it is a wrong time to go.

                    Nancy Astor

---

42   *Major-General Kumar Shri Himmatsinhji Juwansinhji Jadeja CIE (1897–1973) was educated in England and the first Lieutenant-Governor of Himachal Pradesh. A descendant of the rulers of Nawanagar State, he served with the Indian Army and was later a member of the lower house of the Parliament of India.*
43   *Andrew Russell Pearson (1897–1969) was one of the best-known American columnists of his day, noted for his syndicated newspaper column "Washington Merry-Go-Round," in which he criticized various public persons.*
44   *The Cliveden Set were a 1930s upper-class group of prominent individuals politically influential in pre-World War II Britain, who were in the circle of Nancy Astor, Viscountess Astor. The name comes from Cliveden, the stately home in Buckinghamshire, which was then Astor's country residence.*

Comment from Rosina Harrrison, Lady Astor's personal maid: "Arthur Bushel [the valet] and I laughed it off, but he resented its implications. 'A pack of lies, Rose, whoever invented them ought to come and work here for a week as a housemaid. They'd find no Nazis under Cliveden beds.'"

- From *Rose: My Life in Service to Lady Astor* by Rosina Harrison

CHAPTER 39

She Speaks Up

The publication of *Time to Speak Up* doubled the effectiveness of my teaching and sold like hot cakes, especially with the foreword written by Lady Astor and a recommendation by Eleanor Roosevelt added to the cover.

Three of Jessie's public speaking students holding her book,
Time to Speak Up

The art of public speaking is an art which, I think has to be studied. This book gives much help and information, which at this time is very valuable. We are apt to think that expression of one's thought comes easily but as a matter of fact it requires training and real practice. I am hopeful that more and more people in this country will realize that this is one of the important means of communication between people and we must not neglect to train young and old in the ability to speak well in public. ~*Eleanor Roosevelt*

Jessie talking about her book on Cavalcade of Books

I was invited to present *Time to Speak Up* on Cavalcade of Books.[45] The book became my flag and landed me in the middle of speaking and teaching engagements all over the country. Lecture halls filled with two to five hundred women at each location, eager to buy the book and learn to speak.

---

45   Cavalcade of Books was a television series that aired from 1948 to 1974.

From Chicago to New York to Philadelphia to Florida, I encouraged women to use the skills in my book to take the lecture podium and speak in their own communities and beyond. When teaching the majority of my classes in Washington, D.C., the book made it possible to allocate most of the class time for speeches. It increased the need for students to budget their time to do their homework, in this case reading and learning the techniques explained in the textbook.

I received a favorable nod from Kirkus Reviews:

> *An excellent handbook for the women who some time or other will have to accept the challenge of speaking on their feet. The author gives full credit to the number of excellent books on the subject of public speaking, but hers is the first that focuses attention primarily on the specific problems of the woman speaker (presence, voice, manner, clothes, type of material, approach, etc.) and on the woman audience. Every point made is pertinent. No speaker, experienced or amateur, will fail to find suggestion and stimulation in the content of the book. There is some inspirational quality, but on the whole it is down to earth, practical advice, based on the assumption that the reader has something to learn. It is varied enough to have value not only for speakers, but for program chairmen, introducers, those who make or accept presentations, after dinner speakers, etc. Not a step by step, self-teaching course in public speaking, but sound advice on how to be a better public speaker. Some sample material and some practical exercises add to its classroom value.*

And thus, my dream became a reality. A homely young girl from Pueblo, Colorado, escaped to Smith College and, from there, onto the bigger world stage to participate in the excitement of politics and the suffrage movement in our Nation's capital. And after eight years of living in the charm of England, she returned to the United States to write a book to help hundreds of women find their voice.

Reviews for *Time to Speak Up*

Women who are wise are not theorists. They face facts and use their common sense combined with humanity. Mrs. Butler has both and I believe her book will be a Woman's Guide to Useful Citizenship.
~*Lady Astor (The Viscountess Astor, CH.)*

Those whose social political, or spiritual interests bring them constantly before the public will find Jessie Haver Butler's new handbook for speakers . . . a practical and effective guide.
~*The Washington Post*

If you are afraid to speak in public and occasionally find that you must do so, or if you wish to be prepared for a time when you may have to give an address, Mrs. Butler's handbook for women speakers will be helpful. It covers everything from conquering fear to the etiquette problems connected with public speaking.
~*Chicago Tribune*

. . .It has the advantage of a lively instructive method and a great many specific instances and developed illustrations which lift the exposition out of the realm of theory. . . . The book should be useful to the women to whom it is directed, either reading privately or used as a text in a club.
~*Quarterly Journal of Speech*

As an incentive and guide to women to become effective public speakers, as a textbook in public speaking for high school and college classes and as a source of basic information in this field, this book offers excellent subject matter. To those who dread appearing in public or speaking to groups, the chapters on overcoming fear and how to meet various situations will be especially helpful. Excellent directions for preparing and presenting talks are given.
~*The Journal of Home Economics*

The only person not enamored with my book was my old acquaintance and speaking partner, George Bernard Shaw.

Mrs. Hugh Butler
Wardman Park Hotel, Washington D.C., U.S.A.

Dear Mrs. Butler

Thanks for the book, which our friend (Lady Astor) has sent to me. It is a first rate instrument of propaganda. My particular fad, however, is phonetics and athleticism of utterance. My technique as a public speaker was learnt from an opera singer who was the pupil of Francois Delsarte. If I were a platform orator I should not preach at my pupils (you do nothing else all the time) I should tell them that they must begin by learning spoken English alphabet of 40 letters and work on it until they could hit every consonant like a sledge hammer and make every vowel vibrate like a bell.

Also of course to say "Lo! here I lend thee this sharp pointed sword" and not Low herilentheethish arpointedzoared etc etc etc.

The nervous fear on which you dwell so much can be cured by the consciousness of this athleticism.

Without this technical foundation preaching will be useless. There must be no preaching at this stage — nothing to distract attention from phonetics and utterance.

You are right as to people not valuing what they get for nothing. But also the more it costs them the more they value it. Don't teach cheaply. And don't forget that if you teach for less than enough to enable you to live on, you are undercutting your fellow teachers and dragging down the standard fees of your profession.

My late wife's public bequests do not become operative until after my death; and the war leaves me meanwhile only enough to keep up my establishment and meet my standing obligations. Anyhow we are not allowed to send money to the U.S.A. The "dollar gap" overrides all our activities.

GBS
(George Bernard Shaw)

Closing Thoughts by Mila Johansen

Dearest Mila,

Your last letter gave me more joy and satisfaction than I have ever known in my long life. Your letter showed me that you have reached a philosophy with which to guide your life for the future. Once one does that nothing can stop you. You are on the road for the future.

Lovingly yours,
Grannie

I have dozens of letters in the archives going back and forth between my grandmother, Jessie, and me, with news and sincere words of adoration throughout for one another. We were best friends, and I still feel her close to me.

When I went away to college, we wrote weekly to mitigate the deep longing for each other's company—often two and three page letters. Working on this book has allowed me to see sides of Jessie I didn't know. As a young woman, she was very hip and ahead of her time—a dynamic leader of her generation.

Jessie, went on to speak, write, and lecture throughout her lifetime. She delivered her last speeches at ages ninety-one to ninety-three with Gloria Steinem and Marlo Thomas. They invited Jessie, several times, to share the podium with them as the elder suffragette who had paved the way for the women's movement that continues on today.

Sherna Berger Gluck interviewed Jessie for several days and featured her, along with four other notable suffragists, in the book *From Parlor to Prison*. That book has been used for women's studies ever since. The recordings of the interviews are archived and available online for anyone to listen to.

My grandmother profoundly influenced my life and took me along on many of her speaking adventures, introducing me to amazing women, including Gloria Steinem, Marlo Thomas, and

Jane Fonda. I somehow had the presence of mind, at age twenty-three, to spend two weeks recording Jessie's stories for two hours a day to preserve her legacy.

When she passed away, several women from NOW (National Organization for Women) asked if I planned to follow in her footsteps. Being young and terribly naïve, I flippantly answered, "Oh, no. She told me I'm already emancipated from all the work she's done. I'm going to go out and live my life."

Well, as maturity took hold, I became just like her, speaking out against new travesties facing society—pesticides and insecticides, the unnecessary and unacceptable poisoning of our planet—a subject I am certain Jessie would have embraced as well.

An avid walker and swimmer, Jessie kept up her energetic pace until the very end, when she passed away at age ninety-eight in 1985.

> *Dearest Grannie,*
>
> *This letter shall be opened with a statement from my heart, I love you. Of all the people in the world, I would like to sit down with you for a long, long talk about everything.*
>
> *Your loving granddaughter,*
> *Mila*

I still often wish I could sit with her again and talk about everything!

Hollywood to ERA's rescue

TODAY IS SUNDAY

'The ERA faces a tough campaign to gain the three more approvals needed for ratification. Extension of the deadline appears doubtful.'

THREE AGES OF WOMEN: Elizabeth Yarrow, Gloria Steinem and 92-year-old suffragette Jessie Haver Butler.

Jessie and Gloria Steinem featured in article

Jessie and Gloria

Come join us in a

CELEBRATION
FOR EQUALITY

Saturday, June 10, 1978
1–4 pm

at the home of Dr. Cathryn Ellison
415 Georgina Avenue • Santa Monica, CA

Featured Speaker:
Marlo Thomas

Special Guest:
Gloria Steinem

Honored Guest:
Jessie Haver Butler

Unsung Heroine of the
American Suffrage Movement

Guest Hosts:

Polly Bergen   Karen Grassle
Susan Blakely   Cheryl Ladd
Barbara Feldon   Angel Tompkins

Music by Kellie Greene & Co.
Donation: $25 per person
RSVP: 394-1177 or 394-0033

Sponsored by the California E.R.A. Campaign Fund, a special project of the
National Women's Political Caucus Equal Rights Amendment Fund.

Proceeds will be used to support pro-E.R.A. candidates in unratified states.

Jessie was honored at this event - Jessie signed the books
From Parlor to Prison, *which they sold as a benefit for $500 each*

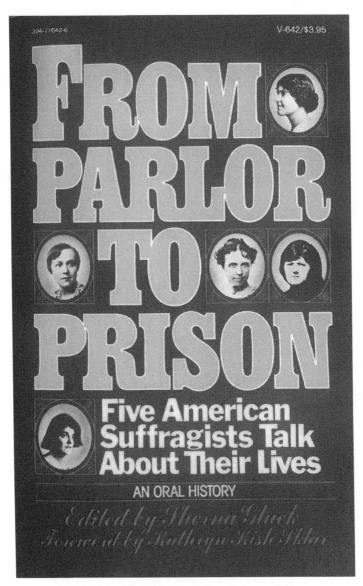

Front cover of **From Parlor to Prison**
by Sherna Berger Gluck—Jessie top right

*Jessie, age 90, with Sherna Berger Gluck,
biographer of* **From Parlor to Prison**

Mila Johansen with grandparents Hugh and Jessie, 1972

Jessie Butler, public speaker

MRS. HUGH BUTLER

NOTED WASHINGTON

EDUCATOR, AUTHOR, LECTURER

•

SUBJECTS

"AMERICA AND ENGLAND IN THE POSTWAR"

and

"TIME TO SPEAK UP!"

•

A VITAL PERSONALITY AND EFFECTIVE SPEAKER

THE LECTURER

MRS. HUGH BUTLER has just returned from a visit to England and France where she re-established her pre-war contacts made when her husband, now Research Director of the U. S. Maritime Commission, was for eight and one-half years Assistant Commercial Attache at the American Embassy in London. She devoted her time abroad to studying the British reconversion programs as they affect children, health, juvenile delinquency, housing and education. Because the national women's organizations are especially interested in the renewal of foreign trade, Mrs. Butler collected information in the pottery towns of Staffordshire, the mill towns of Lancashire, the linen industries in Belfast, the British Industries Fair, and the perfume factories of France. She presents a highly interesting and entertaining eye-witness account of how the American woman stands to benefit from world trade—a key to enduring peace.

Mrs. Butler is the author of "TIME TO SPEAK UP", a speaker's handbook for women. Her public speaking classes have met in the East Room of the **White House** on the invitation of Mrs. Eleanor Roosevelt and Mrs. Harry S. Truman. She has trained more than 200 wives of Congressmen, leading figures of the famous Washington diplomatic colony, national leaders and club women.

In her lectures, Mrs. Butler charts a new course for women in public and private life.

Another "BEST TELLER" of the

NATIONAL LECTURE BUREAU
1811 LARCHMONT AVE.
CHICAGO, ILL.

NATIONAL LECTURE MANAGEMENT
9003 SUDBURY ROAD
SILVER SPRING, MARYLAND

More letters that Jessie wrote home to her family about her adventures with Eleanor Roosevelt

2118 – O Street, N. W.
Washington, D. C.
March 18, 1936

Dear Folks at Home,   (Pueblo, Colorado)
I have had amazing good luck with my classes in public speaking. Had a large class at the Dem. National Women's Club, one in a private home on 16th Street, and am now running one at the Congressional Club made up of Congressmen's wives. They certainly improve with the teaching and seem to enjoy the classes and I love giving them. It has helped make the winter go and through them I have met many lovely people. You know Washington grows on you. I hated it when first we came back last summer and for a long time I felt so uprooted and dislocated; but I notice now that I am beginning to enjoy it again. ...
...Monday evening I went to a banquet of Business and Professional women and heard Mrs. Roosevelt. One of my private pupils spoke. I had given her 12 lessons to make a 5 minute speech. She was the most scared woman you ever saw but that night she made a lovely speech. I was very proud of her. Mrs. Roosevelt spoke well; she is never an orator but very earnest and gracious. The theme was a New Order of Business and she stressed the importance of honesty in business and the difficulty young people have in reconciling business practices which they find with moral codes which they have been taught in schools. It was a courageous talk, I thought.
— No one can understand how Mrs. Roosevelt does all that she does do. She speaks so many times a week; always turns up looking fresh and rested and gives such good talks though they are not at all finished pieces of oratory.

APPENDIX

— Recently I have met Cong. Golden's wife from Los Angeles. She and I have been trying to get the Democratic Women's National Committee to institute some courses in the New Deal for women now in Washington who will soon be returning to their districts and wanting to know how to talk about it. Last Monday they finally called a meeting and are getting under way with the courses. The women's clubs here are more interested in tea parties and social affairs than they are in educational programs. I also found out that if you leave your cards at the White House you will get invited to a White House tea and so Mrs. McCready and I have taken advantage of the opportunity, but I fear we are too late though I am told there is an Easter Lawn Party. I have met Mrs. Roosevelt only casually along with many others but have not had a chance to talk with her alone. Of course here in Washington political talk is not very open among the women. Many women who have been here for a long time belong to the other party; yet are popular and invited everywhere and so the women have learned to be very non-partisan. The other day I noticed that at a cabinet's wives tea Mrs. Wm. Howard Taft was asked to pour. She is quite an old lady but very popular with women of both parties.

— Washington has so many widows in it. When a Congressman dies; or someone in public life; if he has had a home here, his wife is inclined to remain on here and then becomes just another widow. She may go into government work, into public work of one sort, or another or merely live on and indulge in social life of which there is plenty. It is more like London than any place else where we have lived. Many afternoon tea parties.

— Another feature of Washington is the Town Hall, which meets every Sunday night. Many congressional people go to this forum where they have a main speaker and then a panel of some 6 people who cross examine the speaker on his lecture. Then there are questions and discussions from the floor. Some 1,000 people go to these forums on Sundays. When I attended, Mrs. Roosevelt spoke; Sen. La Follette; Mayor LaGuardia; Pres. Hutchins, and others.

*— Another thing that makes Washington different from any
other city is the custom, which prevails here for wives to work for a
regular salary. From the lowest paid workers to the highest, women are
in regular jobs. The costliest living is near the center of town where
people can walk to work, though this year has been a lively building
program of low cost houses out on the edge of town. ... Everyone is like
a bird perched on a tree; ready to fly away at a moment's notice. That
too lends to the instability of the place. Washington is somewhat like
Hollywood, I imagine, exotic, unnatural and yet with a fascination all
its own.*

Dec. 22, 1938

Dear Folks at Home,

*On Christmas Eve, the President goes from the White House to the
Park in front to light the big Christmas tree and we are going to take
Richard, so if it comes in over the radio you can all picture us there
looking at the President and listening to the big band. The next day,
we are going to the church where he goes to see him and his family at
church. We saw him last Christmas Day – and we shall never forget
it. You forget what a cripple he is when you see him in the movies so
you would get a shock if you could see him stumble in on his canes
with his face and neck red with the effort and downright pain which
walking causes him. What a wonderful man to carry his great burden
and yet to be a cripple!*

April 15, 1939

Dear Folks at Home,

*As you know Mrs. Roosevelt came to open my first meeting of
wives of members Congress and was our first speaker. As a result I
had 25 in the winter course and have had 12 since in other classes
besides some private pupils.*

*Last month the Democratic women from all over the country
were in Washington and had me give them a short lecture on Speech
Preparation and Delivery. As a result of that talk, I am to go to
Harrisburg, Penn. in May to the State meeting of the Democratic*

women to give the same speech for $25 and expenses; also to Norfolk, Va. and to Springfield, Mass. and Holyoke, Mass. Don't think I am turning Democratic; I would do the same for the Republicans if they asked me to. (After working with Eleanor Roosevelt, Jessie did become a democrat for the rest of her life.) My desire is to help them all become good speakers. Also the Democratic National Committee here is now assigning some of my speakers to their state meetings; then the speakers come to me for private lessons and so it works all ways around. Hugh says "I have arrived" and it looks as though I have. In a couple of more years by the time Rosemary gets into college, I should be making enough to help out the family budget.

1559 – 44th St., N. W.
Washington, D. C.
Nov. 18th, 1939

Dear Folks at Home

My work has been very fine this fall. I have had a large class with the Junior League made up of some of the most influential women here. How they have enjoyed it. One of them told me on the phone this evening that she was having the most fun of her life in this speaking course. And they are beginning to make excellent speeches too. Then I have another class at the church. Mrs. McNutt is in that. And several other very prominent women; and some club women and business women and others. January 11th I hope to start my winter course with Mrs. Roosevelt as the first speaker. She started us off last year and I hope she will this year. We haven't heard definitively yet. ...

Dec. 17, 1939

Dear Folks at Home,

The coming event of importance in the family is the opening meeting of my winter course in public speaking. Mrs. Roosevelt will be the first speaker and Mrs. Whittington of Miss. will be the chairman. Mrs. Sparkman of Ala. will introduce Mrs. Roosevelt. They were the prize winners of my last winter's course. We have engaged Pierce Hall, holding 400 people and will send out nearly 600 invitations. The subject of the meeting will be Demosthenes' Disciples in a Democracy. Doesn't that sound learned? But we wanted it to be something other than just public speaking and the classes. The date is Jan. 11th. There is a chance that the National Broadcasting Company will broadcast Mrs. Roosevelt's remarks. In that case you may perhaps hear it out there.

... Last week, Mrs. Mary Beard came down from New York to attend a meeting of the Washington Unit of Women's Archives. It seems that history has been slow to record the actions of its famous women. I was cool to the idea at first but I saw the letter that Susan B. Anthony wrote to a questioner as to what the world would be like when women vote. So quaint and full of accurate prophecy, I realized the importance

Sunday Evening
April 21, 1940

Dear Folks at Home,

I have had a great winter. Did you see my name in Mrs. Roosevelt's newspaper column, "My Day", some weeks ago about a broadcast we asked Mrs. Roosevelt to do for my class on the census? She was so grand about it and wasn't she sweet to mention it? (A syndicated column that appeared in 90 U.S. papers for 32 years)

On the afternoon of Friday, May 3rd, I have been asked to speak to the Democratic women — 4,000 of whom are coming to Washington to get pepped up for the campaign and I am to talk to them about preparation of a speech. There is some talk of broadcasting my speech. The day before Mrs. Von Hess, who taught Mrs. Roosevelt, will speak, so watch your radios. I am quite thrilled. In June I am to give a course of 8 lectures on speaking to the Extension course for Farm Women, at the University of Maryland — some 7,000 of them from all over Maryland. I don't get paid a lot for it but it is an important assignment. So my dears, I have a hunch that by the time Rosemary gets into College I will be earning some real money with some steady work in colleges or schools hereabouts. They don't pay as well as my work does now but I spend so much time advertising and working up my classes that the school work will seem wonderful in comparison. And it will roll along like clock work year after year which will help. Went to a luncheon at Mrs. Roosevelt's the other day...

Sunday, March 16, 1941

Dear Folks at Home,

I had my opening meeting with Mrs. Roosevelt as the guest speaker again. This time my dream came true. I had 500 people there; the hall was jammed. Then trouble. First Inauguration. So I couldn't start my classes that week. Then the week I was to start the streets were glazed with ice so I had to postpone the beginning again; so I had to get out 1000 more notices. Heaven dropped a class of business and professional women from the skies, and didn't cost me anything to start. I have certainly put good speaking on the map in this town; but I am not making enough money for the hard work; but as Hugh says I will yet. Then some competitors began to move in. But luckily for me they charged New York prices so people began coming to me with a sigh of relief to find they could get what they wanted for less money. At my opening meeting the elite of the town were there; one speaker said she never saw so many chauffeurs in her life at one meeting. For weeks that meeting was the talk of the dinner tables of Washington. You know what fun they had trying to decide which speaker they liked the best and why.

APPENDIX

Suffrage Timeline

"I desire you would remember the ladies and be more generous and favorable to them than your ancestors. Do not put such unlimited power into the hands of the husbands. If particular care and attention is not paid to the ladies, we are determined to foment a rebellion, and will not hold ourselves bound by any laws in which we have no voice or representation."

~Abigail Adams

"No man is good enough to govern any woman without her consent." *~Susan B. Anthony*

Every woman who was a citizen in the U.S.A. received the right to vote on August 18, 1920. Although certain populations were denied in some states due to race.

Native Americans were granted citizenship and given the right to vote in 1924 under the administration of Calvin Coolidge. But again, some states denied them the right to vote.

Women in England did not receive the right to vote until 1928.

1837 – A young Susan B. Anthony asked for equal pay for women teachers
1848 – Seneca Falls Convention, the first women's rights convention held in Seneca Fall, NY
1850 – 1st National Woman's Rights Convention was held in Worcester, MA
1851 – Sojourner Truth defended Woman's and "Negros' rights" at the Women's Rights Convention in Akron, Ohio.
1866 – American Equal Rights also combined black and women's suffrage
1868 – 14th Amendment ratified, adding the word "male" including Negros.
1869 – National Woman Suffrage Also founded by Susan B. Anthony & Elizabeth Cady Stanton
1870 – 15th Amendment adopted; prohibited states from preventing citizens from voting because of race, color, or previous condition of servitude".
1872 – Republican Party included reference to woman suffrage
1872 – Susan B. Anthony encouraged women to vote using 14th Amendment
1872 – Susan B. Anthony and others attempted to vote – she was arrested
1873 – Susan B. Anthony was tried for "illegally" voting

Appendix

1878 – The "Anthony Amendment" introduced to Congress for women to vote

1885 – Alice Paul, a Quaker, was born

1886 – Jessie Haver Butler was born in Pueblo, Colorado on a cattle ranch

1887 – Senate voted on woman's suffrage for the 1st and last time for 25 years

1887 – Three books published of suffrage movement by Stanton, Anthony & Gage

1890 – Wyoming became the 1st state to allow women to vote

1892 – Susan B. Anthony asks Carrie Chapman Catt to address Congress on proposed Suffrage Amendment

1893 – Colorado gave women the right to vote – first to amend its constitution

1896 – Utah and Idaho gave women the right to vote

1896 – Ellen Sargent started a petition for women's suffrage in Northern California

1896 – Mary Church Terrell and others founded the National Association of Colored Women's Clubs

1896 – Utah and Idaho gave women the right to vote

1900 – Susan B. Anthony asked Carrie Chapman Catt take her place as president of NAWSA

1900 – Carrie Chapman Catt became president of the National American Woman Suffrage Association

1902 – Elizabeth Cady Stanton died

1906 – Susan B. Anthony died

1907 – Alice Paul attended the London School of Economics

1907 – Alice Paul met Emmeline Pankhurst and became a militant feminist

1909 – Alice Paul received a PhD in Economics

1910 – Washington State gave women the right to vote

1911 – California gave women the right to vote

1911 – Jessie Butler organized the Pulitzer School of Journalism with Professor Cunliffe

1912 – Women marched up Fifth Avenue in New York demanding the right to vote

1912 – Arizona, Kansas & Oregon gave women the right to vote

1913 – Territory of Alaska gave women the right to vote

1914 – Jessie Haver Butler helped set the 1st Minimum Wage for women in Boston

1914 – Nevada gave women the right to vote

1913 – 5,000 parade for woman suffrage D.C. with one-half million
    onlookers during Wilson's inauguration

1913 – Alice Paul forms the Congressional Union for Woman Suffrage

1914 – Montana and Nevada gave women the right to vote

1914 – The Congressional Union splits from the National American
    Woman Suffrage Assoc.

1914 – Carrie Chapman Catt and Alice Paul split and lead the two groups

1914 – The first Minimum Wage for women is passed in Boston from $4 a
    week to $8

1915 – Carrie Chapman Catt became president of National American
    Woman Suffrage Assoc.

1915 – 25,000 women marched on 5th Ave., New York for Women's Suffrage

1916 – The National Woman's Party is formed by Alice Paul and others.

1916 – Jessie Haver Butler became the first official woman lobbyist at the
    Capitol

1916 – Jessie Haver Butler got minimum wage legislation passed for entire
    country

1917 – NAWSA officers met with President Wilson

1917 – National Woman's Party began picketing the White House and
    were arrested

1917 – New York State gave women the right to vote

1918 – House passed Anthony Amendment but Senate did not

1918 – The Anthony Amendment became the 19th Amendment

1918 – Michigan, Oklahoma, South Dakota gave women the right to vote

1919 – 19th Amendment adopted by Congress and sent to states for
    ratification

1920 – Carrie Chapman Catt founded the League of Women Voters

1920 – Carrie Chapman Catt and Jessie Haver Butler spoke across western
    states for ratification

1920 – Tennessee legislature ratified the 19th (Anthony Amendment) by one
    vote - Harry Burn

1920 – Women won the right to vote in USA on August 18th –
    Celebration!

1920 – Alice Paul and others create the Equal Rights Amendment

1923 – Equal Rights Amendment introduced to Congress by Alice Paul &
    National Woman's Party

1924 – Native Americans granted citizenship and are allowed to vote

1925 – Nellie Taloe Ross - first female governor in the USA - Wyoming

1928 – Women in England finally won the right to vote

1933 – Frances Perkins - first female Secretary of Labor appointed by
    President Franklin Roosevelt

1941 – Millions of women recruited for jobs during World War II

1961 – FDA approved birth control pills

1961 – Eleanor Roosevelt helped establish for passage in 1963 the Equal Pay Act

1964 – Civil Rights Act established Equal Employment Opportunity Commission

1966 – National Organization for Women – NOW, founded by Betty Friedan and Associates

1972 – The Equal Rights Amendment passes in both houses signed by President Nixon

1972 – Shirley Chisholm was the first Black American to run for president

1973 – Roe v. Wade affirmed women's right to 1st trimester abortions without intervention

1981 – Sandra Day O'Connor was appointed first woman U.S. Supreme Court Justice

1982 – Deadline for ERA ratification expired; final count - three states short of adoption

1984 – Geraldine Ferraro - first woman from major political party nominated as Vice President

1991 – Senate confirmation hearings for Clarence Thomas as U.S. Supreme Court justice and testimony of Anita Hill raised awareness of sexual harassment

1992 – More women ran for and were elected to public office than in any other year in US history

2020 – Jan 15 - Virginia became the 38th state to ratify the ERA, reaching ¾ ratification

2020 – 26 women in the Senate and 101 in the U.S. House

STATES GRANTING WOMEN THE VOTE PRIOR TO THE 19TH AMENDMENT

1890	Wyoming	1912	Oregon
1893	Colorado	1913	Territory of Alaska
1896	Utah	1914	Montana
1896	Idaho	1914	Nevada
1910	Washington	1917	New York
1911	California	1918	Michigan
1912	Arizona	1918	Oklahoma
1912	Kansas	1918	South Dakota

Appendix

Photo Credits

Opposite Page 1. Author unknown, *Women's Club Reception for* Time to Speak Up *by Jessie Butler*, Photographic print, 5x7 inches, Source: Butler Johansen Historical Archives.

Page 6. *Mrs. Hugh Butler Teacher of Effective Public Speaking*, promotional flyer, source: Butler Johansen Historical Archives.

Page 7. *Jessie Haver as a Baby*, photographic print, source: Butler Johansen Historical Archives.

Page 9. *Clara Rehwoldt Haver*, photographic print, 5x7 inches, source: Butler Johansen Historical Archives.

Page 11. *Jessie, Emily and Fred Haver*, photographic print, 5x7 inches, source: Butler Johansen Historical Archives.

Page 13. *Jessie*, photographic print, 5x7 inches, source: Butler Johansen Historical Archives

Page 14. *Jessie, Clara, Edwin and Fred Haver at Home in Pueblo, Colorado*, photographic print, 5x7 inches, source: Butler Johansen Historical Archives.

Page 15. *Article from Pueblo Chieftain May 13*, photocopy of original, source: Butler Johansen Historical Archives.

Page 16. *William Jennings Bryan (1860-1925)*, Geo. H. Van Norman, Springfield, MA, Public domain, Library of Congress LC-USZC2-6259, source: https://upload.wikimedia.org/wikipedia/commons/0/04/William-Jennings-Bryan-speaking-c1896.jpeg

Page 21. *Haver siblings with grandfather, Herman Rehwoldt*, photographic print, 5x7 inches, source: Butler Johansen Historical Archives.

Page 23. *Jessie at family home in Pueblo, Colorado*, photographic print, source: Butler Johansen Historical Archives.

Page 24. *Edwin B. Haver*, photographic print, 5x7 inches, source: Butler Johansen Historical Archives.

Page 24. *Jessie Haver on Pony*, photographic print, source: Butler Johansen Historical Archives.

Page 28. *Pueblo Chieftain headline of death of Stepmother*, scan of newspaper, source: Butler Johansen Historical Archives.

Page 28. *Jessie's Pueblo High School Graduating Class*, photographic print, 8x10 inches, source: Butler Johansen Historical Archives.

Page 33. *Jessie Haver Freshman Smith College*, photographic print, 5x7 inches, source: Butler Johansen Historical Archives.

Page 34. *Jessie's Smith College Dorm and page from Yearbook*, photographic prints, source: Butler Johansen Historical Archives.

Page 39. *MacCallum Mill on West Street Northampton Massachusetts*, 1913, photographic print, source: Special Collections, Hampshire Room, Forbes Library, Northampton, MA. https://www.digitalcommonwealth.org/search/commonwealth:bk129323c

Page 42. *Jessie Haver at Mary Thornton's Wedding*, photographic print, 5x7 inches, Butler Johansen Historical Archives.

Page 42. *Jessie in Smith College Play*, photographic print, 5x7 inches, Butler Johansen Historical Archives.

Page 43. *Jessie Haver Riding in Pueblo*, photographic print, Butler Johansen Historical Archives.

Page 44. *Jessie Haver Portrait*, photographic print, 5x7 inches, Butler Johansen Historical Archives.

Page 50. Bain News Service, *J.W. Cunliffe Abstract*, 1915, glass negative 5 x 7 in. or smaller, source: https://commons.wikimedia.org/wiki/File:J.W._Cunliffe_LCCN2014711041.tif

Page 56. Minimum Wage Decree, recreated.

Page 58. Hine, Lewis Wickes, *Noon Hour in an Indianapolis Cotton Mill*, 1908, photographic print, National Child Labor Committee collection, Library of Congress, Prints and Photographs Division, source: https://www.loc.gov/item/2018673720/

Page 59. Hine, Lewis Wickes, *Operatives in Indianapolis Cotton Mill. Noon Hour*, 1908, photographic print, National Child Labor Committee Collection, Library of Congress, Prints and Photographs Division, source: https://www.loc.gov/resource/nclc.01329/

Page 60. *Jessie Haver Side Portrait*, photographic print, 5x7 inches, source: Butler Johansen Historical Archives.

Page 62. National Photo Company Collection, *Mrs. Carrie Chapman Catt half-length portrait, facing front*, 1909, photographic print, 12.8mb tif, Library of Congress, source: https://www.loc.gov/pictures/item/94504767/

Page 63. National Photo Company Collection, *Sewing stars on Suffrage Flag*, 1920, 1 negative, glass, 4x5" or smaller, Library of Congress, source: https://www.loc.gov/pictures/item/2016827559/

Page 67. Edmonston, Washington, D.C., and New York Campbell Studios. *Mrs. Florence Kelley*. New York United States, ca. 1910. [to 1916] Photograph. https://www.loc.gov/item/mnwp000099/.

Page 68. Jewish Women's Archive, *Josephine Clara Goldmark*, source: https://jwa.org/media/josephine-clara-goldmark

Page 69. *Fatigue and Efficiency by Josephine Goldmark*, digital image.

Page 71. *President Woodrow Wilson*, RCP, Adobe Stock.

Page 72. *Hugh Dewitt Butler*, photographic print, source: Butler Johansen Historical Archives.

Page 77. Albert "Dutch" Roth, *Appalachian Trail originator Benton MacKaye pauses on the A.T. near Newfound Gap*, 1933, JPEG Image, 462 × 674 pixels, University of Tennessee Libraries, source: SOURCE: http://archive.knoxnews.com/news/on-75th-anniversary-appalachian-trail-doing-better-with-age-ep-360274115-356770471.html/ .

Page 78. *Benton MacKaye with Jessie and Hugh Butler friends group*, photographic print, source: Butler Johansen Historical Archives.

Page 82. *Letter of Recommendation from Florence Kelley for Jessie Haver*, 1920, letter, 8.5x11" - Butler Johansen Historical Archives.

Page 84. National Photo Company, *U.S. Capitol, [Washington, D.C.],* [Between 1918 and 1928], 8x6 glass negative, Library of Congress, source: https://www.loc.gov/item/2016826656

Page 90. *Ratification Dates by State,* original design, 11x17", source: Butler Johansen Historical Archives.

Page 94. *Jessie Haver Ready to Paddle the Potomac,* photographic print, 4"x6", source: Butler Johansen Historical Archives.

Page 101. *Mrs. Butler, Hugh's Mother,* photographic print, 5x7", source: Butler Johansen Historical Archives.

Page 104. *Jessie Haver Prepares to Paddle the Potomac,* photographic print, 4x6", source: Butler Johansen Historical Archives.

Page 114. *Letter 1 from Carrie Chapman Catt to Jessie Haver,* February 1920, original, 8.5x11", source: Butler Johansen Historical Archives.

Page 116. *Letter 2 from Carrie Chapman Catt to Jessie Haver,* May 1920, original, 8.5x11", source: Butler Johansen Historical Archives.

Page 118. *Lowell Sun Headline – Suffrage Wins,* August 1920, photographic scan, source: Butler Johansen Historical Archives.

Page 123. Author unknown, *Board of Directors National League of Women Voters Chicago Convention,* February 1920, photographic print, Library of Congress, source: https://www.loc.gov/pictures/item/98511969/.

Page 128. *Weekend Potomac River Hideout,* photographic print, source: Butler Johansen Historical Archives.

Page 141. *Frank Butler, Hugh's Father,* photographic print, source: Butler Johansen Historical Archives.

Page 142. *Letter from Carrie Chapman Catt to Jessie Haver,* November 1920, original, 8.5x11", source: Butler Johansen Historical Archives.

Page 144. *Secret Wedding Article,* December 1920, photographic scan, source: Butler Johansen Historical Archives.

Page 150. *Inscription in book* Back to Methuselah, photo scan of original, source: Butler Johansen Historical Archives.

Page 153. Unknown author, *Anglo-Irish playwright George Bernard Shaw writing in notebook at time of first production of his play "Pygmalion.",* 1914, 967 x 1280 pixels (13.4 x 17.8 inches), LIFE photo archive.

Page 154. *Hugh and Jessie Butler in London,* 1921, photographic print, source: Butler Johansen Historical Archives.

Page 156. *Hugh Butler passport,* jpeg of photo scan, Source: Ancestry.com Special Passport Applications, 1920-21, Volume 18: Military, Civilian, Federal Employees and Dependents, Volume 18: Military, Civilian, Federal Employees and Dependents. https://www.ancestry.com/interactive/1174/32290_620303987_0003-01018?pid=1804301&backurl=https://www.ancestry.com/family-tree/person/tree/81929178/person/342097964629/gallery&usePUB=true&_phsrc=MBp2&usePUBJs=true - ?imageId=32290_620303987_0003-01016

Page 163. *Jessie Butler with Fabian Summer School Group,* photographic print, London, source: Butler Johansen Historical Archives.

Page 167. *Fabian News*, 1922, photo scan of original, London, source: Butler Johansen Historical Archives.

Page 168. *Jessie Haver Butler Portrait*, photographic print, source: Butler Johansen Historical Archives.

Page 172. Bassano Ltd, Nancy Astor, Viscountess Astor, 1923, whole plate glass negative, National Portrait Gallery, London, source: https://commons.wikimedia.org/wiki/File:Nancy-Astor-Viscountess-Astor.jpg.

Page 176. *Butler Home in Golders Green London*, photographic print, source: Butler Johansen Historical Archives.

Page 179. *Jessie Butler Holding Baby Rosemary*, photographic print, source: Butler Johansen Historical Archives.

Page 194. Kay Brighton, *Queen Mary Portrait presented to Jessie Butler*, 1928, photographic print, 5 x 7 inches, source: Butler Johansen Historical Archives.

Page 198. Author unknown, *Jessie and Hugh Butler Presentation at Court*, 1928, photographic print, 5 x 7 inches, source: Butler Johansen Historical Archives.

Page 208. George Grantham Bain Collection, Queen Mary/Mary of Teck Portrait, circa 1925, digital file from original negative, Washington, D.C., Library of Congress Prints and Photographs Division, source: https://commons.wikimedia.org/w/index.php?title=Special:Search&limit=20&offset=20&ns0=1&ns6=1&ns12=1&ns14=1&ns100=1&ns106=1&search=Queen+Mary+portrait&advancedSearch-current={}#/media/File:Queenmaryformalportrait_edit3.jpg.

Page 212. Author unknown, *Cliveden – Lord and Lady Astor's Home*, photographic print, source: Butler Johansen Historical Archives.

Page 216. Bain News Service, Publisher, *Lord and Lady Astor*, 1922, photograph from glass negative; 5 x 7 in. or smaller, Washington D.C., Library of Congress Prints and Photographs Division, https://commons.wikimedia.org/wiki/File:Lord_and_Lady_Astor_LCCN2014714257.jpg.

Page 220. *Hugh Butler with children Richard and Rosemary*, photographic print, source: Butler Johansen Historical Archives.

Page 224. *Hugh and Jessie Butler*, photographic print, source: Butler Johansen Historical Archives.

Page 228. *Emmy, Nanny to the Butler Children*, photographic print, source: Butler Johansen Historical Archives.

Page 230. *Emily Haver in New York*, photographic print, 5x7 inches, source: Butler Johansen Historical Archives.

Page 231. *Butler Home in Needham, Massachusetts*, photographic print, source: Butler Johansen Historical Archives.

Page 236. *Jessie in Beaded Court Dress*, 1928, photographic print, source: Butler Johansen Historical Archives.

Page 238. *Jessie Butler Teaching Public Speaking*, photographic print, source: Butler Johansen Historical Archives.

Page 241. *Letter from Lady Astor*, December 2, 1935, scan of original, source: Butler Johansen Historical Archives.

Page 242. *Letter from Lady Astor*, December 27, 1935, scan of original, source: Butler Johansen Historical Archives.

Page 248. *Hugh Butler Working at Social Security Admin. in Washington, DC,* photographic print, 5x7 inches, source: Butler Johansen Historical Archives.

Page 250. *Invitation to Jessie Butler's Speaking Course with Guest Speaker Eleanor Roosevelt,* 1941, scan of original, Butler Johansen Historical Archives.

Page 252. *Signed Photograph to Jessie Butler from Eleanor Roosevelt,* photographic print, 5 x 7 inches, source: Butler Johansen Historical Archives.

Page 255. *Map of Shenandoah Hideout,* scan of original print, source: Butler Johansen Historical Archives.

Page 256. *The Butler Family at Shenandoah Hideout,* photographic print, source: Butler Johansen Historical Archives.

Page 257. *Jessie Speaking at National Convention of Women's Clubs,* 1948, photographic print, source: Butler Johansen Historical Archives.

Page 259. *Shenandoah Hideout in Flint Hills,* photographic print, source: Butler Johansen Historical Archives.

Page 260. *Newspaper article on Jessie's Canning for War Effort,* scan of original, source: Butler Johansen Historical Archives.

Page 262. *Photo of Jessie's Canning for War Effort,* scan of original, source: Butler Johansen Historical Archives.

Page 269. Author unknown, *Women's Club Reception for* Time to Speak Up *by Jessie Butler,* Photographic print, 5x7 inches, Source: Butler Johansen Historical Archives.

Page 270. *Jessie on Cavalcade of Books with* Time to Speak Up, photographic print, source: Butler Johansen Historical Archives.

Page 276. *Newspaper Photo of Jessie with Gloria Steinem at ERA Fundraiser,* 1978, photocopy, source: Butler Johansen Historical Archives.

Page 276. *Jessie Butler with Gloria Steinem,* 1978, photographic print, source: Butler Johansen Historical Archives.

Page 277. *Invitation to ERA Event with Jessie as Honored Guest,* 1978, scan of original, photographic print, source: Butler Johansen Historical Archives.

Page 278. *Front Cover of From Parlor to Prison,* scan of original paperback book, source: Butler Johansen Historical Archives.

Page 279. *Jessie Butler with Sherna Gluck,* photographic print, source: Butler Johansen Historical Archives.

Page 279. *Mila Johansen with Grandparents Hugh and Jessie Butler,* photographic print, source: Butler Johansen Historical Archives.

Page 280. *Jessie Butler Public Speaking Portrait,* photographic print, source: Butler Johansen Historical Archives.

Page 281. *Flyer for Jessie Butler's Lecture Series,* scan of original, 8.5 x 11 inches, source: Butler Johansen Historical Archives.

Page 297. Dee Anne Dinelli, *Mila Johansen,* "2019, photographic print.

Page 298. *Jessie Butler with Hugh Butler a Rally,* scan of original, 3 x 4 inches, source: Butler Johansen Historical Archives.

About the Author, Mila Johansen

Mila Johansen is a professional director, playwright and writer. She is the author of twenty-two plays and musicals that circle the globe along with two teaching manuals, *101 Theatre Games* and *50 Scenes to Go*. Jessie helped raised Mila, which made her the woman she is today—a writer, historian, activist, and speaker.

All of Jessie's archives were passed to Mila in the late 1980s, but they remained in two file cabinets while Mila was busy teaching, raising her daughter, and writing plays and books. Finally, in early 2018, Mila began the process of organizing Jessie's archives, and began the book that Jessie had always encouraged her to write—the story of Jessie's life.

Mila Johansen has written nine screenplays, several children's picture books, and has one YA historical novel, *The Four Thieves*, finished and ready to publish. She also has three provocative upmarket fiction novels almost completed.

Mila lives on her organic citrus ranch in Northern California with her husband, four dogs, and a cat.

Tribune Photos by Tom Hinkle

PURSE PROBLEMS — Women's lib marchers
Hugh and Jessie Butler of La Verne are
caught up in the spirit as he totes her purse
while she pickets Rep. Wiggins' office in El
Monte Thursday.

*Women's lib marchers Hugh and Jessie Butler
of La Verne are caught up in the spirit as he
totes her purse while she pickets Rep. Wiggins'
office in El Monte Thursday.*

Made in the USA
Middletown, DE
19 April 2022

64333048R00182